Leslie Simon and
Jan Johnson Drantell

A MUSIC I NO LONGER HEARD

The Early Death of a Parent

SIMON & SCHUSTER

SIMON & SCHUSTER
Rockefeller Center
1230 Avenue of the Americas
New York, NY 10020

SIMON & SCHUSTER and colophon are registered trademarks
of Simon & Schuster Inc.

Designed by Deirdre C. Amthor

Manufactured in the United States of America

10   9   8   7   6   5   4   3   2   1

Library of Congress Cataloging-in-Publication Data
    Simon, Leslie, date.
    A music I no longer heard : the early death of a parent /
Leslie Simon and Jan Johnson Drantell.
        p. cm.
    Includes bibliographical references and index.
    1. Parents—Death—Psychological aspects. 2. Parents—
Death—Psychological aspects—Case studies. 3. Bereavement—
Psychological aspects. 4. Grief. 5. Loss (Psychology)
6. Children and death. 7. Teenagers and death. I. Drantell, Jan
Johnson, date. II. Title.
    BF789.D4S55   1998
    155.9'37—dc21   97-35471   CIP
ISBN 0-684-81319-X

Grateful acknowledgment is made for permission to reprint an
excerpt from "Camelot," by Alan Jay Lerner and Burton Lane,
© 1960 (Renewed) Alan Jay Lerner (ASCAP) and Burton Lane
(ASCAP). Chappell & Co. owner of publication and allied rights
throughout the world. All rights reserved. Used by permission.
Warner Bros. Publications U.S. Inc., Miami, FL 33014.

Acknowledgments

First, we want to thank the seventy people who trusted us with their stories. It could not have been easy. It took courage and a special kind of generosity to share their countless gifts with us and, in turn, with our readers. Quite literally this would not be the book it is without them. Thank you.

Thanks to all of our friends who patiently listened, asked questions, offered insights, and never lost faith in this project. So many people generously wrote to and called others on our behalf, recommended people, and went out of their way to help us we cannot possibly name them all here. Thank you.

Thanks to Peggi Oakley, who did most of the interview transcription, and Keith McCandless, who did the rest. Thanks to Pat Rose, who read an initial version of the manuscript.

Thanks to everyone at Simon & Schuster, especially Aviva Goode for her encouragement.

—L.S. and J.J.D.

I want to thank my mother, Rose, whose constant devotion and support carried me through my early years. Although she lost the love of her life, she never lost her love for life. Thanks to my brother Marc whose humor helped us both make the journey back to the day that forever changed our lives. Deep and loving gratitude goes to my husband, Don, my daughter, Caya, and my son, Sage, all three steady reminders of how rich and full life can be. Expert back rubs from my daughter, the perfect ghost-movie date with my son, and good, solid advice from my husband kept me going while working on this book.

And, finally, thanks to the friends and family who kept Charlie Simon stories in circulation.

—L.S.

My brother, Phil, my nephew Christopher, and especially my niece Jessica all provided emotional and moral support through the process. I am grateful to them and my brother Paul for the parts of their stories that appear here, as well as to various members of my extended chosen family for their support. My daughter, Addie, is the one person without whom I could not have finished this book. She has been with it from before the beginning, from the night her father died when she was sixteen. She provided clerical help, insight, and emotional support all along the way. More, she generously and compassionately allowed me to live with the fiction that I was writing this book for her until, in the process, I discovered that I was writing it for myself most of all.

—J.J.D.

Contents

She was a music I no longer heard, that rang in my mind, itself and nothing else, lost to all sense, but not perished, not perished.

—Marilynne Robinson, *Housekeeping*

Preface: The Participant Observer

We are the authors of this book and also share the defining characteristic of our informants: each of us lost a parent before the age of nineteen. Jan's mother died just before her eleventh birthday, and Leslie's father died when she was seventeen. So every time we stepped into someone else's story, we also stepped into our own. We were two authors—investigators and interviewers—in the pose of neutral observers, with our preprinted questions, our tape recorders, and—when at our professional best—our sharpened, active listening skills. But we were also always two informants with our own stories to tell. There was no way we could even play at the elusive role of neutrality. We were, in the language of contemporary behavioral science, "participant observers."

Early on, one of our interviewees inquired if we were going to ask each other the formal questions we wanted our subjects to grapple with. At one point, we thought we might, but eventually we realized it would be anticlimactic. We in fact had been interviewing each other from the day we decided to do the book, and we never stopped. In all-day meetings and countless hour-long phone calls, as we discussed strategies, sources, and work divisions, we were interviewing each other. In the course of writing this book, we went from two mothers whose daughters had been classmates to two good friends who shared a similar childhood trauma.

From the start, we knew we wanted to use our own experiences as foreground for the stories of the people we interviewed. We sought to work the field plotted out by Studs Terkel in his now classic oral histories. But we struggled over how we would incorporate our own stories. We knew we wanted to explain how this book came to be. That process, of course, would involve the description of our participant status. We also wanted to discuss grief and loss more generally, using outside sources as well as our own personal histories. Together, these elements became our first chapter, "Something Died in My Heart."

Our role as participant observers helped us structure the rest of the book. Eventually, we decided to use our own experiences as a kind of frame for other people's stories. Although we never stopped being two girls who had lost a parent in childhood or adolescence, we laid claim to our observer status through the body of the book, limiting our participant voices to the beginning and end of the book. As we let our contributors tell their stories, we took on an editorial role for ourselves, cutting and arranging each narrative to fit a general schemata of early loss of a parent based on research and analysis. We chose to introduce each chapter in our editorial voice, offering insight and interpretation as we commented on each excerpt of oral history. At the end of the book, we invited our personal voices back into the text, in the form of a coda. It gave us a place to talk about the effects of doing this research on two adults orphaned young.

Of course, no role-playing is ever as neat and clean as the process used to describe it. Just as we never lost our participant status even as we played our observer roles, the participants in our study also acted as observers. Their analysis helped shape the book. Even those who have not considered their loss in the context of their professional lives have often constructed narratives of analysis in the form of personal journals and essays or edited collections of photos, mementos, and letters. We felt privileged when they shared those documents with us during the interview or afterward through the mail.

The beauty of the field of oral history is that in it we are all experts. Each one of us has something to offer as we reflect on the events that have shaped our lives. Each one of us has much to contribute to a more general understanding of what it means to be human. To suffer and to survive.

Introduction

The genesis of *A Music I No Longer Heard* was grief—both recent grief and past grief that has lingered. This book was born in 1958 when Jan's mother died and again in 1965 when Leslie's father died and again in 1992 when Jan's daughter's father died and then again in 1993 when we first began talking about writing it. It was also born as early as 1920 when the mother of our oldest interviewee died, and at sixty-nine other times, mostly remembered to the day and hour, throughout most of this century when the people whose stories make up this book experienced the ground-shattering grief of a parent's death.

A Music I No Longer Heard was also born in the hope that, after experiencing an early grief, people can and, as these pages reveal, *do* integrate their grief into their lives. Some of the people in this book are young, just beginning to mark the adulthood passages into college and careers, choosing life partners, starting the journey that will lead them away from their childhood bereavement *and* remind them of it at various junctures. Some have passed the age they were when their parent died. Some have raised children, lived to see their own grandchildren, experienced the subsequent and inevitable losses that life brings, now reflecting back on their early loss from a vantage point of many years. The people in this book talk of grief, but they also talk of rich and full lives, of empathy, independence, creativity, transformation, and hope that grows from their experience.

No one book ever tells the *whole* story on any subject. When we began this book, we looked around for books on related subjects that deal with the story and process of children eighteen (although, in the end, we included two people who were nineteen) or younger who lost a parent to death in childhood. Aside from two academic books, listed in Suggested Reading on page 345, we found little. Then, as our proposal was being submitted to publishers, we discovered *Motherless Daughters: The Legacy of Loss* by Hope Edelman. Actually, we could scarcely help discovering it; it was on several bestseller lists, not to mention on the tips of the tongues of women we knew whose mothers had died. As we worked, we discovered related books, nearly a bookshelf full of them. Some of them, like Edelman's, deal only with a mother or a father dying, but not necessarily in childhood. Some of them, like *Giving Sorrow Words* by Candy Lightner and Nancy Hathaway, include chapters on bereaved children in the context of the more general topic of grieving. We also discovered and/or rediscovered several memoirs that include the story of the writer's parent's death as part of the larger context of their lives. Those we quote from in this book include William Styron's *Darkness Visible*, Alice Kaplan's *French Lessons*, and Suzanne Lipsett's *Surviving a Writer's Life*. As we neared completion of our book, Maxine Harris's *The Loss That Is Forever: The Lifelong Impact of the Early Death of a Mother or Father* appeared. And the books continue, including Mary Gordon's just-published memoir, *The Shadow Man: A Daughter's Search for Her Father* and Stephen Bogart's recent *Bogart: In Search of My Father*. Each one of the books in Suggested Reading contributes in some way to *A Music I No Longer Heard*. The very fact that these books and other similar ones exist now is evidence in our mind of the solace and insight such books offer.

The general theme of being orphaned informs literature, fairy tales, and myth through the ages. There is something archetypal about a child facing the world alone. Such a child faces larger obstacles finding his or her place in life. The odds against happiness, fulfillment, and plot resolution are longer. Charlotte Brontë's character Jane Eyre wouldn't be who she is if she had living parents. Although many novelists who create orphaned characters did not themselves face the early loss of a parent, Brontë and many others did. Yet even given the ongoing theme and mythic proportions of childhood bereavement, we can't help asking ourselves why so many memoirs, oral histories, self-help books, and novels dealing with the loss of a parent in child-hood have recently been published.

According to census statistics from 1930 on, roughly 5 percent of the population falls into the orphaned category, which means having lost one or both parents to death before age eighteen. This is, of course, a relatively small percentage of the general population. How-ever, we see several factors that contribute to the interest in these books, and to the continuing need for them. First, although the or-phan population is small, losing a parent to death in childhood is a life event that keeps on reverberating long into adulthood. It affects not only the orphan grown-up, but his or her spouses, friends, and chil-dren. Personal stories of grief and books about the grief process are of interest to these people, as well as to the professionals, such as psy-chologists or teachers, who work with them.

Our culture has become of late far more conscious of the effects of childhood trauma on adult lives. We are now more willing to talk and read about childhood physical, sexual, and emotional abuse; about the ongoing effects of addiction and divorce; and about the devastating consequences of poverty, racism, and war, on chil-dren. More books and more TV talk shows deal with these issues than ever before. And beginning with Elisabeth Kübler-Ross's pioneering work on grief, death was no longer a taboo subject. But, and this is a big but, if the effects of death and other traumas on sur-vivors—delayed stress syndrome among Vietnam-era veterans comes to mind—weren't recognized in previous generations, it doesn't mean they weren't experienced. As thoughtful people attempt to make sense of their losses, the stories of people with similar experi-ences can and do help in that process.

After Diana, Princess of Wales, died, leaving her two sons mother-less, the conversation of how to help children cope with the loss of a parent became more public than it has ever been. More people became aware of the importance of addressing the differences between how children and adults mourn. Several experts pointed to the same key conclusions we have come to in this book, including the idea that while grief never fully disappears, once acknowledged it can become a transformational experience.

A Music I No Longer Heard looks at childhood bereavement and its effects on adults from the perspective of the people who experienced the loss. (See also the Preface.) Their stories, *in their own words*, comprise the bulk of this book, and that makes this book different from the other books in this market. Both Harris (*The Loss That Is Forever*) and Edelman (*Motherless Daughters*) include stories of others, but by and large these stories are filtered through the authors' lenses. Some anthologies, such as *Loss of the Groundnote: Women Writing About the Loss of Their Mothers* (editor, Helen Vozenilek), collect creative writing dealing with the death of the mother or father. But this book is not poetry or fiction; it allows people to speak in their own words; and it covers the whole territory: men and women, who were boys and girls, who lost either their father or their mother.

We began by asking people about their early lives. If we were sociologists, this inquiry would be called a baseline. We wanted to describe the range of circumstances our interviewees were living in and develop a sense of how different these stories are, and how they are alike. After that beginning, the book considers the entire process of loss and grief, from the moment the children found out about their parent's death, up to their present understanding of how that early experience affects who they are now. We offer commentary on the stories throughout the book, drawing attention to common themes and implied meanings, to the various problems that can arise and to possible ways to deal with them. In Chapter 1, "Something Died in My Heart," and in Chapter 10, "Coda," we share something of our own experience, both of early grief and of the healing value of writing this book.

Here we offer a caution: this is not a how-to book designed to help people forget about the aftereffects of their early bereavement or to help people dealing with children who are recently bereaved avoid ongoing grief. Plainly and simply, no such quick fix exists. Plainly and simply, grief never disappears. It changes. It changes those who grieve. It even allows room for hope, insight, and transformation in a variety of paradoxical ways we'll explore. But it only evolves if we acknowledge its ongoing presence in our lives. One way to acknowledge grief is to tell, read, and share stories. That is what this book is about.

A Brief Note About Process

Our goal was to interview fifty people for this book. We interviewed seventy. We found our interviewees through word-of-mouth. We started close to home. Leslie interviewed her brother Marc and Jan's daughter Addie. Jan interviewed her niece Jessica and her friend William. Other interviewees are friends we've known for years, colleagues from work, writers or others we've admired from afar and were able to contact through acquaintances. Still others came to us circuitously, three or four degrees of separation away.

There were more volunteers than we could reasonably talk to, so we consciously chose a wide age range. The youngest interviewees in this book are just beginning their journey into adulthood, at age nineteen. The oldest look back nearly eighty years at childhood loss. Five of our interviewees grew up outside the United States, in China, the Philippines, Mexico, Norway, and Iran. We also worked to present a representative sampling in terms of race and ethnic backgrounds, sexual identity, and geographic locale.

∽

In the pages that follow, you will meet seventy people. Each time a person's name appears at the beginning of a portion of his or her story, a parenthetical code follows it. The code tells how old the person was at the time of the interview. Then comes an "m" for "mother who died," or "f" for "father." That's followed by the person's age at the time of the parent's death. Like this: Jan (47, m, 11), or Leslie (47, f, 17).

I

Something Died in My Heart

Yes . . . weep now, darling weep. Let us both weep. That is the first thing: to let ourselves feel again . . . Then, tomorrow, we shall make something strong of this sorrow.—Lorraine Hansberry (f, 15),* *The Sign in Sidney Brustein's Window*

The Genesis, Leslie's Version

"So this is where that day has brought me." As I climbed the stairs of Jan's house on the afternoon we planned to begin this book, I paused for a moment before I rang the bell. The day that confronted me on the doorstep was the day my father died, almost thirty years ago, when I was seventeen.

If I'm honest with myself, I must admit that his early death has marked and changed my life in ways I'll probably never completely understand, but until very recently, for a good fifteen years, I think, I had told myself that I was done with it. Mourning was long over, and the small, sharp aches of missing him were usually confined to moments I told a story about him to my children or placed his photo on

*Hansberry's father died when she was fifteen. We use this code throughout the book.

the Day of the Dead altar I've built each November for the past six or seven years. Constructing this physical space in my home—a borrowed ritual from Mexican culture—offers me a way to remember my dead ones.

Remembering my father became my primary goal by the evening of the day he died. In the haze of shock and fear, the belief that I had a job I could do helped to settle me. I told myself I had to remember our father so that my ten-year-old brother, Marc, would experience, when he got older, the pleasure of knowing him—at least by proxy— in ways no ten-year-old can appreciate a parent. Within a few days of our father's death, I sat down at his large custom-built desk in the basement of our house, scribbling notes to myself of funny stories about our dad, smart things he had said to me, and memories of what was important to him—like the deep love he carried for his own father and how he wanted me to know my grandfather, who had died when I was only five. I needed to explain to Marc that, with a few choice stories and jokes, our father had succeeded in giving me an idea of a man I barely knew. That's what I intended to do for him, and Marc assures me I've succeeded. But I don't believe him; I'm convinced I've failed. Perhaps that sense of failure and urge to make it right is one of the reasons for this book.

Another one is my recent realization, with the sudden death of Jan's ex-husband Peter—the father of her teenaged daughter Addie—that you are never done with mourning. To think so is an act of hubris. And secretly I believe the gods have punished me by taking my ability to remember the sound of my father's voice away for acting as though I had finally finished dealing with this first deep sorrow. I wonder, if I do this book right, will his voice return?

When Addie, who is a friend of my daughter, Caya, called our house on the Columbus Day holiday in 1992, her broken voice telling me her father had died the day before brought me back to the day that brought me to this book.

Jan and Peter and I had only really gotten to know each other about six months before he died. We were working together on a campaign to establish an independent public high school for the arts in San Francisco. I liked their midwestern groundedness, Jan's sense of humor, and Peter's political savvy, so when I heard that Peter had died, I was devastated. And the few small circumstances that echoed my own father's death—dying at home of a sudden heart attack on a Sunday—were enough to pick away at my stubbornly buried grief.

As I began to call around to the small school community to give people the sad news, here and there I would mention that the same thing had happened to me when I was a teenager. I remember Barb, one of the other parents, saying, "That's really good. You can help Addie deal with this."

I could identify with Addie. She is a first and only child, a daughter. Even though I have a brother, Marc was not born until I was seven years old, and a friend once told me that if a child experiences the first five years without a sibling, he or she develops much of the psychology of an only child. We feel a strong sense of responsibility and carry a terrific burden to succeed. When I finally talked to Jan, I told her I'd be happy to meet with Addie in the next few weeks. That's when I discovered that Jan's own mother had died when she was eleven, but we both agreed that since Addie and I had lost a father around the same time in our lives, the parallel experience might create a rapport that could help Addie with her grief.

Of course, what slowly crept into my consciousness, the thing that was just now finally occurring to me—what I wanted to tell Addie, but knew I couldn't then—is that you never get over it. The wound lasts forever. A day or so after my father died, a neighbor woman of about thirty, whose father had died when she was twenty, relayed to me conventional wisdom of the healing effects of time. Time does help, but the proverb fails to hold. Time does not heal wounds; it merely helps you get used to them.

In the first year after Peter's death, I met with Addie a couple of times. The first time, I think, worked. At the raw stage of grief, even though shock is still in effect, you can sometimes get to someone. By the next time we met alone, in August, on Addie's birthday, I saw she had begun the process of paving over the gaping hole torn by grief: it's a common way of getting through this thing alive. I can't blame her. I don't want to tell her of my rough experience of a year of repressed grief breaking open into a suicide attempt. Jan knows this stuff; she'll watch for it. Besides, we both agree that our daughters are much more mature than we were at their age. Nevertheless, I hope this book will help Addie push away that fresh cement before it has time to harden.

Later that month, Jan was at our house for my husband's fiftieth birthday, where she met an old friend of ours, Bill Merryman, our daughter's godfather. Within a month, they began seeing each other. And, as I sat at my computer one day, a line that Jan had shared with me from a conversation with Bill ran through my head: "Something died in my heart." He was referring to his reaction to *his* father's death when he was fifteen. Jan and I had talked about the bond the early death of a parent can create between people. The feeling is relief: "They know. They understand. I don't have to explain or hide." What would happen, I wondered, if we interviewed women and men whose parents died when they were children? Could I finally hear my brother's story—the one he seems either reluctant or unable to tell? Would it help if he could read mine? Could a new kind of healing begin for an old and buried pain if lots of us began to talk?

That night I was having dinner at the house of a friend whose husband had died two years before, when their daughter Emma was only ten months old. Before I even spoke with Jan, I talked to Sue about my idea for this book. She loved it. In some ways this book is also for Emma, when she grows up.

It's for my brother, of course, and for my friend Ellen, my oldest friend—the girl who was my best friend when we were girls, and the woman I had remained tied to for nearly forty years. In October, a year after Peter died, Ellen's brother called to tell me that she had just been operated on for a malignant brain tumor.

As I built my Day of the Dead altar a few weeks later, I had the impulse to put something of Ellen on it. Shaken by that quickly aborted gesture, I reminded myself that she was not dead. In the next moment, I reached into the box in which I keep altar objects and pulled out a card Ellen had sent to me a couple of years before—an architectural photograph of the Monadnock Building in downtown Chicago, where my father's office had been located. Ellen and I shared a love for architecture. In her extravagant script, Ellen had written that she was thinking of me and the stories I used to tell about my father. It struck me that she still thought of him, but, of course, Ellen was as close to a sister as I will ever know.

And now she is gone. She died a cruelly short five weeks after being diagnosed. I wonder if during that moment at the computer, when the idea for this book moved through my body and into my brain, that I didn't somehow know I would soon lose her and be left alone with all those stories that no one can listen to as patiently as Ellen could.

The Genesis, Jan's Version

After the first death there is no other.—Dylan Thomas, "A Refusal to Mourn the Death, by Fire, of a Child in London"

My mother died on December 1, 1958, three days shy of my eleventh birthday. That morning, my mother and father left for Minneapolis, an hour's drive from our house. She was two weeks overdue in what has variously been explained to me as her ninth and her twelfth pregnancy. (My family has always kept secrets, sometimes by simply refusing to talk about things, over long periods of time. I remember having exactly two conversations about my mother with my father after she died. And sometimes secrets grew because details were embellished. The result is I don't know simple factual things, like how many times my mother was pregnant.) I think we knew that she would remain in Minneapolis until the baby was born. I later learned that if she did not go into labor that day, her doctor intended to induce it. He administered Pitocin, orally, under the tongue as they did in those days. Her uterus ruptured. She bled to death, nearly instantaneously my medically educated friends reassure me now. Then, I was told she drowned.

The baby, my brother Phillip, was born by cesarean section, in her hospital room, after her death. He was a perfect and beautiful baby. I pieced the former together by eavesdropping on my father's conversations with the adults in the next few days. The latter I discovered for myself when I first saw him a week later.

That same day, Holy Angels School burned in Chicago, killing a number of children and their teachers. I had only recently begun to watch the news. That fire on the ten o'clock news remains etched in my memory. I went to bed edgy. Later, I don't know what time, I woke to the sound of voices. I met my father in the hallway. I think he said, "We lost your mother." But I don't know. It sounds like something he could have said. The fact of my mother's death didn't even begin to sink in until I got to the living room and my Aunt Rosalie put her arms around me and held me tight. We were not a hugging family. At first, I thought she was laughing. Slowly and with great embarrassment, I realized she was crying. This is the first time I remember seeing an adult member of my family cry. If my mother or father, or any of their siblings, cried two years earlier when her father and his mother died, they did not do it in front of the children. I don't remember my grandmother crying that night. I do remember her sitting on the couch, cursing her anger at my mother for getting pregnant, at the doctor, at my father. Somebody shushed her. This early lesson that it's not okay to express grief, especially in front of children, haunts me still, years after I came to know better intellectually.

The next morning, we went to mass. From the altar, the priest announced that the mass would be said for the repose of the soul of Phyllis Johnson, who died last night. I remember the school kids in the front row braving the nuns' wrath by turning around to gawk at us. Although I didn't have a name for it then, I felt the sting of pity stares and knew I was different, an orphan.

I have carried the fact of my mother's death with me through life. In a way, the seed for this book lay dormant in me for more than thirty-five years. In some very real, albeit subconscious, ways, her death affected my choice of spouse. I chose a very mothering man. Our marriage lasted for seventeen years, until Peter needed to leave it to live out his late-in-life realization that he was gay. Then, in the fall of 1992, events took another unexpected and traumatic turn. Our daughter, Addie, was sixteen when Peter dropped dead one Sunday evening. Although Peter and I had not been living together for over three years, he was still intimately involved in my life as coparent, friend, family member whose relationship to me had no name.

When the phone rings at 11 P.M. on a Sunday, it's hardly ever good news. On October 11, 1992, it was terrible news. Addie answered. Peter's friend asked for me. I laid down my book and walked to the phone on automatic pilot. "Don't think about how bad this could be. Watch yourself walk to the kitchen to take the call." By the time I heard he was dead, Addie was at my side. I think she asked. I think I said, simply, "He's dead." We held each other. We were in shock.

Within minutes, I began making my own dreadful calls. I called my friends Amy and Lauren, then Addie called her friend Rachael and her mother, Penn. Within the hour, our house was filled with grieving women. I called my friend Margaret in Minnesota, my brother Phil in Indiana. I tried to reach Peter's brother Paul in Iowa. I was unable to reach him until the next morning. By then, I had begun to panic, thinking that I would have to break the news to their mother myself. That was a phone call I don't think I could have borne to make.

I found myself having to coordinate the many facets of Peter's abrupt death—from funeral plans and logistics for out-of-town family and friends to Social Security and other legal matters. And, of course, I grieved the loss of someone who'd been part of my life for more than twenty years. In those first hours, along with my grief I felt fear, or perhaps "terror" is a more apt term.

In a very real way, I became the totally bereft eleven-year-old I was when my mother died. "After the first death there is no other. . . ." That line, from Dylan Thomas's "A Refusal to Mourn the Death, by Fire, of a Child in London," has haunted me since I first read it twenty-some years ago in college. My mother's death was the first that really affected me. At every funeral I've attended since my mother's, I think of her. I see myself, my eight-year-old brother, and my father, following her casket up the aisle into a cold December church. My father's admonition not to cry, not to make a scene, echoes in my ears. It doesn't matter if they happen in high summer or the dead of winter, I am always cold at funerals. Mothers' funerals, no matter at what age they died, no matter what the age of their children, are particularly difficult for me. I have, in fact, avoided three mothers' funerals—my grandmother's, my mother's sister's, and my godmother's. All these women died in their seventies after long illnesses. I was too far away, too busy, too much in crisis myself to honor their dying with my presence.

Peter was not a mother, but, in many ways, throughout our marriage and especially in his life as Addie's father, he did mothering things. He cooked, cleaned, took care of us both. But more, he simply was a caring, loving presence. My mother was forty when she died. Peter turned forty-six the week before his death. He died suddenly. He left a shock wave behind him. In retrospect, it seems only natural that I would relive parts of that first death at the time of Peter's death.

As I sat that first night with Penn and Lauren, making a list of the things that needed to be done—enumerating tasks, dividing up phoning, making a logistical plan for the next few days—I lost my ability to concentrate. I said, "I just can't do this."

One of them said, "You don't have to. We'll make the phone calls."

"No, I mean," I said, "I can't *do* this. I can't stand for Addie to have the same terrible experience I had. This will affect her whole life." I have wise friends. Penn said, "Jan, you are not your father. Her experience will be different." Lauren reassured me that the only right way to proceed was to trust myself, to let myself feel my grief, and not to try to hide or bury it.

In the days that followed, that's what I did. I cried. I talked about my feelings. I met Peter's mother and brother, my brother, my chosen sisters Margaret and Nancy at the airport. I let my college friend Jim hold me. I let my friends Lynn and Ken rub my back. I let my friends Pat and Amy see that we were fed daily through that first week. I let my baby brother Phil run errands, pay my bills. I cried some more and told Addie, repeatedly, it was okay to cry. I held her hand. I told her how much I loved her. In some ways I could make Addie's experience different from mine. But what I couldn't do was make her pain or shock any less. Nor could I, in the end, avoid the paving over Leslie speaks of earlier. It happens. It has to happen. We can only deal with so much at any given time in our lives.

Plus, especially for children, there's a privacy to grief, a selfishness, some people call it, a part that doesn't want to share the dead parent with anyone. That was surely already operating in Addie's life. And I think that in my attempt to be open about my grief and about how much this death took me back to my mother's, I both scared and angered her. I scared her because she needed a mother, not an eleven-year-old bereft child. I angered her because, in relating my grief over my mother's death to her father's death, I think I seemed to her to be taking something away from Peter and her loss of him. That was, of course, never my intention.

Leslie called me shortly after she talked with Addie. She asked what she could do. She kept asking that question in the weeks that followed. Because of her own experience, one of the things that she could do was talk with Addie. She knew something of Addie's experience. She took Addie out for tea. She gave her books. She invited both of us over for dinner. She became a supportive adult in our world.

I know that it wasn't easy for Leslie. In order to be there for Addie, she had, in some way, to relive her own experience, let herself remember what it felt like to suddenly be without a father. Leslie and I began to talk about our mutual experiences. We went together to a Day of the Dead art exhibit. I told stories about my mother's death I hadn't told, or even thought of, for years. We began to rediscover how strong an impact a parent's death has on a child.

In the days and weeks following Peter's death, I spoke with others whose parents died when they were young. My main agenda, I thought then, was to ease Addie's way. If I gathered enough experiences that were better than mine, I thought I could weave together a net to catch Addie from falling too far into grief, or, at the least, a blanket to comfort her. In the end, I had to accept that there was no making it easier. There was no way her mother could protect her from the harsh reality of her father's death.

Nearly a year after Peter died, I met a new friend at Leslie and Don's house. Bill (who in this book has chosen to go by his given name, William) and I went out to dinner for the first time on the anniversary of Peter's death. As one does when one is getting to know someone, we exchanged the outlines of our lives. Death figured in both our stories. That night William spoke the line that cracked open the seed for this book and let it begin to germinate. He said, "When my father died, something died in my heart."

A few days after that dinner, I was talking with Leslie. Since she and William are old friends, she knew, of course, that his father died when he was fifteen. Neither of us was really surprised that the subject had come up. It has been my experience that people whose parents die young tend to find each other. And when they do, there's an almost instant fraternity-sorority of shared experience. Because William's line so moved me, I shared it with Leslie.

Within the week, Leslie called me. "I have an idea," she said. "I got it in part from Bill's line. I want to do a book about people whose parents died when they were children. And I want you to work on it with me." That was the beginning of *A Music I No Longer Heard: The Early Death of a Parent*.

Memory, Myth, and Storytelling

(Leslie)

Memory is a funny thing, full of both comfort and cruelty, gift and loss. Some people say we delude ourselves choosing to recall only the good times: the revisionist expression "the *bad* old days" is an attempt to poke at the nostalgia that can sickeningly sweeten a problematic past. We put on our pretty colored glasses and make of our dead parents heroes and saints. *Or* we develop a particular form of amnesia and refuse to remember anything about them, running from the pain, which also keeps us from the pleasure of the past.

My brother Marc was almost eleven years old when our father died, yet he claims to remember little of him. That hurts me. How can he not remember a father who adored him? A man who was devoted to him? Marc is supposed to be *with* me in this pain. Isn't that part of the sibling bargain—that we share the good times and the bad? Is it any wonder, then, that a small part of my loyalty to Ellen was that she never forgot the man called Charlie Simon? Now that she is dead, Marc *must* remember. And so this book is for me, also—the selfish act of a loving and still needy daughter. I will interview my brother. He will tell me his story.

Our memories, and the stories that hold them, compose and construct who we are. With memory, we retain identity; without it, we are lost. As we recover our memories and tell our stories, we expand our understanding of ourselves. In the opening of her first novel, *Ceremony,* Leslie Marmon Silko writes: "I will tell you something about stories. . . . They aren't just entertainment. Don't be fooled. They are all we have, you see, all we have to fight off illness and death. *You don't have anything if you don't have the stories.*" (Emphasis added.)

The scientists tell us that memory is a combination of chemicals and electricity. Déjà vu, they say, is merely a misfiring in the brain that occurs when we are tired. But poets prefer other kinds of explanations. And we can offer the oral traditions of many cultures to argue our case. In fact, as we approach the end of a particular stage of the modern era, there are scientists, physicists mostly, who pay homage to the work of some of the world's great spiritual thinkers, recorded in traditional literatures and mythologies: our lives are an illusion created by our minds.

Love predates science; science predicts love. Love is what we miss when the parent goes too soon. Even if that parent would not have given us all that we needed, even if their survival might have meant some abuse or neglect, the fact that we have no person with whom to complete our understanding of the most primary of relationships affects us.

"Storytelling is a lost art," they say. And with that art has gone a portion of our souls. In writing of the value of oral traditions, Frank LaPeña argues that without the knowledge of the elders, a culture loses its strength. What happens when an elder dies before he or she has passed on important information? The loss is irretrievable unless someone else shares the original knowledge. Of course, not all elders are equal, and not all parents carried the best parts of their cultures. That doesn't matter. The child needs to know *what* came before, *which* stories he or she would have heard had the parent survived the child's adolescence. So when a parent dies, we need to try to piece together what they knew and who they were with stories.

I awoke this morning to hear Paul Robeson's voice on the radio: "Sometimes I feel like a motherless child, a long way from home." And I remember the story my mother told me, just within the last year, of how she went to a Robeson concert in someone's home when she was pregnant with me. My mother is eighty; had she died when I was a teenager, or younger, I wouldn't have this piece of family history.

I don't know which stories of my father I have missed. Of course, I'm lucky. My mother, a talented storyteller, has helped fill in certain blanks. But life is no fill-in-the-blank quiz with only one right answer. I'll never hear my father's version of certain stories, nor will my children. But I refuse to let his memory go. However we can, we retrace and recreate our pasts. The music we no longer hear comes back, rewritten but not forgotten.

As I began the work for this book, I was struck by how many writers I know of who lost a parent during childhood or adolescence: Charlotte, Emily, and Anne Brontë, Harriet Jacobs, Hans Christian Andersen, Virginia Woolf, C. S. Lewis, Gertrude Stein, Zora Neale Hurston, William Styron, Mary Gordon, Amy Tan, Brown Miller,

Robert Sward, John Nichols, Howard Fast, Suzanne Lipsett, Georges Perec, James Baldwin, Anna Quindlen, Diana O'Hehir. Am I drawn to those who share this experience, or are adults whose parents died young attracted to the craft of writing—the modern world's story-telling traditions? Do those who lose many of their own stories need to keep spinning narratives and lives of people they create and care for? Or are they trying to complete a conversation they never had the chance to finish?

Poet Audre Lorde called her autobiography "biomythography." In it she interweaves cultural myths and legends with personal history. Coming from the African diaspora culture, a culture ripped from its motherland, Lorde needs to recover those stories. Characteristically, diaspora cultures value language and all its manifestations—song, myth, legend, story. Talk becomes a kind of home. The farther people are from their homeland, the more they yearn to speak about it. People orphaned young also crave information about a dead parent. Sometimes all they can do is imagine.

The mother of songwriter and musician Jimi Hendrix, with whom he spent little time, died when he was a teenager. Hendrix biographer David Henderson postulates: "Perhaps it was the contemplation of his mother's death and her love of music when she had been alive that inspired Hendrix to fall so deeply in love with music—to the extent that he often lost himself completely within its magic." It seems, as Lorraine Hansberry advises, he had made something strong of his sorrow.

Whether it be through story or song, myth or legend, adults orphaned as children often find a way to keep alive the connection with the dead parent.

My brother is a professional photographer. His interest began with an after-school class he enrolled in at age thirteen. A therapist whom he saw in college conjectured that he chose this field because the rare, vague memories he had of our father were ones in which our father had a camera in hand, taking pictures of the family. Whatever the pull, my brother has also gravitated toward stories. Photography, film, and television are the postmodern world's storytelling traditions. The fragmented postmodern worldview recapitulates ancient wisdom: our lives are construct and illusion. We make it up. When we have less matter to play with, we substitute it with mind. And so the stories roll.

My brother did a series of photographs for a solo show when he was twenty-one. About five or six of them comprised a study of doubles: two doors, two phone booths, two stoops. Several years ago, I had my favorite one specially framed. My husband said I should give it to Marc. It records a gray Chicago day, either at the start or the end of winter. The central image is an empty catcher's cage at a park baseball diamond. The doubles are two bare trees: one stands, with branches spread, behind the cage and looks as if it's growing out of home plate; its double, whose branches have been cut shorter by the borders of the photograph, is outside of the cage, off to the right. My brother doesn't remember all the games of catch our father played with him. I told my husband I'll give Marc the photograph when he remembers—a statement full of both love and anger. *Why can't he remember? Why won't he face the pain?*

Will telling his story help him bring the second tree home? That is my wish. And then I can give him back his gift—the power of the storyteller, who makes up some of what he must know in order to remember who he is and what it was that came before him.

In James E. B. Breslin's essay "Terminating Mark Rothko: Biography Is Mourning in Reverse," in which he reflects on having completed his biography of the contemporary painter, he tells the story of his own father's sudden death from a heart attack, two weeks after the younger Breslin, seventeen, graduated from high school. That summer, his father's employer, Western Union, hired him as an office boy. Part of his job was to clean out "the 'dead' matter" in his father's files. Breslin comments on the ironic reversal: "I destroyed my father's papers; I compiled Rothko's."

He briefly alludes to Freud's theory of mourning—that it is terminable, that after bringing into focus each "memory and hope" associated with the loved one, after spending time with it, grieving it, and then letting go of it, you are healed. Your mourning is complete. Breslin likens the mourning process to the work of the biographer, who also "takes in" the person whose life is being examined. Instead of letting the person go, however, the biographer releases the subject into the public realm, so as Breslin's subtitle suggests, "biography is mourning in reverse."

Like many people whose parents died young, Breslin used to worry that he would not outlive his father, who died at age forty-nine. Instead, when he reached that age, he began work on the biography of Rothko, whom he calls his "father's substitute."* Stories and songs and dreams keep our dead ones with us at the same time they help us let them go.

About fifteen years ago, I had a dream about my father. In the dream, he lies collapsed on the floor. I visit a doctor who tells me that we can revive him and keep him alive if we massage his heart twenty-four hours a day. I think, "No problem. We can split the day into three eight-hour shifts. My mother, my brother, and I could each take one." In the dream I call my mother and explain the situation to her. She readily agrees to take her shift. But when I call my brother, he's not so certain.

The way I see it, the project of massaging my father's heart represents the process of keeping his memory alive. And since Marc has little memory of our father, he couldn't very easily participate. But I think *I've* been blocking some important information, and the only way I can really help Marc with his fears is to face what I've buried. I am not the memory hero who will save my brother. We are all in this together. Assigning Marc his eight hours of toil puts me in charge, but it keeps me from getting at my own fears and buried memories, which is what, I hope, this book will do. I hope in that same way it will help others.

Now I remember a dream Marc told me about years ago and again more recently. He is sitting in the living room of my mother's apartment, where she and my brother moved about five years after my father died. Books line the walls and fill the room in aisles as they would in a library. Our father appears, standing with his back to the window with the setting sun behind him. He doesn't speak but with his eyes communicates a message of reassurance that everything's okay, that he's okay. My brother wants to talk to him, but our father's look tells him there's nothing they need to speak. There is a feeling of calm and peace. The dream soon flashes to a night scene in the same apartment. And the books are on fire. My brother panics at the thought of losing our father's legacy, his stories. A man appears with his young son to help him put out the fire and save the books. But whenever my brother tells me the story of this dream, he reminds me that it ends with the books still burning.

*Sadly, Breslin has since died.

Every time we go back to one of our identifying stories or dreams or jokes, it is as if we are taking them in our hands, holding them, caressing them, as we would a favorite rock found at the beach and placed on a shelf so that we might remember the bright sun of the day and the friends we were with and how we felt, why we picked up the stone in the first place. The beauty of dreams and stories is that they do not take up any room on the shelf, and if we no longer need them, we can forget them. But if we tell them to enough people, sometimes they take on a life of their own. Someone else writes them down and offers them up to other people who might get some use out of them. You never can totally know when the story or dream you no longer need is just the thing that will save someone else's life. It pays to talk.

We mourn together. We mourn alone. We finish and begin again. Complete? Maybe. Finished? Never. No matter what, we'll always want to tell the stories. Of the day our mother or father died. Of the time before, and how we have survived since then.

As I sit and listen to other people's stories, I hope I can attend them with the grace and humility that come from knowing my own grieving process has at times been blocked. I want this book to be an ongoing companion for those of us who have lost our parents before we grew up. I want us to bring to these tellings all of our half-formed, partially remembered, and, sometimes, well-rehearsed stories.

My hope is that I can come away from this with something much more true than the original canned talk I had planned to give Addie. That a parent's death *is* a kind of end to your childhood, that you never *do* get over it, that something *does* die in your heart, but that as you go on with the work of shaping your life, something else will come alive.

A Formative Experience

(Jan)

The movie *Shadowlands*, the story of C. S. Lewis's marriage and love affair with Joy Gresham, ends with her death. In one of the early scenes, Lewis recounts to Joy, who is visiting his home for the first time, the story of his mother's death when he was a young boy. He says, "It was the end of my world." When Joy dies, Lewis is once again at risk of having his world end.

In the final scene, Lewis walks through a meadow, saying, "Twice in this life I've been given the choice. The boy chose safety. The man chooses suffering, the pain now is but part of the happiness then." Lewis perceived that he had two chances in his life to know love and suffering, essentially to be open to life at its fullest. The first time, when he was a child and his mother died, he chose safety. This time he was choosing love. He was choosing to be in the world, not closed to it, to suffer his grief in order to remember his love.

"Of course," I almost said aloud, through my tears, in the movie theater. But later I decided I did not agree with Lewis, or at least not the portrayal in the movie. I do *not* think the child can choose love and suffering when a parent dies, at least not for many years. Children can do nothing but shut down. Their world *is* at an end. Something in their hearts inevitably dies.

The child didn't sign up for the good times with the parent, didn't choose the happiness and love, with the knowledge that things change and sorrow may well follow. A child simply can't do that. A child lives in the here and now as if it were forever, and if the trust in the parent is broken by the parent dying, then there's really nothing to do but despair or shut down. The parent is gone. If that can happen, anything can, and it is better, far better, to believe in nothing, to hope for nothing, to bury one's feelings with the dead parent.

My second thought was that the main life task of the child of a parent who dies is to somehow reopen to life. That task can take years, decades, or never be accomplished. Because of the shutting down, the death of a parent is very much a formative experience, coloring everything else for years to come. It's hard work to choose love and suffering, to put away fear, despair, denial, superficiality, and to feel. The adult Lewis, after many false starts, was in the process of doing that, first when he fell in love with Joy and then, later, when she died. I have been working at this task for more than twenty years, and I've come to the conclusion that it can never be done, it is something we keep doing. In talking with others for this book, I began to feel hope from the transformational experience of others.

I particularly began to feel the hope when I talked with my niece Jessica, and later with my younger brother, Phil.

At age twenty-three, having recently graduated from college, full of life and promise, Jessica came to see me, to reconnect with me. Her father, my brother Paul, was halfway between eight and nine when our mother died. He married Jessica's mother, Lynda, when they were eighteen, and divorced her when they were in their early twenties. In Vietnam, something happened to him, as it did to thousands of others. He was never the same when he came home. Although I believe he tried, he was unable to connect to his children, his family, his own life. He withdrew.

When Jessica was sixteen, her mother died, a suicide. Seven years later, Jessica came to me, in part, to connect with someone related to her by blood, and, in part, to have me tell her the *real* story of her mother and father, their marriage. What happened? she wanted to know. How did the darling, childhood sweethearts become grim, worn down, crazy, withdrawn, dead? I told her stories, I shared details: what I knew to be true because I'd seen it, what I believed to be true because I'd heard it from Paul or Lynda, what I conjectured. And conjecture is mostly what I talked about. In the end, my comfort was cold, I think. I said to her: "There is no knowing the all of other people's lives. And since you have no parents to tell you, you have only one choice. You must reconstruct the stories as best you can. You must use your imagination and your spirit."

The comfort may have been cold, but the connection was there, between us, the survivors. We shared stories of her mother, then of my mother, the grandmother she'd never known. We talked about how we felt about our lives, and what we each wanted to make of them and how our mothers fit into that equation. What did we get from our mothers? What did we want to do differently than they had?

Shortly after I began work on this book, my brother Phil phoned one night to say that he and Angela were going to have a baby. After sharing the happy news, he asked a question. They had been to see the doctor. The doctor took a family history. When he heard that Phil's mother died in childbirth, he wanted to know details. My brother called me, figuring I was the only living person who might share those details. The conspiracy of silence my family engaged in beginning the day my mother, Phyllis, died in childbirth, leaving us with a baby Phillip, was still in me, so deeply ingrained that even as I began to tell him the precious little I knew, my gut rebelled. My voice came high and tight from my throat. Breaking the conspiracy of silence with my niece was one thing. But talking with Phil, my baby brother, after all these years of silence, was something else entirely.

In the weeks that followed, Phil and I had several more phone conversations. We talked about what it felt like for him to have to go to a memorial mass for the mother he never knew, every year on his birthday. We talked about how it felt to have a stepmother we all pretended, for "his sake," as my father said, was our "real" mother. (I want to say here that our stepmother, who died during the time this book was being born, was a very fine person *and* the only mother Phil ever knew. However, she could never make up for the loss of my mother, his other mother.) Phil told me about a family party when he was about six. Somebody said something about Phyllis, our mother, maybe that he looked like her. He asked to see a picture of her. His memory is that the whole roomful of adults went silent, a more powerful message than any number of words to a child. He never asked again.

I hung up the phone after that long conversation in which we talked about childhood memories and feelings about our mother—or, in his case, his total lack of knowing her—for the first time in thirty-five years, and I wept. I wept for all the years of silence. And I wept in joy that the silence was broken. Someone should remember Phyllis Johnson, nee Schuneman, out loud.

All of us who have lost our parents before we could know much of them must rely on the stories of others, we must fill in the blanks with what we believe to be true. We must acknowledge that something did die in our hearts. Our worlds have ended. And we must, somehow, start them up again, reopen to life.

Losing a parent to death is *a* formative experience, not *the* formative experience. Of course, all of our experiences as children form and inform our adulthood. Who we are is based not only on the genetic code and personality we were born with, but on the story of what happens next. One good way to figure out our formative experiences and their impact on our lives is, as I told Jessica, to share the stories and to speculate when you don't have "facts." Another good way is to read the formative stories of others. That's, of course, what this book is about.

Reductionism, Dismissal, and Denial

(Jan)

It is not our thesis that adults whose parents died as children are the only ones cut off from emotion. To postulate that would be foolish and fly in the face of the evidence before our eyes—the children of poverty, racism, abuse, and addiction, children who live in war-torn countries, children who struggled with life-threatening diseases of their own. All of these children, as adults, have particular issues to resolve, fears to overcome, losses to grieve. Indeed, as Judith Viorst points out in her book *Necessary Losses,* each and every one of us struggles with loss in our lives. It is, she posits, one of the things that both forces and helps us to grow into adulthood.

Given our predilection as a culture to examine, reexamine, and then look at all of life's problems again, in desperate search for cause and effect—if we know what happened, then we'll know how to fix it—it is far too easy to fall into reductionism. I am like I am, with all these problems, because . . . And then we name the past trauma du jour: my father drank, my mother beat me, I had an abortion, I grew up poor. One might insert here, my mother or father died suddenly or after a long illness when I was three or nine or thirteen. The tendency to attribute all of one's current troubles to past trauma or grief—of any kind—is reductionism. We are not proposing that all adults who suffered the death of a parent at an early age do or even try to attribute whatever happens next in all the days of their lives to that one fact. Yet, some people do attempt to deal with the death of a parent in this way—and never get on with their lives.

Others talk about how their parent died, but it was so long ago that they never think of it. Dismissal of past sadnesses is no better way to deal with them than reductionism. People who dismiss the effects of trauma in their lives tend to dismiss everything else in their lives as well. There are no peaks because there are no valleys. There is no love because there is no loss. There is no joy because there is no grief.

Then there's denial. It has aspects of what we're calling reductionism and dismissal. Okay, fine, so my mother or father died when I was four, or twelve, or sixteen. But I don't remember him. Or I was pretty much grown-up when she died. It didn't really affect me then, and it certainly doesn't make any difference in my life now.

Of all the possible traumas in this life, death is the only inevitable one. We all die some time. What happened to the people in this book is, of course, that we experienced the death of a parent earlier than most people do. We are in the approximate 5 percent of the population who become orphaned before we reach maturity. Yet, it is important here to echo the words of many of the people we talked to. In struggling to explain the effects of their parents' death on their current lives, they repeatedly urged us to remember two things: that this is their life, the only story they know; and a constellation of events, of which the death of their parent is one, has gone into making that life. We respect that message. We have lived it.

The other message we heard time and again from the people we interviewed for this book, some of whom have professional experience in the helping professions, and from others—psychologists particularly—is that it's important to say that this fact of death never goes away. The intensity of mourning diminishes, the effects linger. At a dinner party one night, a therapist of my acquaintance told me, "If you get no other message across in this book, please convey that this never goes away entirely." Her concern seemed to be that people waste an incredible amount of time and energy trying to erase the past, when what they might be doing is incorporating it, transforming it, bringing themselves into their present lives.

Grief is territory in which comparisons are meaningless. Is my mountain of loss higher than his? My valley of despair lower than hers? Do children who lose their parents at an early age suffer more than children who live with the daily threat of bombs? Than children who go to bed hungry at night? Clearly, no. Yet to suffer devastating loss is to suffer devastating loss. And it is in relating the particulars of one's loss and sharing the similarities and differences with others orphaned young that one finds the seed of recovering from that loss.

Leslie and I began to share our stories when Peter died. I met William and the sharing went on. When we realized what happens when people share significant stories about their lives, we decided to do this book. We wondered what would happen if we simply asked questions that led others to tell their stories. What happened is this book.

2

The Way It Was

What a jumble of things I can remember, if I let my mind run, about my mother; but they are all of her in company; of her surrounded; of her generalised; dispersed, omnipresent, of her as the creator of that crowded merry world which spun so gaily in the centre of my childhood . . . there it always was, the common life of the family, very merry, very stirring, crowded with people; and she was the centre; it was herself.—Virginia Woolf (m, 13), Moments of Being

We were always poor, but while my mother lived we children never realized that we were poor. . . . She was a wise woman, and if a wretched tenement was less than her dream of America, she would not surrender. She scrubbed and sewed and knitted. She made all the clothes for all of her children, cutting little suits out of velvet and fine wools and silks; she cooked and cleaned with a vengeance, and to me she seemed a sort of princess.—Howard Fast (m, 8), Being Red

Ask every person if he's heard the story, and tell it strong and clear if he has not, that once there was a fleeting wisp of glory called Camelot.—Camelot

When her husband was shot, leaving her two children fatherless and the nation stunned, the young Jacqueline Kennedy gave her bereft children and the nation a way to remember what came before. She said, "Call it Camelot." The Broadway musical had been a favorite of

Jack Kennedy. Camelot came to mean a time of innocence and hope. To many, nothing would ever seem the same after that event.

The people whose stories fill this book suffered the loss of a parent in childhood, and their lives were irrevocably changed. When we asked them to remember the time before the parent's death, some did describe it as a kind of Camelot—cohesive families with plenty of love. Others told us they experienced no such golden place or time. There may have been abuse or neglect, or perhaps a prolonged illness, with death bringing relief, albeit a relief mixed with guilt and shame. Still others had had troubled childhoods that became more lonely or even less protected after the main event. Some, too young to remember much, can only cherish the traces of memories they do have, memories often bolstered by stories from a surviving parent or older sibling.

Every tragedy has its "before and after." One day a child's life feels normal, and the next day it feels as if the world has torn apart. The death of a parent becomes a defining event in personal history. Afterward, the child or adolescent can always be identified as the girl or boy whose parent died. But somewhere in time, a little girl still dances with her mother, and another rides horses with her father. Somewhere a young boy sits at a kitchen table telling his problems to his patient mother, while another buys a special birthday present for his quiet, reserved father. Still another suffers daily beatings from his unhappy mother. Whatever the circumstances, by telling their "before" stories, the people here begin to come alive as real people, not simply orphans, statistics, or curiosities. The past counts. It's part of who we are. It matters. No matter if it comes through the blurred lenses of tragedy and time. We need to know the "before" so we can make sense of what came "after."

In this chapter as in all the chapters, you will meet a cross section of the seventy people we interviewed. Some in small snippets like black and white snapshots; others, in a bit more detail, like a full-color photograph. This chapter provides an opportunity to get a feel for the wide range of people we interviewed, and it also offers a sampling of the kind of settings early loss interrupted.

Varieties of Camelot

No childhood is perfect. But some are definitely happier than others. We cast a broad net as we collected these stories under the Camelot heading. What ties them together is not only a strong positive feeling for the parent who died but also a home life that provided a solid base to help people cope with what came later. For example, although Horace Silver and Lauren Muller came from very different circumstances, they both felt a special bond with the parent who died, and remember their early years with affection.

After nearly sixty years, Horace Silver still speaks of his mother's love and support. A renowned jazz musician and composer, he wrote a tune called "My Mother's Waltz" about the times the grown-ups filled his mother's kitchen with music and dance. He has said that he hopes that tune reflects his mother's inner beauty.

Horace Silver, musician (66, m, 9)

I was living with my mother and my father in Norwalk, Connecticut, where I was born. We lived in an alley in a poor people's dwelling, where there was no hot running water. We had electricity and a toilet in the house, but it wasn't modern—it was just a wooden toilet with a chain. Dad worked in the Norwalk tire factory, where they made tires for automobiles and rubber soles and heels for shoes. And Mother did part-time domestic work. She tried to teach me right from wrong, and my dad always taught me not to be prejudiced, regardless of how the white race treated the black race at that particular time in history. I loved my dad, too, but Mom was always my favorite, because I could sit down at the kitchen table and pour my heart out to her. She was really kind to me. She was understanding, and she listened.

の

Lauren Muller treasures the memory of her father's unique blend of responsible citizen and rebel. She describes her earlier years with her flamboyant parents as close to perfect.

Lauren Muller, writer (34, f, 11)

I was living in Sewanee, Tennessee, a small town of about 2,000. We lived in a house out in the country overlooking a bluff. I had three younger sisters. My father was a doctor, the surgeon, the person who delivered babies. He was a Christian who believed in service, so he wanted to work in a rural area where he would be needed. He gave me horseback-riding lessons, and he was very strict, but he would also get really excited by how good I was. My parents loved to have a good time. My mother had been Miss Alabama and a runner-up for Miss America. My father had very blue eyes and sort of curly hair. He looked a lot like Paul Newman. Some of the Newman movies, like *Cool Hand Luke,* made me think of him. Luke, of course, was very much a rebel. I thought my father was as well. I think he was sort of a rascal in a way, as well as a hero-saint. There was a feeling about those days, as if it were a golden time in our lives.

༺༻

Despite the pain and natural disorder that follow tragedy, Deborah Nagle, Robin, and Teresa have not forgotten the special times they shared with their beloved fathers.

Deborah Nagle, writer (46, f, 12)

I was living in Wayland, Massachusetts, which is seventeen miles west of Boston. It is a secluded, wealthy area, along Paul Revere's trail. I grew up in a little idyllic childhood, the oldest of seven. I was the only one who had a real relationship with my father. I was the one who looked like him, and I was the smarty. When the new encyclopedias would come, he and I would sit and face each other, start at opposite ends, and just read. I used to sit down on the floor beside him when he was in bed watching something like *Victory at Sea,* and he would explain to me what was going on, so we shared a lot of private moments together. My dad was involved in eastern seaboard Democratic politics. He brought John and Robert Kennedy around to different places in the late fifties and early sixties and he also brought them to our house.

Robin (46, f, 8)

We lived in an apartment in Chicago, and my father used to take the bus to work. When he walked home from the bus, I'd sit on the radiator and look out the window, waiting for him. He was the neatest man who ever lived. He was funny. He was loving. He was my protector. My mother tells me that my father couldn't sing on key. But I used to love to hear him sing. When I got sick, he would sit with me. And when I was cold, he would slide my feet underneath his seat. We used to go on walks together. I just remember being Daddy's little girl, really attached to him. And wanting to do for him, wanting things to be special for him.

Teresa (32, f, 8)

I was the oldest of five children. We were living in a cotton and tobacco town in Virginia. My mom taught home ec before I was born, but she stopped when she got pregnant with me. My dad worked at a country club. He started out as a caddie, then he moved from caddie to waiter, and from waiter to bartender to maître d'. He was managing the dining room when he died. One of the strongest memories I have is of my dad shaving in the morning. I used to go into the bathroom and he would have a cigarette on the toilet tank, a cup of coffee, and a little transistor radio. He would take forever to shave. I remember being in there with him, and I would sit on the toilet seat and watch him shave. I just thought this was the coolest possible thing in the world.

∽

Camelot stories often emphasize the stability, strength, or spirit that the parent who died had represented.

Rose (87, m, 13)

My parents were both still greenhorns, who had been living on the Lower East Side, and my mother took boarders in from Europe. One day, my father quit his job and went looking for a place to open a tailor shop. He rented this spot right across the street from Columbia

University and opened up his shop. My mother took all the measurements and did all the bookwork. She was very smart. Everyone came and asked her advice. She was also a disciplinarian, which was probably good for all of us. I admired her. She wasn't beautiful in a conventional sense but was stately and had nice features. As long as she was well, it was a nice life.

Gloria Anzaldúa, poet and writer (52, f, 14)

I was born on Jesús María Ranch in South Texas. We moved around from a series of farms that were rented out by Rio Farms Incorporated, in a kind of sharecropper system. When I was about eight, my father decided that we would no longer be migrants, because it kept me out of school. So the family stopped migrating, and he continued on his own without us for a year or two. I remember my father on the tractor or in the truck, feeding the animals, being with the horses, playing around with us, taking us to the beach, being silent. He was a quiet man, who never had to raise his voice. All he had to say was "Quit it" if he wanted us to stop doing something.

∝

A number of people, when asked to recall their mother or father, returned to moments when their parents were in motion: from riding a horse to gesturing intensely during a conversation. By visualizing a parent's specific movements, the orphaned child, now grown, can know for certain that the mother or father had really once been alive and was not just a framed photograph on the bookshelf. By revisiting the dead parent's sense of style or humor, their love for books or people, the adult holds on to what the child once knew.

Doreen (36, m, 10)

We lived in the same house all my life prior to going to college. My father was working full-time for the Springfield Armory in Springfield, Massachusetts. He was, I think, at that time, a toolmaker or a model maker. My mother returned to work when I went to kindergarten. I don't remember for sure, but I think she was working at the book bindery. I have some positive memories of the time before she died. I remember dancing with her in the living room. She had been a really good dancer, an incredible dancer. She had won lots of awards for lindy-hopping. She was hot stuff. So we were always practicing the latest dances.

∽

When a single parent dies, the hole they leave can be especially wide.

Detta (47, m, 17)

My parents had a stormy marriage and were divorced when I was in eighth grade. My mother, brother, and I moved to Philadelphia to be near her big extended Italian family. They all viewed my mother as this wild free spirit. At some point, before my parents were divorced, she had gone away on a business trip with my father and come home a redhead, which was just horrifying to her family. But she looked good as a redhead. She was not the first to be divorced in the family. But she was the first one who thrived on it.

Joe (28, m, 12)

I guess the most vivid memories are scenes of my mother dancing. She had a great spirit and a great sense of humor, considering what she had been through during the war in Europe. There's one story that really shows my mother's positive spirit. She had a fake breast, one of these prostheses, because she had one of her breasts removed because of the cancer. She was waitressing one day, and one of the older golf pros started to touch that breast. She obviously couldn't feel it. He's thinking he's turning her on, but she was totally oblivious, paying attention to other things. Here was a woman who had lost part of her sexuality—one breast was gone; the other, partially removed— and she had all these scars, yet she could tell that story and laugh.

Daniel Meyers, filmmaker (34, f, 18)

I grew up in Southern California with my parents and sister. My fa- ther, a poet, taught college. We spent a lot of time together and were very affectionate with each other. He had enormous confidence in me and treated my ideas and thoughts as equal to his. He would debate me, challenge me, at nine, ten, eleven years old. He gave me books on Lao Tsu, he gave me the Bhagavad-Gita, the Old Testament, the New Testament. We read from the Koran together. We read Zen koan stories.

But he had a negative side also. He had had a very bad childhood. His mother used to spank him, beat him, and he was sent away from home, abandoned. As an adult, he had a ferocious temper and extreme mood changes. He'd explode at me for whatever reason. Sometimes he'd hit me. I was never seriously hurt, but it's something you shouldn't do. Fortunately, I knew he was crazy in his own way. Every time after he sent me to my room or spanked me, he would come in tears and apologize, saying he was so sorry, he couldn't help it, he didn't know why he did it. Occasionally, he'd say his mother had spanked him. One day, I remember lying there in bed, crying a little bit, thinking, "It's not my fault, it's his problem, he's nuts, this is his thing, and a lot of it has to do with his mother." From that point, it didn't bother me as much. I had a lot of compassion for him.

Monica (30, m, 10)

We lived in rural Mexico, in a tiny town in the mountains. My mother owned a grocery store and a house. She built her store from scratch, all by herself. She tried to do her best, but she had six kids. My dad had left her when I was six months old. In those days, if a man in Mexico left a woman with her kids, and she was single, she was considered a loose woman, so my mom couldn't go to church. The way she used to pray was that she read the Bible a lot. She used to teach us different prayers. She used to tell us stories, but I never knew until I became a woman that they were actually Bible stories. She would say that she knew these people named Samson and Delilah.

We rode horses, and she owned a gun for protection. We used to go through this river, near a big green rock, and she always used to aim at it. You could hear the sound of the bullet echoing through the whole canyon. I remember one time we were coming back from another town. All of a sudden, my horse got scared and reared up. When I turned around, the only thing I recall seeing is my mom, pulling the gun out, aiming, and shooting at this snake, all in one smooth motion.

My mother was generous. When the holidays hit, she'd cook big-time, for the homeless. We had a book, pages and pages of accounts, people who owed her a lot of money. She never bothered to go and ask them to pay, because she knew they didn't have money. But not everything was positive. I forgave my mom for the way she released her stress. Unfortunately, all my sister remembers is the whippings.

No Sweet Paradise

We knew we didn't want to fill this book with stories of idealized parents, so we watched for any tendencies to mythologize the dead. On the other hand, when some people reported a pretty happy childhood before the death, we didn't want to relegate those stories to the land of fairy tale or fantasy. Instead, we honored them. Despite the precarious footing childhood memory must depend upon, those stories still seem to stand. Daniel Meyers and Monica gave realistic portraits of their less-than-perfect parents. But, in their stories, the good provided an antidote for the bad, so we called them a kind of Camelot. The following narratives, however, focus more on pain. In some situations, parental alcohol abuse clouded the relationship these children had with their parents, and, in others, physical or sexual violence caused damage, giving these people a particular kind of sorrow to deal with after the death.

Patricia, Mary J., and Edward's fathers all had problems with alcohol. Patricia gave up on her father early on. She recalls what was lost before the final loss.

Patricia (48, f, 13)

My father worked probably ten hours a day. He was a milkman, initially, so he'd get up at three-thirty in the morning and not show up back home until three and then sleep all day. Some of my earliest memories are of sitting on the curb waiting for him to come home. I saw that the fathers of other kids would come home and hug them and smile. The dad would pick up the child and throw them up in the air, or whatever. There was some sort of ritual about arriving home. We didn't have anything like that. My father would get out of the car and go in the house, as if I didn't exist. After a while, you kind of catch on, even when you're tiny, that somebody doesn't really care a whole bunch about you. So, around age five, I think, I decided I wasn't going to sit on the curb anymore and wait for the bastard. It just wasn't paying off. So I stopped. I think I wrote him off about then. I think he was still an active alcoholic.

Mary J. (early 40s, f, 18)

My father was an alcoholic. He had been drinking since he was a boy. He was a farmer when he was sober, a flower farmer. I think my mother felt a lot of animosity towards him for making her life so miserable in the United States. She had come from this wealthy family and was very well educated for a Chinese woman. But her husband had this flower farm, where she had to work from morning to night. She left him when I was seven. He would threaten her and us. Once when she was fighting with him, she locked us up in a bedroom. He had this big cleaver hidden behind his back and was trying to get her to come out. But when he was sober, he was really wonderful. Very intelligent. Very creative. Very giving and loving. He'd give me flowers to bring to the teacher. On the farm, you cut them at the very bottom. They were bigger than I was.

Although Edward shared some good times with his father, he now realizes his father's alcoholism affected him.

Edward (30, f, 17)

We'd visit my father before he had the accident. We used to fly back, usually during the summer, and spend several months with him and his wife. I remember that he read a lot. For hours on end. I remember climbing up on his arm and trying to get him to go outside and do something with us. I remember watching the Watergate hearings with him. What a great Generation-X memory—to be with your single parent watching the Watergate hearings. That was how my dad and I bonded. But as I got older, I started to question why he took my brother and me to the bar at the Ramada Inn in the afternoon. I was about seven or eight. We would eat popcorn and run around on the floors and play James Bond while he sat in the bar and had a drink with the bartender. I have real mixed feelings about being introduced to the alcohol culture that way.

∽

When physical or sexual abuse marks a person's childhood, the adult survivor needs to make some sense of it. David Joseph speaks painfully of the regular beatings he suffered from his mother, who died in a car accident.

David Joseph, poet (40, m, 14)

I was living with my mother, father, and two brothers, about a mile and a half outside of Mt. Vernon, Washington. We lived in a little rented house with a barn and chicken coop, and also orchards and a garden. My father was a shoe salesman for most of that time, but he got a job in cattle insemination, and my mother was a grocery clerk. There was a lot of strife in our family. My mother would constantly talk about how unhappy she was and how she thought she should get a divorce, and how she was going to kill herself. My father was usually very silent and didn't say much, while my mother was yelling at the top of her lungs. And most of the time my mother physically abused my brothers and me. Despite all this, I guess my mother must have been a very talented person. Before she died, she took some art courses at the local community college. I was just amazed that she was doing all this great stuff, but she would look at it and say, "This is all really terrible, I hate all this stuff." All of it was destroyed by a fire the summer before she died.

∽

Laurie believes that her mother's illness contributed to her father sexually abusing her. She may be right, yet, sadly, many well mothers don't protect their daughters from sexual abuse.

Laurie (38, m, 13)

I was six years old when my mother fell off of a counter she had been standing on to clean some shelves. When they did a brain scan, they discovered she had a tumor. My mom had three major brain surgeries and had metal plates put in her head. Every time she'd come home from the hospital, she was a little bit less there. She had a hospital bed, and I did some of the care. Often my job involved preparing the meals for her, or giving her her medicine, or putting her on her commode. My dad rigged up this hydraulic lift, and I could lift her out of bed and put her in her wheelchair. It was pretty intense, caring for someone like that when you're eight years old.

My parents didn't really have a normal sex life, whatever that is, which I think came out in all of these weird ways in my father—exhibitionism, molesting kids. Also, I think he was shell-shocked from the war, the Korean War. You know, I was numb my whole childhood. Not to myself—I felt deeply. But I didn't express anything. Not to people. I cried while I held my animals, but privately, so no one could see me. I was angry and frustrated that my mother was sick, and there were times when I did lash out. I have a lot of sadness about that. But I feel my mother was very sensitive, which is the best of what I got from her, and if *I* understand why that happened, I know *she* did.

The situations of Eric Marcus and Melissa contained elements of confusion and chaos. Marcus reports how life with his mentally disturbed father, who ended up committing suicide, was difficult.

Eric Marcus, writer (36, f, 12)

I lived with my brother, who is two and a half years younger, and my sister, who is four and a half years older, and my mother in a one-bedroom apartment in Kew Gardens, Queens, in a 1930s apartment complex. The two years before my father's suicide when my parents were separated seemed the most normal. We saw my father every weekend or every other weekend. But I knew he was taking tranquilizers, and one of those days when he took us, he drove down the exit ramp of a highway thinking it was the on ramp. I didn't tell my mother because I was afraid that if she knew, she'd never let him take us anywhere. Years later she told me she was afraid that something terrible would happen to us, that we'd get killed every time he left with us, because she knew he wasn't well.

∽

Melissa, whose father killed her mother and then turned the gun on himself, frankly confronts the mixed portrait she carries around of each of her parents. She struggles with building a balanced view of both of them. Her anger at her mother, a battered woman, is not uncommon. Children often resent mothers who don't flee violent situations. The reality is that it's sometimes nearly impossible for women to escape, and the resulting tragedy speaks to the culture's need to provide more support for trapped women and children.

Melissa (28, m, 9, f, 9)

We lived in an upper-middle-class suburb near Los Angeles. My father was in construction, and my mother was a teacher. My father's personal decline was really marked by his increasing inability to keep a steady job. He was violent with my mom. He only turned on me once, which was very close to the end, but he was violent towards my brother and threatening to my sister. But I don't get to just be angry at him, because he had a lot of redeeming qualities. He taught me how to draw, which is one of my most treasured memories of him, just sitting there with him, and drawing. In a lot of ways, it was my job to take care of Daddy after he got home. I brought him his martini, sat down with him, and we'd take out the pens. We would just draw ellipses for an hour. Things like that. My mom was the primary care-giver. She organized it so that we'd all have responsibilities. I never remember her making a lunch for me. It was always a do-it-yourself household, but she made sure we had the tools to do it ourselves. She was a good mom, and there are parts of her ideas about raising children and just being in the world that I really agree with. But I don't get to just have those feelings. I always temper them with the reality that she didn't get us out of the house. What kind of mom would do that to her kids?

Traces of Memory

When a child under the age of eight loses a parent, often the memory of that parent is vague. Mary Montgomery, Suzanne Lipsett, Brown Miller, and Jan B. all have only small scraps, as Lipsett calls them, of memory. And, like Lipsett, they all seem to treasure these remnants, constructing from them a version of the time "before."

Mary Montgomery, who was only three when her father died, recalls the pieces of her father's clothing that her mother saved—his scarf, his hat, and his spats. It's almost as if a familiar ghost emerged as she spoke.

Mary Montgomery, writer (61, f, 3)

I don't remember much about my father. But I do have a memory of sitting around a stove looking at men in overalls, one of whom must have been my father. I have only the vaguest memory of him teaching my brother the Lord's Prayer. He was a kind of cowboy farmer. My mom saved a silk scarf of his, some gray suede spats, and a big ten-gallon cowboy hat.

ॐ

Although Suzanne Lipsett keeps this only surviving memory alive, she admits it might be inaccurate. She cherishes it, nonetheless.

Suzanne Lipsett, writer (51, m, 4)

I have a kind of memory or memory scrap, which I've always treasured, of being stung by a bee and having my mother take care of it. I remember her hands. Actually, I haven't thought of her in a long, long time, but I remember someone taking the bee stinger out and touching me wherever it was, maybe on my arm, but it's one of those close-ups on the hands. It may not have been her.

Brown Miller, poet (51, m, 6)

We lived in a small town where the summers are very hot, so in the evening, when it was cooling off, I would lie by my mother's side in the backyard on some lawn furniture, and she would sing to me. There's a specific song I remember her singing about the moon. That memory sort of illustrates the closeness, and a sense of her understanding my needs. That's maybe my most pleasant and most tender memory.

∽

Around the age of eight, generally, children experience a more secure sense of their own identity, and memories often become more clear.

Jan B. (50, f, 8)

One memory that I have of my father is really dear to me. It's real sacred and real vivid, too. And I'm sure I built a whole mythology around it. We were in Washington, in Spokane, and my mother flew home to Omaha because she was pregnant. My father and I and my sister drove home. And one night, late at night, as we were driving, I was sitting in the front seat with him, in my mother's place—this is probably real Oedipal—and a shooting star came up. My sister was asleep in the back seat, so it was one of those memories that he and I had together. And that is very precious to me.

Barbara Smith, writer (49, m, 9)

One of the things that I always tell people about my relationship with my mother and what her death meant to me is that I really hardly knew her. Like most black women, she had to work. We were brought as slaves and we've been working ever since. My sister and I got to spend very little time with her, except on her days off. But I have vivid memories of being about four or so, and she'd come home around the time it was time for us to go to bed. I do remember eating breakfast with her in the morning. And I remember she did take us to the library when we were six. She took us to get our library cards. That was a very special day, and a very special trip because it was a grown-up thing to do.

∽

Some people who were preteens and adolescents when their parents died, long for a stronger relationship with their mother or father.

Most of them, however, have managed to preserve a comforting memory of their dead parent.

Tron Bykle, artist (51, f, 14)

I grew up in Norway. My father lost his parents when he was three. He was dragged off on a sled by his older brother to this orphanage. I remember one story where they put buttons between their teeth when they got caned so they wouldn't cry. Having grown up in that orphanage, he had a pretty flat emotional life, except that he would get angry. He was like a silhouette or a shadow going through everything. I remember one time when I was eleven and he was about fifty. I had been working, barking this kind of timber. I made enough money to buy him this silver-plated cigarette case with the Scandinavian countries engraved on it, which I thought was absolutely gorgeous. I gave it to him for his fiftieth birthday. That was the only time I remember him actually trying to figure out what was I all about.

Sandy (46, f, 16)

I remember so little about my dad, which is a terrible loss to me. But I do remember him as a very hardworking, honest, ethical person. He wasn't formally educated beyond high school, but he cared a great deal about learning and read a lot. He worked night and day in a gas station, pumping gas. He used to have these terrible shifts, and I remember reading in the paper sometimes, "Gas station attendant held up," and it was my dad. There was a lot of scary stuff. He was always kind of grubby-looking. When he'd wash his hands, he'd have to scrub with real gritty soap for a long time. But I have a picture or two of him standing in front of the gas station with a nice smile on his face. His eyes kind of crinkle a little bit. He looks like a nice man.

Mariam (39, f, 13)

I'm the youngest child in a large family, and my father was much, much older than I was. He was from a very small town in Iran. The family was very traditional, and my father wouldn't really see the kids. So my brother, who was only one year older than me, and I were not really that familiar with him. He was living in the same house, but, mostly, we would only go whenever he came home to kiss his hand and say hello. He'd talk to us for a few moments, and then he would leave. Otherwise, he didn't get involved with children when they were kids. When my sisters were grown-up, they would go to his room and talk to him every night for an hour. Sometimes when he needed them, he would call them and they would come to his room. But, for me, basically, I knew he was Father and he was living with us. And that was it.

Shadows

A parent's prolonged illness can damage an otherwise normal childhood or adolescence. The child's "before" identity is shadowed by what would come after.

Emilia (62, f, 12)

We were originally from Cebu, in the Philippines. My father really was a jack-of-all-trades. He was a carpenter by profession, but he could do anything: fix a piano, make guitars, fix a violin. He liked to play pool and billiards. He was a gambler, too. We were not rich. I remember one time dancing with my father. I can remember the dress I was wearing, its colors. I can remember walking with him. But those good times didn't last. When Honolulu was bombed, eventually we had to evacuate farther into the hills. Before long, my father was arrested. In fact, lots of people were arrested in that area, whether they were civilian or not, including my oldest brother, who was only fourteen, fifteen years old. My brother never came back. My father was in prison for about six months. After he was finally released from prison, he developed beriberi from lack of vitamin B. And then one time when he came home after fixing a piano, he told my mother he had spit blood. He had contracted tuberculosis when he was in prison.

Janette (19, m, 12)

I remember I was five or six living in San Francisco when my mom was diagnosed with breast cancer. All through my life, often in school, everybody would say, "Oh, Janette's mother is sick. Janette's mother is sick." The teachers would always know, so if anything was wrong with me, they'd just say, "Oh well, you know, her mother's sick." I never really understood. All I knew is that it would end in death.

Rich (36, m, 14)

No one ever told me that my mother had cancer. No one ever really prepared me. She had periods of being very ill and then getting better and coming home from the hospital and seeming to resume a normal, although more limited life. But that last illness probably was real confusing to me because no one said anything to me, you know, that she's not likely to come home. I visited her almost every day, until the last couple of weeks. I'm not sure why I stopped, but it was right before my junior high school graduation. I had all these exams, and also it got pretty painful to see her in the condition she was in. She was unable to speak the last few weeks. I have one very vivid memory from, I think, the last time. And it's something that sort of haunts me because I have a lot of guilt about that memory. I went to see her in the hospital right after the junior high graduation awards ceremony. I had won all these awards. I knew she was the one person who would articulate that she was proud of me. Even though she was unable to say anything, I could see it in her eyes. But I felt guilty because it seemed that throughout the period she was ill, I kept needing her support. And, you know, even though I was a kid, in retrospect, I feel like I was real selfish.

∾

Ken Burns and Beto spoke of how they lived with the pain of knowing their mothers would die young.

Beto (52, m, 14)

I was living in Nogales, in Arizona, the border town, with my father and my mother and two brothers and a sister. Before my mother got sick, there had been some good times, some funny stuff. I remember her just hanging around, cooking, or sitting at the kitchen table, talking to her friends. She loved visiting with her friends. She liked to tell stories, she liked to laugh. She had a good sense of humor. She liked to be with her family. But after my mother got breast cancer, and she had a mastectomy, it was very depressing. With radiation treatment, she managed to stay alive for about three years, but in the last year she was bedridden. It was a very tough, very sad place to live. I had been very close with my mother. When she got really sick, I used to stay away a lot. I did not come home until two or three in the morning. I was always hanging around the streets. The worst thing we did was steal a car, and one time we set fire to a water tower. We didn't hurt anybody. We didn't carry guns, and we didn't smoke dope. But we did get into trouble. My mother was concerned and wanted me to go to church a lot. I used to lie, and say I had gone. My mother was happy to believe I was going to church, but I still was getting into trouble.

Ken Burns, filmmaker (41, m, 11)

My mother had had a radical mastectomy, and that was a shocking part of growing up. I remember she was in pain a lot, and I gave her back rubs and foot massages. I spent most of my childhood so terrifically tense about my mother's illness, and some foreknowledge of the doom of it, that I have very little memory of her love or her warmth or her smell, which my younger brother does. He remembers the smells, he remembers a sense of security. I remember I couldn't go on school trips because I would get stomachaches. I didn't want to leave home. We'd go off on a school trip, and I would get sick and have to be sent home. I would come home in tears, and my mother would comfort me.

The Way It Was

Just as historians from every perspective rewrite the Kennedy years, so we refashion and rethink our own personal history. Sometimes as the years pass, revision brings the illusion of a more accurate truth. But whichever version of the story we select, idealized or not, in every telling some aspect of the truth emerges. The way it was or the way it seemed is all we have. And while these stories sometimes feel fragmented, they continue to make us who we are. As we listen to the stories of early loss that follow, we need to remember that people who lost a parent much too young had a starting point. A jumping-off place. And from that place, they move on, to tell their private stories, first of disaster, and then, gradually, over many years, of survival, knowing that what they lost did not completely disappear. Knowing that the integration of the before and the after is part of their life's work.

3

Ground Zero

That moment was the end of a phase in my life. I was old before my time with grief of loss, of failure, and of remorse. . . . That hour began my wanderings. Not so much in geography, but in time. Then not so much in time as in spirit. Mama died at sundown and changed a world.—Zora Neale Hurston (m, c. 13), *Dust Tracks on a Road*

I saw the pigeons floating and settling. I got a feeling of calm, sadness, and finality. It was a beautiful blue spring morning, and very still. That brings back the feeling that everything had come to an end.—Virginia Woolf (m, 13), *Moments of Being*

He was only ten years old and had felt so alone . . . there was that memory, that awful visual image that returned to his nightmares, of the Kraus family plot in the Milwaukee graveyard buried deep in drifting snow the day they buried his dad. Ice. The frozen-hard ground into which they lowered the casket . . . that awful February day twenty-five years ago, the day that was the end of his childhood.—Randy Shilts on Bill Kraus (f, 10), *And the Band Played On*

The place where the bomb hits. The day the parent dies. Whether it's preceded by a prolonged illness or comes unexpectedly, the ground shakes and nothing remains the same. In Leslie Marmon Silko's novel *Ceremony,* the shadow of the atomic bomb testing at Trinity Site,

New Mexico, colors the entire story. The bomb literally poisons Indian land and it serves as a metaphor for the damage done to Indian culture by European America. But the bomb can also be read as a metaphor for the loss of the protagonist's mother, who abandons him when he is four years old and dies soon after. Silko captures the devastating moment when a child experiences incomprehensible loss and realizes that there's no turning back: "He remembered [that hollow feeling] from the nights after they had buried his mother, when he stuffed the bed covers around his stomach and close to his heart, hugging the blankets into the empty space of loss, regret for things which could not be changed."

Brown Miller, one of the writers we interviewed, talked about how his poetry has helped him come to terms with his mother's death, which occurred when he was six years old. His collection *Hiroshima Flows Through Us* includes the poem "Is That Hiroshima or My Mother?" where he imagines his mother trying to comfort him, explaining how she died. She becomes catlike, applying a loving tongue to his body. But the poem ends by saying that his mother and Hiroshima stand in for each other. And the devastation he experienced at her death cannot so simply be licked away.

Yet we do recover. The world trembles, powers rebalance, and we survive. Some of the healing comes from telling the story of the day the flash struck through our childhood. By reexamining what the ground looked like, by describing just how we experienced the bomb, by reminding ourselves of how we managed to get through it, we begin to make sense of the event that changed our lives forever. The recollection of the details of the death and its aftermath can be difficult, cathartic, and comforting all at the same time. We are reminded that we are not alone, even though most of us felt we were at the time. Most of us have so much to say about the day the bomb crashed through our lives. We remember every detail, although sometimes we wish we could forget. Or we remember very little—sometimes nothing—and wish we could reclaim our memories.

The age of the child when the parent dies is an important part of the picture at ground zero. People who were adolescents, going through adolescence's natural, but painful, separation from the parents, felt guilt, while younger children felt confused and sometimes excluded. Those whose parents had suffered an extended illness admitted to a mixed feeling of grief and relief and thus a different kind of guilt. In one case, when an abusive parent died suddenly, the child felt a kind of peace alongside sorrow. Funeral rites had various effects on the bereaved children. Some enjoyed the attention and the party-like atmosphere. Others felt disbelief: how could the body in the coffin actually belong to their mother or father? A couple of women, ten and twelve years old when their mothers died, spoke of wanting to be buried along with them.

We heard the "before" stories, and now we turn to the event that divided one side of these people's childhoods from the other.

The End of a World

In the natural order of the life cycle, children are supposed to survive their parents, but parents are supposed to live long enough to see their children grown, perhaps even with some children of their own. The child robbed of the second part of nature's contract feels the earth has cracked open. Nothing will ever be the same again. For most bereft children, there is a day in time when the world really was ending. In James Agee's *A Death in the Family*, Mary, the recently widowed young mother, draws her children to her: "'My darlings,' she said; she looked as if she had traveled a great distance, and now they knew that *everything had changed*. They put their heads against her, still knowing that *nothing would ever be the same again. . . .*" (Emphasis added.)

Jamie (45, m, 19)

I had the sense that my whole world had been shattered.

Patricia (48, f, 13)

I said to myself, "Your childhood is over."

Rob (44, f, 15)

There was a feeling that the whole sense of innocence was gone.

William (54, f, 14)

Something died in my heart.

∽

For Barbara Smith, the date of her mother's death holds a special power. When spoken, it almost feels like a mantra, used by a supplicant for prayer and meditation, a way to steady or center oneself in the face of terror.

Barbara Smith, writer (49, m, 9)

My mother died in 1956. It was the year the world changed. I remember overhearing a telephone conversation my aunt had with the doctor. He said our mother was sitting on a volcano seat—that it was touch and go. And then it came. The most horrible day of my life— October 16, 1956. My twin sister and I always came home from school for lunch. And it was very hot that day. I remember what we had on, I remember what we had for lunch. We were sitting at the kitchen table eating, and we heard a car pull into the driveway. We saw our uncle, and his wife, and our other aunt get out of the car. They came in, and our grandmother had this kind of upset look, you know, how somebody kind of turns their head in anticipation, a kind of like "what are you going to tell me?" look. And they said, "She didn't make it." That was it. I remember crying all afternoon. We just dissolved. We dissolved into tears.

Paul B. (53, m, 11)

I overheard my mom and dad talking about the swelling she had in her ankles. I was a pretty sensitive kid, real close to my mother, so I knew there were problems. I can remember the day she came back from a doctor's appointment when it was very clear that the situation was serious. The doctor wanted her to go directly to the hospital, and I was very scared. I can recall that fear being present, as I went to my aunt's. I remember going swimming with the other kids, which used to be a real exciting, fun thing, but I remember just feeling kind of an emptiness inside. I didn't want to get in the water. I didn't want to do anything. I had this impending sense that something bad was going to happen. She was in the hospital about three to four days. The only time I saw her—and this was over the Fourth of July—was the day after she was admitted. I remember my father drove me there, and she waved to me from the window. That's the last time I ever saw her. They couldn't get her kidneys to work. My brother was taken by cesarean. He survived, but she died there, a couple of days later. When my aunt came up the stairs to the bedroom and told me that my mother had died, her words were—and I'll never forget them—"The Lord took your mother tonight."

Eric Marcus, writer (36, f, 12)

The day my father died, my mother took me into her bedroom and sat me down on the bed. I can picture this scene as if it were yesterday. I don't remember her saying anything. I just remember my reaction. I remember she was sitting, looking at the bed; she was sitting on the right, I was sitting on the left. I remember her being a very big person, but she's tiny, so it makes me realize how small I must have been. I think I screamed, "No!" I just remember this searing, shocking pain, as if someone had taken a baseball bat and just hit me across the head. I ran through the apartment to the one place that I could always get away to, the only room where you could lock the door— the bathroom. I slammed the door, locked it, turned around and pulled all the towels off from the back of the door, and crumpled to the floor and just screamed into the towels.

Rose's grief was even more intense because her mother's illness had brought the two together.

Rose (87, m, 13)

The surgeon had made a mistake when he operated on my mother, so for five years she was in and out of hospitals, until finally my father insisted on having another doctor, who operated on her again. She recovered beautifully, and we were all so happy that we could be leading a normal life. But it only lasted a year. She was a brave lady and tried very hard to put on a semblance of feeling okay. The last time she came home from the hospital, I was only twelve, and my father couldn't get help. The stool would come out through the incision, and I would have to clean it. My mother was, well, you know, mothers are sometimes very partial to sons, but at that time, she said to me—it's something you don't forget—"It's good to have a daughter." That year, we were able to go up to the mountains. We were having a wonderful time, but around Labor Day things just seemed to go bad. She had to be taken home to a hospital. She died September the fourth. And it was very, very rough.

Shock

Shock is one of the most common reactions to trauma. Physical shock threatens the proper functioning of the body's systems. If the situation is not reversed, the condition can become fatal. The word "shock" has passed into common usage as a stand-in for acute emotional stress. We say a person is in "a state of shock," and it is as if he or she has departed for another country, far away from the place where the tragedy hit. He may return to school the next day. She may attend her best friend's birthday party. The reality of the loss has been suspended, and the expression of grief, which can be likened to a necessary bodily function, has temporarily shut down. Shock can last for moments, days, or years. In the latter case, it moves into the realm of repressed grief and can cause deep, but often silent or invisible, harm. For now, we are interested in the kind of shock that commonly hits at ground zero.

The received wisdom is that a prolonged illness can prepare survivors for the death of a loved one, but that's not always the case. Often hope continues to linger along with the illness so that when the bomb hits, it's no less of a shock.

Danny (30, m, 16)

The day my mom got sick for the last time, I was in school, and somebody told me to come to the office. They told me that my mom had a stroke. I was pretty much in shock. She stayed alive for about a week,

I think. My dad and his fiancée took me to visit her on a couple of occasions. She couldn't talk much, but I talked to her. She communicated with me by grabbing my hand. She slurred her words, but she said she loved me and all, and grabbed my hand, sort of kissing it. I was really scared at the time because she was obviously passing away, so, to this day, I feel bad because I kind of had to pull my hand away. I was so scared because I didn't want to accept it, I think. Earlier, my dad had been trying to explain to me that my mom was probably going to die. I remember walking home—it was five miles to my house—and I walked home. They said, "Be careful. Don't get hit by a car because you're not thinking clearly." I remember walking all the way home, and it didn't even seem like time—there was no time. She passed away, I think, the next day. I felt pretty numb. I had a kind of sunken feeling, but I didn't really think about what I had lost yet. I was still kind of in shock. I think the grief came later.

Some people remember every detail of their mother's or father's last day, but the shock of his father's murder blocked Walter's memory for the first few days. If we were to go back in time to that eleven-year-old boy's life, we might see him walking through a "normal" few days, but the emotional trauma has forever erased his memory of that time.

Walter Liggett, poet (70, f, 11)

My father had been a newspaperman, investigating a corrupt governor who had ties to the underworld. He was killed by a professional gangster. I heard the shots that killed him. I was in the apartment listening to the radio. I thought it might have been a car backfiring; then a second later my younger sister Marda ran into the apartment crying, "Daddy's been shot! Daddy's been shot!" I immediately rushed outside, and there was my father, in the alley behind the apartment, lying dead on his back beside a car, my mother bending over him. He had been shot five times around the heart with a Thompson submachine gun and killed instantly, or nearly instantly. My mother and my sister actually witnessed the killing. They were both in the car at the time. I remember all of that, but then I had a blackout for the next two or three days.

Tim (35, f, 17)

It was a Sunday afternoon. When I came back from playing football, there were about seven or eight cars in the driveway. A friend of my parents came up to me and said, "I'm sorry your dad's gone." I was shocked. At the time that I got there, my mother was already over at the hospital, so there wasn't anybody there except friends of the family. The absolute worst part of it all was coming home and someone telling me my dad's gone and not saying he had died or anything.

Lisa (28, m, 12)

The last time I saw my mom was special because it was Christmas. I had wanted this jean jacket—all the girls had them and I had to have it. Every Christmas my mom always got everything we wanted, but she couldn't find that jacket for me in my size. So I didn't think I was getting it. When she handed me the box and I opened it up, I freaked out, I was so happy. I just knew in my heart that she would never let me down. We were very poor—she had been a single parent and my father never really gave any child support—but no matter what, during the holidays she pretty much gave us everything she could. I don't know how she did those Christmases, but she did. Getting that jacket really hit me inside. I had just a warm, incredible feeling. But my dad came shortly after that to pick us up. He honked the horn, so we kind of left abruptly. I hugged her and thanked her for the present and all that, but I just wish I could have spent more time with her.

She died, with my stepfather, on New Year's Eve in a car accident, and I found out New Year's Day. I think when I was told, I was just in shock. My father tried to do the best he could, but he just said, "Your mom went to heaven." I thought, "What the hell are you talking about?" because I wasn't five years old. I guess maybe the way he said it shocked me. And then when it sank in, I just cried a lot.

Guilt

Both early and late adolescents, in various stages of separation from parental authority, may experience feelings of guilt, regret, or disappointment when a parent dies. They may feel remorse about trouble in the relationship and regret at never being able to see it through to completion.

As you hear Jim's story of his painful guilt, you wish you could somehow go back in time to comfort this very young man. If he only knew how scary death is to everyone, and how hard it is to confront the death of a parent—especially when you're supposed to be moving away from your parents anyway, starting to establish your own adult identity—he might not have been so hard on himself. Jim regrets not being more attentive to his dying mother. But he faced an adult world blocked by its own dishonesty. No one gave him any tools to deal with his feelings. Although they encouraged and even pressured him to visit his mother, they didn't help guide him through the complex emotions he experienced in connection to her imminent death. She had left him in the care of his grandmother when he was six years old, and he had never entirely gotten over his feeling of abandonment.

Jim (61, m, 16, f, 18)

My father told me not to tell my mother she was dying. He said, "Don't tell her. The doctors opened her up and she has inoperable cancer and only a year to live." At that time she was sick in her bed in the back bedroom. For that entire time, I couldn't stand to talk to her. I was afraid I would break down. I don't know what it was. I was just stunned. It was like she was my mother but she wasn't my mother. She was someone who was dying, and I didn't know what to do about it. I had already gone through a long, long thing with my grandmother when she died. It was really bad. I was trying desperately to ignore it by playing hard with my friends and becoming a very good student. Then my mother went into the hospital for a long time. Aunts and uncles and my father and others kept saying I should go visit her, but I didn't want to. Finally, someone convinced me I better go. I was scared to death. She was in an oxygen tent, and she was being cared for by a nurse who was brushing her hair. Even though she was sitting up, she was very weak. I remember that her hand reached out from underneath the oxygen tent, and I broke down. I couldn't talk to her. That image just kind of stays with me, and, in fact, I still feel it now. I feel terribly guilty, I think, in a lot of ways for not having spent more time with her. But it was a dreadful situation. I hadn't forgiven her for leaving me with my grandparents, leaving me behind, when she went to work. I understand that she couldn't help it, but I didn't get it then. I was still trying to punish her in some way by not being close to her. And then she left again.

✎

Deborah Nagle loved her father, but the spring before he died, they tangled over an April Fool's Day prank she had played. Her developing sexuality and a culture of blame in her family added to her feelings of guilt.

Deborah Nagle, writer (46, f, 12)

My father had gone into the hospital to have some surgery and came home a couple of days before April Fool's Day. Early in the morning on April Fool's, I had changed the salt to the sugar and the sugar into salt. My father was always waited on. He never was in the kitchen. But that day he decided to make himself a bowl of cereal, slice strawberries on it, and then sprinkle sugar over the strawberries. I was absolutely apoplectic because I was unable to tell him he was putting salt all over his cereal. So he sat down, with great fanfare, to have his bowl of cereal. He took one spoonful, threw the spoon, and then the bowl. My mother had my little newborn brother in her arms. My father got so angry he started to run after me. He picked up a shoe to hit me with, and I was never hit as a child. We ran downstairs, and then down another flight of stairs into the cellar. I was terrified and crouched in the corner of the cellar. My mother was screaming his name at the top of her lungs, for the first time that I ever remember. Soon after that, he went back to the hospital.

In June, there was a dance that was very important for me to go to. At the dance, my boyfriend, who I was crazy about, kissed me, and I also started my period that night. When I came home, it seemed there was nobody in the house because it was so dark and silent. But when the phone rang, my grandmother answered it and then told me just to go to bed, so I did. The next morning my mother came into the bedroom and told my sister and me that my father had died the night before and we were to go to mass. She told us that Daddy's name would probably be announced at church. It was Father's Day, June 18, 1961. From that point on, what I did was to put together that my anger at my dad for hurting me like that, and my kissing my boyfriend, and my bleeding were all connected. In fact, my grandmother blamed me for my father's death.

∽

Adolescent anger at parental authority is natural. But a healthy adolescent doesn't really want the parent to disappear, so if the father or mother does actually die, the teen often blames himself or herself.

David Z. (52, f, 13)

My father and I had had this series of on-and-off fights for a year about stupid issues. About two weeks before he died, I had had one of my arguments with him, and I told him to drop dead. I don't remember the words, but it was something like, "I wish you were dead." Then the first day of Rosh Hashanah, the start of the Jewish high holy days, came. I had for some reason decided not to go with him to the temple because we were once again arguing about something. That was the day he died. I saw him collapse in the street from a heart attack.

∽

Jessica had to contend with her mother committing suicide, a kind of death that produces guilt reactions in most survivors no matter what their age.

Jessica (24, m, 16)

Right before my mom died, she had been really depressed and hadn't shown up around the house a lot. She had lost a ton of weight, and she was not taking any interest in anything—whether there were groceries in the house, whether we stayed out late. At one point, I was looking at her car and found an empty bottle of painkillers, and I think an old razor blade. She would wake up before we did and leave in her car and come back after dark. Then she'd either come into the house and not say anything to us and just go to her room, or just not come back at all. I think it was the night before she died I happened to look out the living room window and see the car parked outside, so I went out there and found her sleeping on the front seat. I woke her up and asked if we were going to go clean somebody's house the next day—she was trying to start a housecleaning business. And she said, "Yeah," and to leave her alone. So I closed the car door again and left her in there. That was my last interaction with her.

I guess my brother and I both knew she was going to kill herself. She hadn't talked about it. But I say "I guess" because I don't want to feel guilty about it. I think I told my best friend and my boyfriend that I had found this stuff, but I didn't say, "I think my mom's gonna kill herself." I just sort of knew. I had also had a dream earlier in the summer in which I was semiresponsible for my mom's death, which was really violent. There was this dream boyfriend, not somebody I was actually dating, just somebody who was part of a cult in this dream. I found out he was part of a cult that killed people by throwing axes in their heads, so I decided I would break up with him and then he went with his cult and killed my mom because I had broken up with him.

❧

Deborah H. was also sixteen when her mom committed suicide. She is twenty years older than Jessica and has been able to come to terms with her guilt. Part of this resolution seems to stem from her understanding of the reasons her mother was threatened by her sexual activity.

Deborah H. (45, m, 16)

I didn't always understand what I was feeling a lot in the guilt department. I had had this huge screaming battle with my mother about a day and a half before she died. When I went into therapy in my twenties, it still didn't feel right because I kept saying two things. Number one, I don't feel mad at her. I really feel like she was in so much pain she did what she had to do. Number two, I did feel responsible. And nobody is going to talk me out of that. In more recent years, I still make those same statements. But what's shifted now for me is that I don't feel guilty. But I do understand what about me triggered old pain in her. She was raised in an orphanage and was sexually molested there as a young child. I was a very sexually active teenager, so I was a trigger for her feelings of sexual unsafety.

Peggi (56, f, 19)

I had some guilt around my father's death. He had taken to sometimes lying down for a nap on a cot in a back room of his drugstore. I sort of thought he was just working too much, but maybe he did have some heart trouble that tired him; he never went to a doctor. I used to work in his drugstore mostly as a soda jerk, but I didn't go that evening. I felt guilty for not going to help him because it was the night the trash had to go out, and it occurred to me that maybe it was my fault because I didn't help him.

∽

Guilt is sometimes linked to shame. It's the feeling of "I did something that I am ashamed of, something wrong."

Leslie's brother Marc felt shame around what he perceived to be his inappropriate reaction to his father's death. If anything, the adults and friends around him who joked with him on the first night would have done better to encourage him to cry. The real shame is that many people who lose a parent young don't have the tools to deal with their grief and sometimes have to carry with them feelings of guilt, responsibility, and shame for many years. Unresolved, these feelings can add to the pain of grief.

Marc (39, f, 10)

It was a Sunday afternoon, and my sister and I were both coming home at the same time from different places. We met in front of the house and went in the back door. I had forgotten to return something to a neighbor, so I left and my sister went in the house. I heard her scream. She had found my father's body, which I didn't know then, but I hesitated, and I've always felt shame over that, and embarrassment, that it was a cowardly thing to do. I did finally run back into the house. It was a pretty ghastly thing to see. His eyes were open, and he was just lying there. I never had seen a dead body at that point in my life, even in a coffin or anything.

I still feel shame about that day, and I think I always will no matter how much I come to understand it. I think I violated some primary thing. In the basement at the first neighbor's house I went to, I had been crying pretty much inconsolably, but I got exhausted and drained from crying. When I went to my friend's house where I spent the night, they were making jokes. We played a game, and I remember the name of the game and everything. By the end of the evening, I was laughing and having a good old time, and then it was time to go to bed, and I remember lying in bed and feeling such guilt and horror over having had a good time and playing the night my father died. And I still do. I don't, to the extent that I understand what happened, but I still can't get over feeling a horrible shame from it.

Kristy's feelings about inheriting her father's comforter upset her. The comforter meant a lot to her. Paradoxically, it provoked the initial guilt, but also provided the eventual cure. What was especially interesting to us was that it seemed as if the very telling of this story helped ease her pain. Notice how in this brief story, Kristy moves from the feeling of guilt to "It doesn't feel as bad now" to "how perfect."

Kristy (25, f, 13)

I felt so guilty about this thought. I walked in, saw my father dead, dead on the bed, and I remember thinking, "Oh good. Now I get to use his comforter." I wanted to have his comforter. It was a nice brown comforter with this soft interior. And I remember feeling bad because it was material. I guess that could be symbolically looked at also. It's nice voicing this; I haven't done this in years. It doesn't feel as bad now. But, I mean, how perfect, my father—I can wrap up in him.

Relief

David Joseph's mother beat him on a regular basis, and when she died, he felt mostly relief. But because he had begun to fight back and had had a strange premonition before she died, he also felt some responsibility for her death. Even now he says, "I don't *think* I caused her death." Of course, there is no way that he could have. But these lingering doubts speak to the powerful ties—positive and negative—between parents and children.

David Joseph, poet (40, m, 14)

The story was that my mother was driving to work, and I guess she was late. She had had problems making it on time. We lived on the other side of the tracks, isolated, on this road, with only one way to get in or out. What would often happen is trains would come and stop right there, and there would be no way to get in or out. At the time, I thought it was probably suicide, because she was very unhappy, but over the years I've come around to the opinion that it was probably not suicide, it was probably an accident. She was trying to get across the tracks and thought she had time, or didn't know if she did or not but was going to take the chance because she had to get to work on time, and she didn't make it. The train couldn't brake in that small space.

There were a couple of other interesting points about it—one was that I actually had a premonition on the very spot where she was killed almost exactly a week before she died. She was killed on Friday, December 13, 1968, which brought in a superstitious element. Also, I had started to fight back against my mother's continual abuse just before she had her accident, which kind of introduced guilt feelings on my part, but also feelings of relief. I felt a lot of relief not to have this relationship in my life anymore. I also felt like I had caused the accident, but I don't think I did.

The long illness of Beto's mother gave him a chance to tell her goodbye, but his relief that her suffering was over also caused him some anguish.

Beto (52, m, 14)

My mother and I were alone in the house, shortly before she died, maybe a month, or a couple of weeks before. And I just walked into her room—she was in bed and she couldn't really talk at that point. She looked cold and sweaty. She was going through some terrible shit, and I just went up and hugged and kissed her, and that was it. And that's the way I said good-bye. But, yeah, it was good-bye. I didn't really know it at the time, but I felt better for having done it.

Her actual dying, the whole thing, was anticlimactic, even though, of course, we were all sad when it happened. But the weird thing is that I was glad it was over. It's common to feel that way, I guess, but Jesus, I felt terrible that I was just glad it was over. I wasn't glad about her death, but I felt guilty. So it took me years to figure it out, that it really was a good thing it was over, because she was hurting a lot. I mean she couldn't breathe sometimes, and her skin was always clammy, and the last several months it was terrible. But after she died, I started feeling bad and guilty.

∽

Shannon and Jeff B.'s mother had prepared them so well for her eventual death from cancer that they felt relief without any guilt or shame. Jeff B. remembered their mother saying, "You know it's okay if you're mad when I die."

Shannon (24, m, 19)

My mom got cancer at the end of 1981. And it came back a few years later. She was really, really sick for about a year and a half. First, she left work early, and then began to just not go to work at all, and then she became basically bedridden, for a long period of months. She had actually talked to us. She had always been that kind of mom, very honest. About a week before she died, she talked to both Jeff and me individually to say, "I'm ready for it, and it's going to happen soon. And I want to talk to you before the time comes that I won't be able to anymore." After she died, we were very supported, and a lot of our support was in the form of humor. I think the fact that it had been so long and the last six months had been especially hard that it was a kind of relief because she had been in so much pain. We were all feeling that finally she's not in pain and we won't have to watch her go through that anymore.

∽

Two people who were adolescents when their fathers died recall moments in their fathers' hospital rooms, before and after the deaths, when they experienced a sense of completion. Their relief felt almost like a form of release.

Daniel Meyers's father died in his arms. Daniel's description of this last hour together, except for one frightening moment, speaks to the love between them and the relief he felt now that the ordeal was over.

Daniel Meyers, filmmaker (34, f, 18)

I was holding my father when he died. He was not conscious, as far as I know. There was this one just ghastly moment, about twenty or thirty minutes before he died, where he was lying still, breathing slowly, heavily, and he bolted upright in the bed, off the pillow, and half sat up on his arms, looking straight ahead, with his eyes wide open, and made a horrible sound. Some sort of gasp. It was horrible. I don't know. Did he see his life pass before his eyes? Did he see the future gone? Who knows what he saw? Maybe he saw God and God was an ugly creature, a Minotaur with a ghastly face. Then he sank back onto his pillow and he started breathing deeper and softer, and I went up to him and held him in my arms, and he slowly expired. So that was the scene.

My mother and her parents and my father's mother were there, standing by the side. They just looked on and I knelt beside him there and held him. A nurse came in at one point and tried to inject something in to keep him alive, and it didn't work. He faded away. And then we closed his eyes. His mouth opened slightly and one trickle of blood came down the corner of his mouth, and I took his wedding ring off his hand and put it on mine. And we all decompressed or something.

∽

Sandy never got to know her father as well as she had hoped, and her presence at his death allowed her to bridge the divide between them. Moving beyond an old fear liberated her. Sometimes a small gesture in these defining moments of our lives can take on a numinous quality.

Sandy (46, f, 16)

After my father's stroke, he was basically comatose for nine days. I was there the night he died. I was there for the whole business. I was a very shy and inhibited kid, and just not at all in touch with my emotions. After he had died, before I walked out, I went over and touched his left hand. My father had lost half of his finger around the time I was born, and it had always been a little bit scary to me. I'd always hoped that when I grew up, I would be able to bridge that gulf, all the fears and all the distance. Somehow, touching the left hand, which was the scary part, was very, very important.

Confusion and Exclusion

While adolescents typically experience feelings of guilt in connection with a parent's death, younger children feel more confusion about what is happening to their world and sometimes exclusion from it. A particular sorrow and pain stems from this bewilderment. In some cases, if the adults could have been more present during the crisis, the children might have been better able to cope with their emotions. By bringing young children into the process as gently as possible, adults can help the children ease their way into the new world that confronts them. Of course, some confusion is inevitable.

Only two when his mother died, Lawrence has some vague memories, but mostly he felt very lost.

Lawrence (35, m, 2, f, 16)

From what my sister told me, my mother had high blood pressure, and at that time, over thirty years ago, they didn't have the money or the correct medicine for her. Although I was only about two years old, I do have some memory of the day she died. It was a strange day. I remember being in a little cracker-box house and my oldest sister and my dad coming through the door in tears. My dad was saying, "She's gone." I didn't understand why they were crying. My sister was in tears, but my dad was really going at it. I was very confused. I didn't know what was happening. They wouldn't let me go to the funeral.

I have two brothers and two sisters, and only my oldest sister went. The rest of us were too young.

෴

Rachel doesn't remember anyone talking to her about her father's death at the time. She has only this one story from her family history, and she holds tightly to it.

Rachel (47, f, 5)

I have no memory of being told that my father had died, and it has not been part of the oral history of my family, so I have very little data regarding that period. All I know, historically, is that my father came home from work, had chest pains, told my mother he didn't feel well and was going to lie down, which was very unusual. My mother became concerned that it might be his heart and called the local doctor, who said, "Oh no, he's too young and too strong. He must have just pulled a muscle." Then, apparently, he said something like "It'll pass" or "Keep him warm." As the evening wore on, I don't know, but I'm assuming there were other symptoms because my mother called back and they called for an ambulance, which had to come probably fifteen or twenty miles, but by the time it arrived, he had died. Except for that story, it was just not processed in my family. I have no memory of what happened, and I've never been told. I know that there was some service, but I don't know what it entailed. I know that I was not present. That was an era when death was not something children were to be part of.

෴

Eight-year-old Jan B. also felt confused and even in the interview kept repeating, "I didn't quite get it."

Jan B. (50, f, 8)

My father had a heart attack at age thirty-two. We woke up in the middle of the night and there was an ambulance at the front door. I never saw him after that, and I never said good-bye. My mother, who was pregnant, went in the ambulance with him. Some man took my sister and me in a car. We followed the ambulance. I was real aware of the siren and lights. When we got to the hospital, my mother and grandfather and my sister, who was five, and I were sitting in a waiting room. And the family doctor came down and told that gathering of people that my father had died. I think as an eight-year-old I didn't quite understand what had happened. All I knew was that my mother was crying, and my grandfather was really sobbing. But I didn't quite get it, except I was very aware that those two adults were crying. My grandfather took my mother and my sister and me in the middle of the night to my grandmother's house and then there was this big uproar of people coming. I had this sense of really not getting it, just real confusion about what had happened to my dad.

∽

When Brown Miller's father used a euphemism to give the news of his mother's death to his sister, Miller didn't even understand what his father was saying. He had to take his cues from his sister.

Brown Miller, poet (51, m, 6)

You know, while my mother was in the coma, they took me to see her one time. I was old enough to know it was serious. Although I didn't understand it fully at the time, it was pretty traumatic. Anyway, at one point, my father came home, and was looking sadder than usual, and my older sister, who is six years older, asked, "How's Mother?" And he said, "She won't be coming home." I didn't know what that meant exactly, so I looked at my sister, and she fell on the bed crying, and said, "Mother's in heaven." And then it started to sink in. That's how I was told. There was a funeral, but I don't have a clear memory of it. I don't even know if I went. I really don't know. I don't have any memory of the funeral.

∽

Sometimes a surviving parent did try to explain the death to their child, but the child's cognitive development was not advanced enough to take it in. Four-year-old Diana, injured in the same car accident that killed her mother, was completely bewildered. All she could say to her father was, "Do you mean I'll never see her again?"

Diana O'Hehir, novelist and poet (72, m, 4)

I remember being in the hospital. And then I remember being told that I couldn't see my mother. I kept asking for her. I don't think I saw her at all after the accident. I'm not sure. Theoretically, she just had a small cut on her forehead. But, apparently, the wound on her forehead, which was very slight, got infected, and she is listed as having died of meningitis. There were no antibiotics. It was 1927, I guess. I think it was my father who told me she was dead. Certainly, I remember asking him, "Do you mean I'll never see her again?" And he said, "No, you won't ever see her again."

∽

Although the adults tried to prepare Jeffery K. for his mother's death, he was left feeling confused and alone. Like Miller, he has no memories of a funeral service. But a powerful memory does persist—coming home one evening on the freeway and realizing that his mother wouldn't be there. It was a moment of clarity in a very blurry time.

Jeffery K. (22, m, 8, f, 18)

I remember when my mother went into the hospital, and I remember visiting her in the hospital, and I remember how she couldn't talk. I remember coming home and my grandfather and my brother sat me down. They told me that my mom was going to pass away, and explained it to me. I was only eight years old, so I really wasn't aware of what was going on. I knew she was sick, but it was the first time I had learned anything about how serious it was. So I just kind of went off in my own little world, I suppose. I don't remember a service at all, to be honest. But, for some reason, I remember coming home one evening on the freeway when I first realized that my mom had passed away and that she wasn't going to be with us anymore.

∽

There was little clarity for Melissa and Kenyetta. Melissa's father shot her mother and then himself. Kenyetta's father was stabbed by the ex-boyfriend of her little brother's mother. There was just no making sense of what befell them.

Melissa (28, m, 9, f, 9)

We had just moved into a brand-new house in a suburb of Los Angeles. The new house was upper-middle-class, with five bedrooms and three baths. One night my father cornered my mother downstairs in the dining room and shot her with a shotgun and then turned the gun on himself. I used to try to remember whether or not my mother had given me a kiss good night, or if this had been one of the evenings they had been fighting. I don't know, but the events following the incident are very clean and very crisp in my mind.

My brother and I stayed on the stairs. We weren't allowed to go into the dining room where my parents were, and when the police came, they helped us find our shoes. They left the lights off. One of the police officers knew the neighbors down the street and took us there. I remember looking at the clock. It was about three o'clock in the morning. I couldn't sleep and kept looking at the clock. My sister came at around seven or eight. She came with my mother's best friend from college to take us to the friend's house.

Together, they told us in the car that my mother and father were dead. I didn't feel like I knew what to do. What does that mean? Am I supposed to cry? Am I supposed to just take it? What am I supposed to do? So I decided that the most appropriate response would be to hug my sister. And then my *sister* cried. She had been crying all night at the police station.

My grandmother came down later on that afternoon. That night she and I slept in the living room together, and I was really scared she was going to leave me, too. But I was also really angry because I never liked my grandmother. When I was small, she made it clear she did not like the way my mother was raising me. She thought I was very spoiled. So I was angry that here I was with my grandmother, but I was really struggling to hold on to somebody.

Although Kenyetta was older than the others who reported confusion, the circumstances surrounding the death of her father would have pushed anyone into a confused, disturbed state.

Kenyetta (20, f, 18)

I saw my father on a Thursday and he got killed the following Saturday. He had given me money for some groceries and asked me to
meet him for lunch on Saturday. He told me to just call him to let him
know I made it home. That was the last I saw him. Saturday, when I
was supposed to meet him for lunch, I went over to my aunt's house,
and everyone was hysterical. I didn't know what was going on, because they had been trying to get in touch with me when I was on
my way over there. My grandmother, my father's mother, was there.
When my aunt told me, it was a bad moment. She told me my father
had been stabbed several times by an ex-boyfriend of my little
brother's mother. He died on the way to the hospital. The funeral was
real hysterical. We were trying to find out all the answers to what was
going on and where the man was, and why did he do this. I had a nervous breakdown. I felt alone. I felt betrayed. I just felt like there was
nothing else for me, that I just might as well give up.

No Closure

Even though a prolonged illness is a terrible strain, it can sometimes
help a family prepare for the loss. Janette, whose mother died of cancer, talked about the chance she had to say good-bye: "A couple of
days before my mother died, she called from the hospital. She wanted
everyone to be there. She told me that I would always be her angel
and to always be good and take care of my dad." Like Shannon's
mother, who also died after a long struggle with cancer, Janette's
mother could give her family the chance for a final visit. But most
people did not feel they shared a proper good-bye with their parents.
It's one of the tragedies of early and unexpected death.

Gloria Anzaldúa, poet and writer (52, f, 14)

One afternoon, my uncle came to the house and said they had found
my father in the highway, with the truck overturned and part of its
back on him. After they did the autopsy, they found out he had had
a heart attack, his aorta had ruptured, and he had died at the wheel.
The truck had kept on for a little while with the bales of hay he was

taking to the gin, but when it got to the second curve, it turned over. He was thrown out of the cab, and part of the dumpster fell on his face, so his face was all broken. I remember when he walked out the door earlier that day. He had been in the kitchen, the door slammed, he got in his pickup, and he said, "I'm going to go to the gin." I felt incomplete because it was a normal day, the sun was shining, and he gets up and walks away and that's the last we hear of him. It felt sort of like "no closure."

⁓

Athena tried to bring some resolution to a damaged relationship with her father, but she didn't have enough time to do it while he was still alive.

Athena (19, f, 17)

I was seventeen when my dad died. He died on my birthday. We didn't have enough time to deal with him having AIDS. I think he was in the hospital for two weeks. The last week I was there, I held his hand and told him I didn't hate him, so I tried to mend it up. We didn't have a good relationship because I kind of hated him for what he put us through. But, you know, he didn't give me any feedback. So I couldn't tell how he felt. And I didn't know how I felt either because I was torn. I had this resentment for him, but I also loved him. So it was really weird.

⁓

Marc, too, is pained by the lack of a proper ending to his relationship with his father.

Marc (39, f, 10)

My father had had a heart condition for years, but we had no warning. He hadn't been in the hospital recently, or anything. It was just a sudden thing. I don't remember my last interaction with him, which feels pretty bad. It seems, as part of the whole thing does to me, incomplete. My relationship with my father doesn't seem finished, or sealed.

The Funeral

There is evidence of funeral rites dating back tens of thousands of years in human history. Cultures all over the world have developed their special ways of honoring the dead. The funeral usually involves a ritual that celebrates the life of the person who died. The funeral is also a way for people to come together in their grief. One of the purposes of funerals is to give the bereaved a sense of closure. Some funerals work. They help survivors say a final good-bye and get through the first week of grief. But others don't. They feel bizarre or useless to the bereaved. For some of our interviewees, the funeral reassured them that the lost parent was a good person, esteemed by the community. But others were alienated or felt only despair.

Robin (46, f, 8)

There were a lot of people at the funeral because my father had a lot of friends. Schoolteachers were there. My aunts and uncles were in from New York. Being eight years old, everything was kind of mystical. There were a lot of people crying, but what I really loved about it was that everybody was telling me how wonderful my father was, and that was very reassuring.

Kristy (25, f, 13)

I remember crying a lot. I remember that smell of crying, almost like a smell of blood. I remember the house was a mess. We had clothes hanging up everywhere, and there was always food around and flowers. People would come and we'd talk about my father. They revealed things to me about their parents dying, and, if I ever needed help, that they were there. There was a part of me that loved this attention, but I didn't understand it. I also felt like I was taking care of people. They were telling me how great my dad was, and this is supposed to be a hard time. I didn't know it was hard. It just was the space I was in.

⁓

Adolescents are sometimes expected to participate in the funeral preparations. Adults presumed that William would take on responsibilities that overwhelmed him.

William (54, f, 14)

My mother was pretty much in shock for several days, and although I had an older sister, I was the male of the household, so I got to go along making the arrangements, choosing the casket, grave site, and that sort of thing. I was struck then and I'm even more amazed today at that whole system. I was pretty much numb. The grief scene was not allowed for me. It's the way boys were brought up in those days, and I knew the rules perfectly. I'd been set up to shoulder my responsibility. Every man that came up to me said, "Well, you're the man of the house now." There was stuff about taking care of my mother. Of course, I stepped into the breach as the head of the household. I'd been in Boy Scouts and had Catholic training. I knew what was expected of me. But I did not know one thing about how to do it.

Gloria Anzaldúa, poet and writer (52, f, 14)

My mom took my father's death very hard. She cried and cried for months. It fell on me to deal with stuff when we went to the mortuary. The funeral home where he was embalmed and where they fixed his face, because it had been cracked and stuff, sold the coffins and these half-suits, fake suits. We had to pick a coffin to bury him in and a suit, and the suits didn't have any backs. It just had a white shirt with little ruffles, and then a black, kind of fake top, and a tie. My mom wanted to get the best, and I had to kind of say, "Mom"—he had an old suit that he would use for funerals and weddings—"we can use his old suit." But she wanted the best for him, so we were in debt, paying for the funeral expenses for the next four years.

Detta (47, m, 17)

After my mother died, we had to decide on what clothing she should be buried in, so we went into her closet. She made most of her own clothes and had some wonderful stuff. My aunts had sort of picked out two things they thought she would like to be buried in. I don't know how people know that. One was a gorgeous teal-green wool suit that she had worked on very hard. And one was a white wool suit. Her clothes fit me, and I decided I didn't need the white suit, and I thought she would look better in it, so we selected it, and some coral jewelry. And then they said, "What shoes do you want her to wear?" I remember thinking it was stupid to put shoes on a corpse. The aunts were haggling with me, but ultimately I won. They put her in the white suit, and they didn't put shoes on her, although they folded a blanket over her legs so no one would know that I had committed this gaffe.

&

In Emilia's case, traditional funeral rites could not be observed because it was wartime. She deeply regrets that her father was never properly buried.

Emilia (62, f, 12)

When my father was dying, he could not go to the air-raid shelter, and my mother would say a novena every night, beside him. When he died, we were able to call a priest, but we were not able to bury him in a cemetery. We just buried him in the cornfields under a *cainito* tree, like a star apple. I always wanted to put his remains in the proper cemetery. But there's a house there now. So, anyway, that was that. He died just three days before the Americans landed in that particular island of the Philippines. There was no time to mourn, because he died and three days later there was bombing.

&

For Ken Burns, the funeral offered no consolation. He longed for catharsis, but there was none.

Ken Burns, filmmaker (41, m, 11)

There was a perfunctory funeral at a funeral home. My mother was cremated. About 90 percent of the way through the thing, I realized that my mother was in the box. I had blocked it. I immediately shut down. I didn't deal with it or try to relate to it. And I think that was it. There was no grief.

What's strange is that my father is an anthropologist, and one would have thought that the sense of having ceremony or ritual would have been there, but it wasn't. For some reason, he never even picked up her ashes from the funeral home.

∽

For others, important cultural traditions shaped the funeral. Gloria Anzaldúa and Beto, for instance, described Mexican funerals in Arizona and Texas.

Beto (52, m, 14)

We had the wake at the house. My mother's casket was there in the front room, and a bunch of flowers. It was a Mexican funeral. A lot of people, lots to eat. Women just brought over all kinds of things to eat.

Gloria Anzaldúa, poet and writer (52, f, 14)

People came over to the house with food. They brought different casseroles, and lots of drinks and beer. The house was just full of flowers, and they brought my father back from the mortuary for the memorial, for the wake, and he was at the house for about three days. The men would drink, the women would be wearing black, with these veils over their faces, praying with their rosaries.

∽

Doreen's extended African-American family provided the children with comforting distractions. The mix of laughing and crying was healing for her.

Doreen (36, m, 10)

When my mother died, we cried a lot, off and on. Yet, in some ways, it was also kind of a happy time because we got to get clothes for the funeral. I remember I had to wear white, because children didn't wear black to funerals. I went shopping for the first time without my mother. I got a white dress that I loved and a wonderful coat that I wanted. It was really a wonderful, extravagant thing, that usually wasn't part of the mix. There was lots of doting. Lots of favorite foods showed up. The food story was amazing. The cakes alone were out of this world. There were three days of wake where lots of people came to view the body. We heard lots of stories about my mother and met childhood friends of hers, which was really nice. I remember laughing, and playing with other kids. There's a large extended family, lots of cousins, kids our age. It was a mixed bag, the sadness along with the happiness of just being together. People you haven't seen in a while, family sharing stories.

Bob (58, f, 16)

An uncle took me for a ride during the time they were getting ready for the funeral. He let me drive his car. We stopped at various bars, so he could go in and have a drink. He didn't chat with me. He just drove. The wake was pretty dramatic and the secret to "getting through" wakes was to get smashed. The uncles would have bottles in the back. Even the funeral director might have one. From their point of view, I was too young to drink. My brother was my hero then, of course, and when I watched him drink, I thought that was part of the Irish funerals and Irish wakes, which, of course, it is.

Addie (19, f, 16)

My father was a Quaker. I've always related to Quaker funerals because they seem very respectful and they do something for the people involved. You sit in silence and when people have something to say, or feel like they want to share something about the person, a story or poem, whatever, then they can do that. And I think that's nice because you get in a very safe way sort of a sampling of what people are feeling, and how people related to him and what sort of different lives he had with other people. And it's a real understanding of that rather than a clear-cut one religious view of one person's life.

Laurie had to contend with her family's racism at her mother's funeral. What happened frightened her out of any expression of feeling.

Laurie (38, m, 13)

In the South, when a person dies, they take the body, fix it up, and then the night before the funeral, you go to the funeral home and all the family and friends come. When I looked in the coffin, I thought, "Who's that?" That did not look like my mom at all. They had put a ton of makeup on her and did her hair in this weird way that she would never wear it. It was creepy and shocking and really hard to say good-bye. There was a half-plastic person, and everybody was saying, "Oh, doesn't she look beautiful?" It was just painful to see everybody thinking that that was my mom at her best. It was sort of surreal, and bizarre.

The next day, there was a funeral. The one person who surprised me was Edna, our maid. You know, some white people in the South are pretty controlled and don't express emotion very well. At least that's my family. I was sitting in the pews before I knew Edna was even there. I heard somebody crying, "Oh, Miz Dorothy! Miz Dorothy!" She was really grieving, but the next thing I heard was this man's voice saying, "Get her out of here!" And then that was it. She was gone. The funeral was the last time I heard her voice. I didn't ever get to say good-bye to her. But, you know, when I think about it and look back on it, she was probably the healthiest person there. She wasn't ashamed to express what love she had. I think that is a point where I just decided that it was not really safe to cry. So a lot of the grief that I had for my mom was immediately pushed down, way, way down. And I never expressed it with my family.

～

Mariam just didn't know enough about her culture's funeral traditions and so ended up feeling alienated from the whole process.

Mariam (39, f, 13)

In a Persian funeral, the first three days are a big deal, but I was at my uncle's house at that time. The seventh day is another big ceremony, and my mother wanted me to be there. She made a black dress for me, and I went with them to the mosque. My father was pretty influential when he died, so there were different things in different mosques, but the real funeral was where he was buried. There was food, but basically they sit around and cry and do prayers. Men and women are separate. There are special prayers, but I don't know any of them. I would go only for a couple of hours.

∽

Tron, Monica, and Janette broke down at the burials of their parents. It took Tron by surprise.

Tron Bykle, artist (51, f, 14)

I was quite impressed by the amount of people that showed up, lots of family, lots of my father's colleagues at work, union representatives. I was trying to be a tough kid and not cry. My sister, who's older, elbowed me, telling me to cry, but I couldn't. I cried the day, or the evening, when he had died, for a little bit when I walked my dog through a park. But after all the singing and ceremonies, as the coffin was disappearing, I broke down. It was a very strange thing. I was totally in the world of tears. I couldn't see. I couldn't focus on anything.

∽

Both Monica and Janette were their mothers' youngest children, and each experienced utter despair and loneliness at the burials.

Monica (30, m, 10)

The funeral was really hard. In rural Mexico, they didn't have any funeral homes. They kept the person at home, and I was not kept away from that. At the same time, nobody bothered to come in and kind of explain to me what was going on. I think the most torturous thing was to see a person who you loved so much just lying there and not moving.

After a few days, they come and put the person in the coffin and take them to church and the priest goes through his procedures. Every time somebody died in that town, we'd see them going down the hill with the coffin, because my house was in the middle of the town, and the church was less than half a mile in front of my house, higher up the hill. And that day—usually the doors of my mom's store would be open—that day her store was closed. I can still see those closed doors, and everybody just carrying her down the hill where I used to see other dead people being carried. It seemed like the whole day turned gray. Her coffin was gray, the day was gray, everything seemed gray. Everything. I don't remember seeing any green. Nothing. We had to walk quite a long time. It was about a half of a mile to the cemetery, and people took turns carrying the coffin. When we reached the place in the cemetery where she was going to be buried, that was the hardest thing. People encouraged me to throw her some dirt to say good-bye, but the only thing that I wanted to do was throw myself inside with her. I remember this friend of my mother—they were very close—she was the only person that I can remember, just feeling her hands, squeezing me, and holding my arms, because I wanted to, I was thinking I wanted to jump.

Janette (19, m, 12)

I think my mother was in the funeral home for three days. The whole time, it kind of still didn't hit me because, I guess, her body was still there. But as people walked by me at the funeral, I just felt pitied, as if they looked down on me. When they actually put her casket in the ground and I saw the reaction of my family and everybody, that's when I really felt it. They didn't want her to go, and before they had closed the coffin to bring her in, her aunt had kept grabbing her, trying to take her out, like she didn't want her to go. I just remember that when they put her down, I just felt like I was being buried with her.

Sacred Memory

Somehow the death of a parent early in a child's life seems both holy and profane. Profane, because it feels like a violation of the basic promise from parent to child: "I will be there for you"; holy, because it inducts the child at an early age into what some cultures have described as a sacred mystery.

Lauren Muller, writer (34, f, 11)

I felt like I grew up a lot. I think, in a way, it felt like a really holy time. I had to think about death and God in ways that I hadn't. It was really touching rock bottom and sort of knowing the truth in a way. I had lots of conversations with adults about death and God. My mother and I became very close. I think for both my sister Heather and me, in a strange way it's, I think, an exalted time. It's sort of like it's the most terrible but the most wonderful thing that could happen because it's a sense of rock-bottom knowledge.

Ground Zero

Why do people old enough to remember still indulge in the story of where they were when Kennedy was shot? Why do survivors of an earthquake or flood endlessly repeat the story of how they made it through? To heal from trauma, we must remember as much of it as we can in order to make some kind of sense of the fear and grief, the shock and sorrow of the first hours and days of a disaster. We turn this way and that, reshaping the ground beneath our feet and the air above our heads. Going back is not going backward into retreat. It's about revisiting, retelling, and sometimes revising the story of the events that forever change our lives. Our narratives make us who we are and remind us we're still here: different, changed, but still alive. And with an understanding of how each of us got to where we stand now, our stories bind us to one another. By opening up a view into the days surrounding childhood tragedy, the people here have allowed the rest of us to recall our own time of mourning. Each story is different, but each one contains a common element: we survived to tell the tale.

In Jane Smiley's book *A Thousand Acres,* Ginny, whose mother died when she was fourteen, talks about "early grief, when the fact that you are still alive and functioning is so strangely similar to your previous life that you think you are okay. It is in that state of mind that people answer when you see them at funerals, and ask them how they are doing. They say, 'I'm fine. I'm okay, really,' and they really mean, 'I'm not recognizable to myself.'" What Ginny calls "early grief" affects many mourners at ground zero. During the first year after the death, other reactions begin to set in. We turn now to what some cultures call the official year of mourning.

4

The First Year

The world was already rearranging itself. It was like a big gym with everyone who had a mother standing against one wall and the few of us who didn't standing against the other wall.—Kyoko Mori (m, 12), *Dream of Water*

There is no despair so absolute as that which comes with the first moments of our first great sorrow, when we have not yet known what it is to have suffered and be healed, to have despaired and recovered hope.—George Eliot (m, 16), *Adam Bede*

I was plunged into nothingness. All the threads were broken; I fell, on my own, without any support. The parachute opened. The canopy unfurled, a fragile and firm suspense before the controlled descent.—Georges Perec (f, 4, m, 6), *W, Or, The Memory of Childhood*

That the dead stay dead is a daily surprise. The initial shock wears off, and our lives go on. In the first year after our parent's death, we acclimate to a different world. Whether we were two or seventeen, whether our caretaking parent, our breadwinning parent, or our noncustodial parent died, we endure, encounter, and process mind-boggling changes. The world as we knew it is different.

The people whose stories fill this book talk about how their world changed with their bereavement, as if it might have been yesterday. Yet they speak with the perspective that comes with time. In their voices, we hear echoes of the sadness, numbness, and anger they felt. In the adult we hear the child. Who will take care of us? Who will buy our clothes? Who will cook and clean? Who will pay the rent? Where will we live? What roles and responsibilities will we be expected to assume? Or take upon ourselves? Who will love us now that our mother or father is dead? And we feel again, through memory, the "plunge into nothingness": the lack of support, and, then almost always, the parachute opens. We do not, as it turns out, fall to our death.

The stories in this chapter evoke that first year in which many of us lived with permeating grief and sadness, whether our feelings were encouraged or not. The word "numb" came up a lot. People who were teenagers tend to be able to articulate the extent and nuances of their grief, and their inability or unwillingness to share it with others in the first year.

Some talked about their anger, not necessarily at the parent who died. Sometimes it was anger at a God who would let such a thing happen; at an adult who tried to help (and often fumbled); at the surviving parent for simply being the surviving parent, or for abandoning the child in the face of his or her own grief.

How the world sees us and how we see the world when we are children is inalterably and inevitably changed by the death of a parent. Relationships with teachers, other important adults, and peers are transformed. In Spike Lee's autobiographical film *Crooklyn,* Aunt Maxine brings the newly motherless Troy new clothes to wear to her mother's funeral. "Aren't they pretty? I picked them out myself." Troy remains impassive, but Maxine persists. "Troy, why don't you at least try them on? I know this is hard for you. It's hard for everybody. But you have to wear something nice. Don't you want to look all pretty like Aunt Maxine? Carolyn would be so proud of you." Troy responds with obstinate anger, "Listen, my mother hates polyester. She would never let me wear anything like that." Sometimes other adults attempt to enter the picture, but the child resents anyone who tries to take the lost parent's place. If continually rejected, most adults unfortunately stop trying within the first year.

Some children began to work out their grief in dreams during the first year. These were often, but not always, recurring dreams. In some, the dead parent reappeared and life was made whole again.

Others were horror dreams in which the dead parent taunted the child.

Some of us were forced into adult roles too soon; some of us avoided adult roles for years. Others talked about trying to fill the emotional void, the emotional center of the family, and feeling unequal to the task. Some children tried to fill a gap left not by their dead parent but by their surviving parent's abdication of his or her role in the family.

In the story "A Tidewater Morning" (from the book by the same name), William Styron (m, 13) writes: "We each devise our means of escape from the intolerable. Sometimes we fantasize it out of existence." In a chilling echo of Styron's story, several people talk about their various ways of pretending the mother or father had not died. One man went so far as to repeatedly deny his mother's death to people calling on the telephone or knocking on the door, to adults who inquired how he was doing, and to curious friends who asked, "Didn't your mother die?"

No matter how old we were, our sense of home, whether it was a safe haven or a battlefield, inevitably changed. And to say that we were unprepared for what this year brought us is an understatement. But we coped.

I did it. We did it. You did it. He, she, and they did it. Did and do. We live with or try to recover the feeling memories of the first year. In as many ways as there are people and stories in this book, we strove and strive to discover who we are now that we're orphans.

Many Ways to Mourn

Various religious traditions and cultures have formal periods of mourning. Sometimes these traditions become a way of dealing with grief. Sometimes we don't know what to do with our feelings, and we act out in various ways, or withdraw. And as we mourn, our very senses play tricks on us. The imagined sight or sound of a dead person in a crowd is so common it's almost a cliché.

Tron Bykle, artist (51, f, 14)

I missed my father, I missed him a lot, it was a tremendous loss. I'd be listening for his footsteps. It was surreal because sometimes I'd hear them on the stairs, and I would hear the key in the door and the door open, but nobody came through. We lived on the fourth floor, and you had to walk through this wooden walkway into the backyard before you came up, and I would hear his measured steps at certain times, coming up, but he wouldn't be there. I remember going behind this bush with my dog and crying, really crying. I felt, in a way, deserted, and strangely lonely. I was very perplexed by people's behavior around me, because it didn't make sense, a lot of stuff that was going on. But the main thing was a tremendous loss.

Paul B.'s reaction is extreme, yet it is shared with several others including Brown Miller and Eric Marcus, who failed to tell people about his father's death because it was supposed to be a secret that his father committed suicide. If we don't tell people our parent has died, then we might be able, for at least a while, to pretend it isn't true. Paul's fantasies are an attempt to change the fact that his mother died, or at least to take control so nothing that terrible will happen again.

Paul B. (53, m, 11)

The early memories after my mother's death were of great pain and an ache or an emptiness that I first dealt with by denying that it had happened. If someone asked me where my mom was, I would say "She's at work" or "She's shopping." Literally! I remember making up stories to friends, and I can remember some other kids saying, "Well, your mother died, didn't she?" And, "No. No."

The whole thing was complicated by the fact that I also had a tiny little baby brother that I had some real ambivalent feelings about. He came home, she did not. I didn't cry. Maybe just brief episodes, but it would be quickly shut down. I just ached. There was this great sense of loss, and I just went on. Kept going to school. But I really changed. I was no longer a confident kid. I was no longer assertive. My self-esteem was poor. I was fearful of things. I was embarrassed when my father had to sign my report card and when my mother couldn't come to PTA meetings. I remember going through a period of being fearful of getting sick and dying. And that persisted well into my adult life.

I spent a lot of time alone fantasizing. I fantasized a lot about my mother in the hospital. I fantasized about becoming a great physician and saving people that were terminally ill. I developed a lot of rescue fantasies. I played alone a lot, acting out these fantasies.

≈

After Jim's mother died, he continued to live with his father until his father died, too. The image of the spider, which he recounts so vividly, is perhaps indicative of one of the ways we deal with grief. The spider he shouldn't have been frightened of at his age seems to have become a replacement object for his larger fear, the fear of death, a fear he could neither name nor cope with. As he says, after all, this was 1950. People did not talk about their feelings, they did not acknowledge them.

Jim (61, m, 16, f, 18)

One of the images I have about that time was coming home and seeing a white garden spider having built a huge web over the steps leading up to the house and being terrified by that. I mean I was a young male, sixteen years old, and I shouldn't have been terrified, but it just seemed somehow to symbolize what had happened to me.

When I got into college, I couldn't focus very well. I did all right the first year, and then when my father died, I could hardly pay attention. I'd look at a page of a book and I'd read it, and then I'd realize I wasn't thinking about it and I hadn't absorbed any of it, and I could force myself to learn something if I read something three or four times. I never stopped going to school. I don't know why. It was like home, though.

There was no discussion of grieving. This was 1950 and working-class. So, the idea of therapy or grieving or mourning, or any of this stuff that I know about now, you just didn't do it. There was nothing, none of that. Nobody knew about it. My friends were all teenagers and that wasn't an issue amongst us. In that milieu, at that era, people generally didn't talk. I was just a working-class kid. We didn't talk, we stuffed it in.

∽

Art was a child of the Depression. When his father died, the family's focus was on earning enough money to live on and doing the work that needed to be done. Art seemed almost puzzled when we asked about feelings of grief, but he did remember the story of the piano and the dog, symbols of mourning.

Art (70, f, 17)

After my father died in December, I graduated from high school in February. I don't remember a lot, but nobody was real happy. We had a dog at that time, a terrier. And he could howl along to music on the piano when my sister played. And one of his favorite songs was "Claire de Lune," and that's kind of a gloomy song, if you think about it, the wail of the loon. And, she played that a lot, and the dog never stopped singing. He even knew where the pauses were. That was maybe the most mourning anybody ever did, with my sister and the piano and the dog. No one sat around moping. There was work to be done.

∽

Nan's story, set in roughly the same era, echoes Art's in one particular. Music became a comfort and a way to express feelings that otherwise went unexpressed.

Nan (79, m, 13)

My oldest sister was seventeen. She cooked for us and we went to school. I have to say this. We had beautiful clothes. I had an aunt in L.A., and she had two daughters, and one of them was a private tutor to the movie stars. They sent us boxes and boxes. I mean there was no problem really, food and clothing, because it was during the Depression and everybody else was in the same situation.

But do you know that everybody was giving my dad advice as to what to do and not to do with us? And he finally told them all to bug off, in so many words. It wasn't that exactly, but they sort of left us alone.

We kind of supported each other. We had a lot of music in the family, so I think music is the answer to a lot of things. We went to church, and we knew all of these Protestant hymns, and we sang a lot. Music was just a part of our lives. We lived in the country, but this lady that lived down like, oh, a half a mile away, she could hear us singing. We sang when we did the dishes.

∽

Jim, Art, and Nan lost parents in an earlier era, when death may have been taken more for granted as a natural part of life, but few people knew how to help children cope with grief. When Jessica's mother died in the 1980s, our culture allegedly understood more about dealing with grief, about allowing children their feelings. Jessica had what Jim didn't, a relatively close extended family to talk to her. Yet, as her story so poignantly shows, in the end, we all grieve alone. And sometimes we need to pretend it doesn't hurt.

Jessica (24, m, 16)

I could tell you in retrospect why I felt like I needed to keep my distance from my family. I don't think I knew why at the time. I was feeling very selfish about my grief. I think grief is a selfish thing. I had more of a parental role with my mother in the last couple of years of her life, making sure she was okay, and that nobody was upsetting her. So when Mom died, I didn't care how anybody else felt. I didn't think they had the right to grieve her. She was my mom, and the only other person who might have the right to grieve her the way I did was my brother. But then he wasn't as close to her, so I said to myself it's okay for my brother to feel as much pain as I do, but I didn't think that he should. I didn't want to share my pain, and I didn't want anybody to tell me to get over it.

I just wanted to pretend that I wasn't in pain. I was badgered to cry. My grandma was after me for days and days. She didn't think it was natural that I wasn't crying or grieving, but I think that I was just numb. I know that many of my mother's family friends, my boyfriend's mother, who was a psychologist, my best friend's mother, who was a psychologist, and plenty of my relatives suggested I deal with the fact that my mom had died. I didn't, though, for probably almost a year. Then I saw a therapist and had sort of a breakdown.

Addie, who is Jan's daughter and Jessica's cousin, later talked with Jessica about their shared experience of wanting to keep their grief to themselves.

Addie (19, f, 16)

I was very encouraged to talk. I wanted to talk some about it, but mostly I wanted to really keep it sort of controlled. I was very into keeping the grief controlled, and I did it. I knew what was going on, and I wasn't into sort of just sitting down and sharing grief. It's just not something I do very well in general, and I think it's also something that was a reaction to how my dad would deal with grief, or how my dad dealt with feelings in general. He sort of shut off and felt like everything was going to be okay, or was okay. He was willing to talk about it but not really get into it, sort of scratch the surface a lot. And I guess I sort of slipped into doing that. I don't know if that's a function of remembering him or wanting to somehow replace that in my life and become that or something, I don't know.

The support was there, but I didn't want it from a lot of people. I took it when I sort of felt like I needed it, like from my godmother and godfather, and their whole family who we stayed with when we went to Minnesota after he died. They all have a history with my father, so they were definitely very supportive. Most of the time when I wasn't getting support, it was because I wasn't asking for it and I didn't want it. Talk about my father mostly made me feel worse unless I initiated it. And I think people caught on to that pretty quick and stopped initiating it. I'm sorry that I sort of alienated people I think. But I also think I don't need to apologize for things that I did either.

Sometimes traditions, even if they are the traditions of our heritage, hold no power to help us mourn.

Rich (36, m, 14)

Someone told me, and I guess I didn't know this before, that when a parent dies, the eldest son is supposed to go to synagogue every day for a year and say the mourner's Kaddish. I really felt, and I know that I was made to feel, that I owed it to her. Since I had such strong feelings about my mother, I tried. It was a very strange experience for a fourteen-year-old kid who never went to synagogue. The first few months I went almost every day. And I'd show up with all these old men who didn't know me. They never said a word to me. I'd sit there through the whole service and then stand up when they did the Kaddish, then sit down, and that was it. And throughout that year, I would go occasionally.

∽

Martin Yan grew up in a different culture from anyone else in this book. For him, many of the same emotional issues just didn't apply. Yet a tradition did hold some power and meaning, so much so that he continues it to this day.

Martin Yan, chef, writer, TV personality (43, f, 3)

As soon as I was born, Communists already basically took over. About 1950, they started to nationalize and take away all the private business. And nobody behaves any differently toward me or toward anybody else. Nobody cares about you lost your father. Even if your father's around, you don't really make that much more, you're not that much better off than any other people. It's not like I'm brought up in America. Then my father's death would probably have an immense impact on my future, psychological as well as emotional, and physical. But, you know in China, basically, under Communist doctrine, your father is the Party, the official. Not your father, per se. And you basically follow the rules.

My mother would always remind us to remember, to pay respect. She has an altar in the house, just like most Asians do. And we would go to see my father's cemetery twice a year to pay respect. And even today, every year I go back I do the same thing. It's become an instinct.

∽

Beto's story about mourning demonstrates the power of tradition, if that tradition is an integrated part of someone's life. His Mexican heritage called for a full year of formal mourning. This tradition flies in the face of the "get back to normal as soon as possible" school of thought. But sometimes removal from daily life can help us back into daily life.

Beto (52, m, 14)

My father wanted us to be in mourning for a year, a very Mexican thing. I didn't go to a movie for a year, the television wasn't on for a year. No parties, nothing, for a year. We dealt with it in a very traditional way. It was not a bad way of dealing with it. There is a reason for those traditions. That year of mourning did help.

Feeling Angry

We asked people whether they felt angry at their parent for dying and abandoning them. We asked about anger, of course, because so much of the psychology of death and dying includes anger as one of the stages of grief. Many of the people we talked to did *not* feel anger at their parent for abandoning them. Paul B. did mention in the interview that he has tried to get in touch with his anger, which he's pretty sure is there, under the surface, masked by his overwhelming feeling of sadness, depression, and numbness. That, of course, raises another point about anger. It could be that people simply aren't remembering their childhood anger, perhaps because it was so frightening to them. Anger *is* a frightening emotion. Being angry at a parent is like being angry at the gods, those who have the power to control our lives. Even young children feel the strength of anger. If they are angry and allow themselves to feel or act angry, bad things are likely to happen.

However, people did talk about feeling anger at a number of other things. The stories here reflect some of the many different ways children express anger. Some, especially younger children, remembered "acting out," and on reflection, attributed their actions to anger, although not necessarily at the parent. It was often anger at the situation or at someone who tried to intervene, like Jessica's anger at her grandmother for "badgering" her to cry.

Jeffery K. (22, m, 8, f, 18)

I remember a little later I was playing in a baseball league, and my dad and his fiancée were there. I obviously was still angry. It was probably a year after my mom's passing. They put me in to pitch, and I beaned three kids in a row. I remember throwing fits between eight and ten years old.

Brown Miller, poet (51, m, 6)

During the summer after my mother died, I went to stay with my eldest sister, who had small children of her own. She fancied herself somewhat of an amateur psychologist. She had Dr. Spock's book and all of that. She spent a lot of the time talking to me about things, and that maybe helped a bit. I feel like after that summer I was better. In a vague way, things were better, but there was still that ungrieved grief, that delayed grief, that I was carrying around in me. At that age, I was writing all over furniture, fences, and walls, and I remember there was a makeup case—it had spilled red nail polish in it—that my mother had owned, and I had written "Death to You" and skull-and-crossbones all over it.

Horace Silver, musician (66, m, 9)

I stayed back that year in school because I became hostile. I wasn't belligerent in class, but I just refused to do my work. The nuns were nice to me and sympathized with the fact that I had lost my mother, but I had a resentment against God, you know. I thought God was unfair to take my mother away from me. I didn't really rebel against my dad, but I rebelled against my schoolwork. I didn't do my studies, and half-did my homework. And then the next year, here I am a big, tall kid, and I'm with these little, shorter kids, and I was kind of embarrassed, but I had to struggle through. I finally applied myself more scholastically, the next year. And then I moved on, and I never stayed back since then. But that particular year, I was very bitter and hostile. I refused to cooperate with anything.

∞

Nan, who was older, remembers being angry at God as a child and then angry again later in life when her husband died and one son was killed.

Nan (79, m, 13)

This was a famous expression then, "God knows best." And I said, "Well, if this is the way he feels . . ." I went through this belligerent attitude. "Why should this happen? Here's all of these people, and you see these other families, and why should it be us?" You just can't hardly cope with it.

∞

It is a not uncommon experience from childhood to carry memories so vivid there's a feeling of being there in the retelling. That's the quality Rachel's story had. She got angry all over again in the telling. Children also tend to interpret things in ways that adults might not. One explanation for the weight of Rachel's memory could be that terrible feeling many of us had that we had no power. We had no power to change the fact that our parent was dead, and we had no power to convince the adults in our lives to recognize situations from our point of view.

Rachel (47, f, 5)

Probably my most defining moment of rage about my father's death came in Brownie scouts. We had to make a Father's Day card. I was the only child there that did not have a present dad. And so I did want what I think then, and what I think now, was a reasonable thing. I wanted to make a Father's Day card for my mom because she did both roles. I remember the Brownie teacher telling me that my mom was a woman and she couldn't be a dad, so I couldn't make her a Father's

Day card. I can remember it was the closest I had ever come to flat-out rebellion. I mean I wanted to destroy the whole Brownie room. I can *still* feel that rage.

She made a Big Scene. She would not allow me to make a Father's Day card for my mother. She finally made me make it for my uncle. And I still am angry at myself for complying. I remember that was invoked, that whole "Well, Rachel, you've always been so well behaved." And I can remember then thinking, "It's just not right. It's my card!"

Feeling Different

Edward didn't want to be marked or named as different. At the same time, he recognizes the hostility in that reaction. His attitude was not unusual among the people we talked to.

Edward (30, f, 17)

I remember going to see a shrink for the first time in high school. The three of us, my mom and my brother and I, all went together the first time, and I remember this guy saying to us, "It sounds like you've had a pretty hard life." And I remember saying to him, "What do you mean?" And he said, "Well, you know, your parents got divorced and your father died." And I was just shocked by this, because for me it was my life, and I never thought it was exceptional or tough. This is just the way life goes. I think most kids probably feel that way up until a certain age, when they start to get a sense of other people's lives. So for me it was what happened and you dealt with it and you moved on.

I don't want to make it sound too extreme, but sometimes I felt like I was being placed on a slide and slipped into a microscope. It was like, So my dad died, big deal. I mean, maybe I didn't want that kind of concern or something. I think there was a lot of hostility involved in that. I didn't want anyone to feel sorry for me because I didn't think there was any reason for that, you know what I mean?

∽

The extra attention that can come when a parent dies is often not welcome, particularly in regard to Mother's and Father's Day. These are the days, like birthdays and holidays, that we all remember in the first year. A holiday without a parent is bad enough. A day designed to honor that parent adds another element to the loss. When the child is specifically singled out on that day, and marked as different, it can feel like salt being rubbed in the wound.

Laurie (38, m, 13)

My dad was already an alcoholic, and he was pretty lonely. My mother was really the reason that people had ever come to our house. My sister had died of breast cancer at age thirty-four, five years before my mother died. Christmas and all the holidays had always been a big deal, because my mother was bedridden. So everybody came to our house. When she was gone, those visits stopped. Nobody wanted to come see my father because he was such a strange one, so it was dramatically different. The warmth and the heart of the home was gone.

My mom died around the time of Easter, so Mother's Day was soon after. At Sunday School every Mother's Day when you came into class, they would pin a red rose on you to honor your mom. I came in, and they pinned a white rose on me. It was so hard to wear that white rose and see everybody else with their red ones. I hated it. I just wanted to rip it off. Theirs were red like blood and vitality, and for me white was a symbol of wearing the death. It was pretty traumatic. I had to wear it through the whole time, so everybody who saw me would pity me or something, and say things that I didn't know how to accept. I just pushed everybody away. I wanted to be invisible. I just didn't want to be noticed as, you know, Child of the Dead Mother. Thirteen is an age when you don't want to be different. It was hard enough all those years, living with my mother, who was an invalid. She never was able to come to school or church or anything when everybody else's mother did.

☙

Barbara Smith told a very similar story.

Barbara Smith, writer (49, m, 9)

I hated the attention that people paid to us, in particular, at church. There was always the kind of public pity. Like I mean, "Oh, there go the Smith twins." See, we were a spectacle anyway, because we were twins, and we were dressed alike. So it's not like anybody could miss us, or ignore us. I attribute it to our being so visible, but I'm sure it would happen if we'd been singles.

Oh, I hated it! Hated it. I've said this to many people who really know me. They know how shy I am at bottom, and the thing is, despite all the public kinds of things that I've had to do and learned to do, in my later life, if I could have had a choice about how I would have gotten through, it would have been to have made no waves and to have no one pay any attention to me on that very basic level of physical notice. It never happened that way. My sister and I arrived, and it was like every eye in the room turned to us. I used to hate Mother's Day.

∽

Not everyone who recalled feeling different was quite as upset about it. Michael remembered it as one of a constellation of feelings.

Michael (43, m, 9)

I recall feeling a lot of emptiness, and also loneliness. I think I remember feeling sad. I do. And I remember feeling strange, like how are the other kids going to act? It's going to be weird not to have a mother. And sometimes it might not have necessarily been a negative feeling. But it was like "This is going to make me different," but I wasn't worried about that.

There was always some discomfort about not having your mother, sort of embarrassment and discomfort. I do remember feeling that way, especially things like Mother's Day. So much of what you do in school that you used to think was fun, the stuff in school is so geared towards making this for your mom, or doing this and bringing it home. And her death kind of took the fun out of all of that.

Dreams as a Way to Cope with Changes

It's hard being a child, or even a teenager, and having to cope with change, because we have no real say in how our lives will be altered. We are moved here or there. We are expected to fit in to new rules and situations. Dreams can offer comfort, enhance memory, and help our psyches understand our parents really are dead.

Robin (46, f, 8)

The first year, I dreamt that my father was still alive. I had two entirely different lives. When I went to sleep, I dreamt that we were a normal family, that it was my father and my brother and me and my mom, and everything was right. When I was awake, he wasn't there, but I convinced myself that the *waking* time was when I was actually asleep, and the sleeping time was my actual life. So I just kind of turned it around. I don't think I really came to understand what I was doing until I was around ten or eleven years old.

Lisa (28, m, 12)

After my mom died, I moved with my brother and sister to Napa, where my father and stepmother lived. My father has a daughter with my stepmother, and she has three kids. There were nine of us in the house altogether. There was a lot of violence. If you did something wrong, you got a beating for it. There was a lot of screaming, and it was just very, very different. It was just crazy. I guess the worst part of it was being taken out of my environment. I was raised with my mother in San Francisco, and she was very liberal-minded, and my father is just totally different. He's very strict and close-minded and couldn't see beyond his own beliefs, couldn't see what was happening to his kids. That as well as being in the Napa Valley, where there was a lot of racism, as opposed to being raised in San Francisco, a multicultural city.

I had a dream that my mom showed up in the deli my father and stepmother owned. I was in the deli and she drove up with Richard, her husband, my stepfather. He was a very incredible man, a very nice man. They pulled up in a sports car, which is funny because we were poor, and my stepfather had this big huge jalopy car. I guess the idea of the dream was that they were away, they weren't really dead, they were away, and they had come back and they have money now and they're taking me away! So it was kind of depressing to wake up. I had a lot of dreams that were pretty much like that.

∽

Like Lisa, Horace Silver had recurring dreams that his mother came back. He remembers how the dream made him feel more sad when he woke up, but, as a coping mechanism, it allowed him to feel his mother's presence.

Horace Silver, musician (66, m, 9)

That first year, the main feeling I had was sad. I started sleeping in my dad's bed. And I would have these dreams, not every night, but on and off for maybe a year or two. It wasn't always exactly the same, but the dream, principally, was that she had gone away but she was coming back. And I would wake up, and I'd realize she's not coming back, because she was dead. And then I'd just lay there and cry. This happened over and over, for maybe a year or more. Maybe giving me that dream was her way of saying that she's not really dead, she's in another dimension, you know. But I was too young to understand that.

∽

Because of her living situation after her mother's death, Detta began to feel she couldn't do anything right, including grieve for her mother. Her dream, not a recurring one, was a nightmare, a horrible way to realize, finally, her mother was dead.

Detta (47, m, 17)

I know my aunt was worried because she didn't think that I had grieved enough over my mother's death. One day when I was on my way to school, I got onto a bus, and a woman got onto the bus and sat in the front by the driver. She had red hair, she was wearing the same trench coat, she looked just like my mother—to the point where I almost went up to her and asked her if there was any chance that she knew who I was.

That night I had a really *horrible* nightmare. I dreamed that I was in a laboratory full of frogs. I was walking down the rows, and all of a sudden one started screaming, "Come look at me! Look at me! I'm your mother, I'm your mother!" And I woke up screaming. Then my aunt considered that it was okay, that I had grieved enough, and I had finally had whatever it was that she decided would push me over the edge into being able to really cry a lot about missing my mother.

Doreen's dreams, like Detta's, gave her a way to realize that her mother simply was not coming back,

Doreen (36, m, 10)

I was just mad my mother was gone. I felt that my mother had abandoned me, she had left—not that she had any control over that. Everyone else was feeling guilty, and I was angry. I felt much more abandoned, later on, as I realized that she really wasn't coming back. I was having dreams at that time that I called at some point the *"nanh na-nanh nanh-nanh"* [singsong] dream, where she would pop up and say "I was just testing you, and I just wanted to see if you guys could handle it, without me," and, "it was just a joke." I had these dreams for a long time.

I remember what made me really, really realize that she was not coming back, probably eight months after she died. I was at camp, and I loved it. I think I went six weeks because it would give my father a break. It was a rest hour, and I was lying there on my bunk, and I could not conjure up my mother's face. In my mind's eye, I could only see pictures of her, the way she was in particular photographs. It was the difference between that frozen moment and being able to conjure up like I can right now what my little girl looks like with her eyes moving and animated. That's when I knew she was dead. And I really cried. That was the real grieving time for me. Mindy, my counselor, really supported me and helped me go through that. I cried all night. I remember I had to let go of the *"nanh na-nanh nanh-nanh"* dream because that wasn't gonna happen. And she was really gone.

Memory as a Way to Cope

Melissa went from a large home where she lived with her parents to sharing a bedroom at her grandmother's house. She needed to make an effort to remember all she could, since no one was talking about the life she'd been wrenched from because of the circumstances of the deaths—her father murdering her mother and then committing suicide.

Melissa (28, m, 9, f, 9)

I've always felt ashamed of the way my parents died and ashamed of my grandmother because she wasn't very clean even. My mother had been a very clean and organized person. My grandmother also couldn't attend to any of the psychological issues that were around my parents' death. And I couldn't touch on feelings about my father because, out of everything that had happened, there wasn't anybody to defend him.

When I was ten, every night I went to a lot of trouble to go over everything I could remember about both my parents and about living with them, to remember everything and go over information on how to get different places and different streets in the town that we lived in and the house that we lived in, what was it like to be here, what was it like to be there, remember when this happened, remember when that happened. I was trying to remember good things. Later on, I guess it was about high school, I decided that the memory of bad things wasn't so bad, and that if I was going to remember anything, I was going to try to remember everything.

↺

Although Melissa's story is more traumatic than many, her brutal removal from her prior life puts in relief the need to remember what quite a few of us experienced. Maybe the adults thought talking about our dead parent would make us feel worse. Maybe it was too difficult for them to remember. Maybe they thought we were young and would "get over it" faster if we didn't hear stories. Yet many of us who were robbed of our memories by silent adults have devoted much of our adulthood to retrieving them. Terry, part of whose story appears later in this chapter, talked about his struggle to conjure memories. With awe in his voice, he told us how he had just recently seen a home movie in which his mother appeared for a few seconds, walking across a room. It was like a confirmation that someone he couldn't remember, someone who nobody would talk about, did exist after all.

Growing Up Too Soon

In the previous chapter, William recalled several adults telling him he was the man of the family. It was a message especially prevalent in the stories of men who are now middle-aged or older. One can only hope that is something we now know not to say to bereaved boys. It may have been intended to comfort, to give him a sense of responsibility to somehow make up for his loss. But William recalls feeling bewildered. What was he supposed to do? Other men, like Tron, despite their young age, tried to take on more adult roles on their own.

Tron Bykle, artist (51, f, 14)

I remember walking and talking to a friend—I was in eighth grade—and I was walking with him and saying, "Well, now that my father is dead, I have to drop out of school and get a job to take care of my mother and family." He said something contrary to that. But I was dead set on it. That's what I thought I had to do, which was fine by me. Of course, I had no idea what to do. In the wintertime, I'd go and get the coal and the wood for the apartment. I felt I was the oldest man in the house.

Sometimes very young children will try to take on an adult role.

Jan B. (50, f, 8)

I think for maybe a year I was awake all night. Many nights. You know how you lie in bed and you see cars driving by and the lights on the ceiling? I have these vivid memories of that. I was protecting the house from being broken into. I never spoke about it. I think I identified with my father. He had died, so I was in charge of protecting the house from anybody breaking into it. But he hadn't been able to protect us from death, so how was I going to protect us from death?

Given the circumstances, Deborah Nagle didn't have much choice but to take on responsibilities well beyond her years.

Deborah Nagle, writer (46, f, 12)

The summer my father died we went to the Cape and we took a cottage that had seven bedrooms, horse stables, a stocked fish pond, and a stained-glass library with miniature books, really gorgeous. My mother was doing a lot of crazy things, was heavily into drinking and tranquilizers. None of us had realized she was having such a bad time. We just thought we were having fun.

That fall I started ninth grade, and the entire school year was a blur. I was trying as hard as I could to take the place of my father by keeping the house running when it seemed as though my mother couldn't. I even had moved upstairs into my father's bed, with my mother in her bed, and we would sometimes talk late into the night while Johnny Carson droned on in the background.

The following summer (1962) my mother was in a very bad car accident, which crushed her from the chest down to her feet. She was drunk when she left the house that evening, and about ten o'clock I got a call from a policeman who asked if he could speak to my dad. I told him my dad wasn't here and then said my dad died last summer. When I heard how bad my mom was, I moaned and started to cry. I grabbed a dish towel and covered my mouth so no one would hear my sobbing.

My mother was in the hospital forever. I tried to keep the house together for about, I don't know, a couple of weeks. I then split the kids up for the summer. Some of them went to godmothers, some to neighbors, some to grandparents. I didn't realize that my brothers and sisters thought my mother had died. My four-year-old sister showed the worst of the trauma when she no longer would eat or cry.

I believe my mother came home sometime in November. She was in a full body cast from the neck down to her toes. The furniture was moved out so that a hospital bed could be put in the dining room. I took care of her, emptied her bedpans, gave her drugs, and massaged her head. I'd do the food shopping and I sent the laundry out. When Christmas came around, my twelve-year-old sister and I did the shopping for the kids, getting a Christmas tree, collecting money from an aunt or a friend. I had a taxi come and pick us up, which was odd in the suburbs. All my brothers and sister have absolute memory loss for three or four years. Nobody was being treated, there was no intervention, and everybody was really young.

∽

Deborah H. coped by taking care of business and by taking cues from her father.

Deborah H. (45, m, 16)

In the sort of classical sixteen-year-old-with-two-younger-brothers kind of way, I did things around the house. I had been a little-mother kind of kid anyway. Took care of the neighborhood kids. So I knew a lot about caretaker stuff. My mother's death probably changed the most my relationship with my eight-year-old brother, because he was eight years younger than I and he already felt very little to me. With him waking up in the middle of the night, having nightmares, and missing Mommy, and crying "Mommy," and I would go to him and hold him and he would call me Mommy and I would be Mommy for him in those middle-of-the-night times. So I went from being clearly older sister to mommy substitute for him for a while. I wasn't home for much longer. I was a junior in high school.

When I went back to school, everybody was very deferential. I got the best grades of my high school career the following semester through no change in either ability or work level because people felt sorry for me, or bad for me. I think that the emotional leadership in my family spilled over to school, and I already had that leadership ability, but then it really blossomed. I became class president the next year. I did reverse acting out. I got all of my attention by being more good and more responsible and, you know, wise. I remember feeling incredibly wise.

∽

When the single caretaking parent dies and a house must be closed, the child faces another loss, a very concrete loss of childhood. People deal with that loss in different ways. We talked with Shannon (m, 19) in her crowded apartment. At one point, she gestured around the room, pointing out all the things that had been in her childhood home. She talked about fiercely protecting her and her brother Jeff's interests, trying to ensure that their childhood was not thrown away.

Detta had a different experience. She told us how in her adult life she's become a collector.

Detta (47, m, 17)

Closing the house was pretty hard. My aunts wanted to get rid of all this stuff. They decided what I should keep, and what would be thrown away. And what they wanted, they took. I think they just took little mementos, which was really fine. My mind wasn't on what to do with the stuff, and I was surprised at their emphasis. Although I can understand, they pretty much packed up and threw away my childhood—all my dolls, including the glamour one my mother had sewn clothes for. They didn't really understand. I have built a mythological ancestor out of other people's mothers' things to make up for the stuff that my family took away from me.

When the surviving parent isn't capable of taking care of the child or there is no surviving parent, things can get even more complicated. Jessica (m, 16) opted to live with friends of her mother's so she could stay in the same town she'd been living in. Joe made a different choice. Both of them had to learn to take care of themselves at an early age.

Joe (28, m, 12)

There was sort of a struggle between a friend of my mother's who wanted to take me, and my sister. And my sister won out. She wanted me to stay with my family, with her or my brother. At the time, I was actually interested in living maybe with this other person because it was an older woman and there was a father and they had a dog and they had a house. I guess it was good in the long run because I learned to be self-sufficient. And this is no criticism to my brother and sister—they were so young, especially my brother, being twenty-one. Right now I'm seven years older than he was when he had to take care of me and I can't imagine taking care of me in seventh grade. I think he got a Social Security check for me, but he was somewhat irresponsible with money at the time. There were a lot of issues over my missing that sort of family structure, that parental structure, because it wasn't there. So a lot of times I had to cook for myself because he just went to Burger King. I don't know where I got this, maybe from my sister, but I had a sense of "I've got to eat better." And there was a lot of conflict around it. I don't remember a lot of it, but I remember complaining to my sister about how I didn't like it. So I started spending a lot of time away from our apartment, wherever we lived, with friends, or I'd go spend the night at my sister's once in a while. I know it was hard for my brother. He wanted to take care of me, but he also wanted to live his own life.

Surviving Parent

Our relationship with our surviving parent changes in many ways. Many children feel some need, which they often resent, to try to protect their surviving parent. Others fear abandonment by that parent as well. Mariam grew up in a vastly different culture from many of the people in this book. Because she scarcely knew her father, the impact of his death on her life was reflected in her relationship with her mother.

Mariam (39, f, 13)

This is kind of unusual—my father had two wives. He had another wife before he married my mother, and my mother was much younger than my father. Basically, he was living with us, and he would visit them on weekends. I had never seen my stepmother, and my family was always afraid of them. My father had farming land that was very difficult to manage. After he died, my mother had to take care of it. She had never done it.

I started going to school in my hometown. I kind of felt like she needed help, but I couldn't help her. I was really afraid, especially because she became sick after my father died. I couldn't help her, and, at the same time, I would feel lonely, and I hated my hometown because it's a small town and you have to be very careful how you act. And my mother was busy. Instead of being nicer, I would be more obnoxious, and then I would feel guilty being obnoxious, but then feeling guilty I would be more obnoxious.

I remember I had a problem with Arabic, which you had to study, and I hated it. I had to repeat it again in the summer, and everybody was so busy with the whole situation that they didn't have time to get me a teacher or teach me about it so I could catch up. Finally, my mother got this person to come as a private teacher, and I hated it because he was a mullah, wearing clothes like a religious person. She asked me to wear the veil when I go to the room and he comes to teach me Arabic. I was really, really upset and I was crying, crying how I didn't want to go. That was the only time she got really mad at me, and she said, "Oh, you didn't cry that much when your father died, and you are crying for just wearing the veil and going to the room."

∽

Monica's surviving parent was a father she'd never met, a man who, along with her older siblings, was ill equipped to take care of her or help her deal with her grief.

Monica (30, m, 10)

I saw my dad for the first time. He was an old-fashioned man. He didn't want females to dress a certain way, which my sisters, who were teenagers, didn't like, so he threw them out of the house. Then it was just my dad, my youngest brothers, and me. My oldest brother wasn't around much. I mostly felt lots of rejection. I tried to force myself to like my father, but I didn't like him. He was very different compared to my mom. My dad was a very cold person. He tried to take my brothers' money to gamble at the racetrack. I got hit a lot, too, for talking about my mom, and I think that that's why I never asked about her. I remember my sisters used to say, "Well, you're not going to bring her back!"

Jamie (45, m, 19)

We were lost, but things functioned okay. My father set up a routine, and the house was taken care of. I think he asked me to come home for the summers until my brother was out of school. He relied on me a lot. I'm the only daughter. Holiday functions, and social functions. Growing up in the Navy, I think, had an effect on that, too. I had been groomed for that.

He didn't withdraw affection, but he was withdrawn, I have to say. I think that he really tried, especially in the year following her death, to share with me some of the things about their relationship. Partly probably so he wouldn't lose them, and partly so that I would have maybe a more adult understanding of the value of that.

So in some ways it was an opportunity to sort of be the emotional center and help hold things together and not lose my place in the family. Things like taking care of going down and buying a wedding present for so-and-so or going to a party occasionally with my father were not problems, or doing the holidays. I mean I just did it because that's the way we did. But in another sense, it was a big burden that I really felt in a lot of ways inadequate for.

∽

The death of a breadwinning parent can cause serious financial hardship, like that Mary Montgomery spoke of, when her mother was forced to sell the farm, in the pre–Social Security days of the Depression. For others, like Jessica, Paul. J., and David Z., Social Security provided a safety net.

David Z. (52, f, 13)

My mother was a very serious caregiver for me at that point. When we moved to Florida, she bought me a relatively new car. She overdid it, constantly buying things for me and for my sister. But she did not want me to participate in her economic life at all as I think about it now, did not expect me to work, although I did, and raised me with a lot of love and care, a lot of spoiling during that period.

She was terribly destroyed by all of this and would regularly cry. She relied on me to the extent that I would walk by and regularly find her crying in the bedroom or something. And she'd give me a hug and she'd say either one of two things, either "What are we going to do?" or "Everything's going to be all right." But I remember primarily "What are we going to do?" But then when it came to doing, she handled it, for better or for worse.

I recollect saying to myself, periodically, "I killed him. I killed him," sort of fantasizing that you could kill someone just by wishing it. I remember saying to my mother, "I killed him, I killed him." And she would say, "No, no, don't be silly. It's not true. You didn't kill your father." She was supportive in saying "That's silly." If a kid has an injury and says, "Is my leg going to fall off?" you say, "Don't be silly, that's ridiculous."

∽

Nan talked about how her relatives thought her father incapable of taking care of children. The idea that men can't take care of children, especially daughters, may not be as pervasive now as it was in the days Nan was a girl. But Doreen, who is considerably younger, had a similar experience.

Doreen (36, m, 10)

My father really came up to the mark on this one. He was really there for us. But he was really sad. I remember him crying. He was alone in that big bed all by himself. I remember one night he came and got in bed with me. He couldn't say anything. All he could do was cry. And I didn't know what to do to comfort him. And I just cried, too. And we cried. Because he couldn't get in the bed by himself, he was so lonely. I held him, he was my *daddy*. We'd just lost our mother.

I remember there was talk that maybe it was not appropriate that he would keep me and my sister, being that she was fourteen and I was ten, that maybe we should be with a woman. But I don't know where that came from. All I know is that I remember overhearing this kind of talk. I was always kind of afraid that something would happen, what they were scared would happen, that something incestual would happen. I didn't know what to do with that information, other than to be fearful. And when he came in my bed, I remember feeling a little bit like, "This is not right," but then when he cried, he was so lonely and sad that I knew it was okay. We were all lonely. We needed each other, that's all we had.

✑

The fear or the fact of abandonment by the surviving parent came up again and again. Mary Montgomery's fear started at a young age and persisted throughout her childhood, an instance which shows how difficult it sometimes is to divide our lives into neat packages of time.

Mary Montgomery, writer (61, f, 3)

My mom was very much there. However, she has never been an affectionate woman. I think because she always said "I have to be both mother and father," she was even less affectionate than she might have been because affection means softness. I wasn't as bothered by this as my brothers. They got spanked a lot. But I tried to be the perfect kid, so I avoided all that. I never gave her any grief. I took on that role right away, I think.

We knew that she had given up almost everything to raise us. But there were a lot of mixed messages. Sometimes she'd say, "If I didn't have you kids, I would have this." Or, "I feel like running away and never coming back." So I was always afraid that she might. I still remember one night. I must have been about in third or fourth grade. She taught at a country school, and we usually knew about the time she was coming home, and she didn't come home. And I can remember sitting there, on the front porch, just absolutely devastated and sobbing. I mean I thought she wasn't coming home.

I feared abandonment more than dying. I'm really not casting blame on her, but I'm sure it was because of those remarks. I do know that I never talked to my mother ever about my feelings. If I said anything to her that was a concern of mine, and I remember this from earliest childhood, she would say, "Now, that just gives me one more thing to worry about." And so I never took anything to her if I could possibly avoid it. Again, it was trying to be that perfect child and not giving her any more things to worry about. And it carried over into my adult life as well.

✑

Several people talked about their surviving parent, often a mother, grieving deeply and for a long time, and becoming, almost as a by-product, closed off to the child. These people were taken care of. They had meals and clean clothes. But mothers who had previously stayed at home needed to go to work, putting another demand on their time, leaving less for the children. Even for older children, that feeling of being abandoned can cut deeply.

William (54, f, 14)

My mom was quite overwhelmed by the responsibility. I guess I suspected or noticed that she was just busy or distracted, but I didn't feel like she'd really withdrawn her love. I had plenty of attention, but I was missing the hugs. Talking about this, I'm reminded of something on the first day. It was very influential in my relationship with my mother. After she'd been put to bed and I'd done the dishes, I went to check in on her. I knocked and I opened the door to the bedroom and a couple of her women friends were with her. As I came in her room, she sat up and said, "Oh he looks just like his father," and fell back, sobbing. Her friends kind of waved me off. I backed out the door and closed it.

Now I don't look anything like my father. I look like my maternal grandfather. That was just a hysterical reaction. I knew that, but the next morning I was very conflicted as to whether to go see her or not. I wanted to go to her, and I needed Mom, you know. But I didn't want to trigger that reaction. Finally, she called me to her room. I went in very gingerly, and she was okay. And she said to me, "Why didn't you come and see me earlier?" I made some apology. But after that I was very skittish, or I guess careful, around my mom. So there was a kind of a separation that got set up.

I do remember a particular evening that she was angry. You could see it, but it was subterranean. She was tired and angry. Three kids at the dinner table, and she was hustling work. She was working as a teacher's aide and made very little money. She said, "I'm going to the movies and you can come or not." It's the first time that I ever heard her say anything like that. She'd always say, "We're going to the movies tonight." You know, *we* are. And it was clear the way she said it, I didn't go, as much as I loved the movies. Emotionally, I felt that she had abandoned us.

∽

To get the whole picture, it is important to note here that William went on to say that later in life he developed a warm and close relationship with his mother that lasts to this day. But in the first year he felt like he'd lost his mother as well as his father.

Mothers are more apt to be the "emotional center" of the family, the ones who listen to stories, soothe wounds, and show love in the daily ways a small child understands. From fairy tales to recent books on childhood bereavement, we get the idea that it's harder to lose a mother than a father. That may or may not be true. By and large, it seems a social construct that is pretty useless to the motherless or fatherless child.

But we do expect a lot from mothers and tend to blame them when things go awry, perhaps in a different way than we blame fathers. And, as Patricia points out, often when the father dies, the mother may essentially disappear from the child's life as well.

Patricia (48, f, 13)

Everybody assumes that when you lose someone like a father it's such a sad thing. But the real issue for me, and I think for lots of kids, is that when fathers die, mothers go away. They're not emotionally available to their kids. Whole chunks of history are lost because of that. I mean I'm very aware of not knowing things. And my mother's relationship with me is fairly nonexistent at this point, for lots of reasons, but certainly one of them is that she chose not to talk to me and made it real clear that I'd better not after my father died because she couldn't say anything. She couldn't talk at all. She viewed that as an intrusion. She was just emotionally unavailable. And when mothers are emotionally unavailable, good-bye. Kids are left on their own to figure it all out. Life. The future. And I resent that.

∽

In contrast, Lauren Muller was able to forge a new, closer relationship with her mother after her father's death.

Lauren Muller, writer (34, f, 11)

I got the impression that my mother especially had to grow up after my father died. I think she certainly had her own personality, but she was probably very much also the wife. I think for her it was that everything was really ripped out from under her and she had to re-think it all. She also had to learn about finances. I think in some ways my father was a gambler, so a lot of what he had was on credit and we had to sell the farm. She also did run a ballet school before he died, so she had some income. She taught ballet at the university. I think we started getting Social Security. And then she remarried two years later. I'm amazed at what my mother accomplished. I think I was amazed by her strength and sense of needing to redefine herself. I always felt she was quite remarkable.

I also know now that I mothered her a lot and that she relied on me a lot. There would be conversations where she was sobbing and I would offer some sort of bit of wisdom that she would find very consoling, and I think that I probably thought I had some wisdom. I do think children can have wisdom in a way. I revered my mother very much. And I guess these conversations brought us a certain intimacy, but there was also a way in which I know that she was very dependent on me.

∽

Mary Montgomery became the good child as a way to ensure her mother wouldn't abandon the family. Lauren Muller does not mention any explicit fear of abandonment. But perhaps her mother's dependence on her is a kind of insurance policy: if she depends on me, she won't abandon me. The conventional wisdom, of course, is that adults should not depend on children. However, as Muller points out, some dependence can make a child feel wise and needed, especially if that child is not being asked to assume roles or caretaking tasks far beyond his or her years.

In other families, things just seem to fall apart. Janette experienced a particularly painful double bind: feeling that no one was there for her, but that she had to take care of things far beyond her skill level, while at the same time feeling that if she let on what was happening, people around her would "look down" on her.

Janette (19, m, 12)

When my mother died, I felt like I didn't have anyone. I was close to my sisters, but they were closer to each other. My three sisters are older, but I was the one who was expected to take over. I was never close to my father. When my mom died, she was my life. I was connected at the hip with her. I never really knew my father. He was there, but he wasn't there. We all grew up to be scared of him.

My dad wasn't doing too good, I guess, because the insurance didn't pay for all her medical bills. She was in there for so long, he was left with over a hundred thousand dollars' worth of medical bills. He had to take care of that and take care of all of us, and he owns a store. It put a whole different burden on all of us because we were used to always getting what we wanted. And then it was all gone.

It was just too much for me. I had to clean the kitchen and do everything. And I kind of felt bad. I felt like I had to do it for him, but later realized that I had to take care of myself, you know? I love him, but I have to take care of myself. I think everybody kind of knows, they know my dad, but I felt that if I showed them I was hurting, I would be looked down upon again, the way people pitied me at the funeral.

∽

Terry used strong imagery to describe how bereft he felt after his mother died, especially since his father was suffering so intensely and left so much about his mother's death untold. For example, he was an adult before he even found out where his mother was buried.

Terry (38, m, 6)

I don't think that we blamed my dad. I think that we clung on to him a lot more for fear of losing him, too. I think of the analogy of these kind of drowning rats clinging on to some piece of wood out in a stormy ocean. He was dealing with his own stuff. He couldn't really be there that much for us. But still he was all that was there. He was the semblance of a family or what was left of it.

Recently, I was talking to my aunt and my grandmother, who are his sister and mother, about that time and how he felt about my mother. They were telling me a story that I hadn't heard before about after we were in New Mexico. He had visited and then he went off somewhere on a train. He saw someone get on a train that looked just like my mother, and he was trying to follow her and lost her in the train or something. Later, he had come back and told them that if he had met up with this woman who looked like my mother, he would have just gone away with her and never come back.

I related this story and this album that he used to play called *Black Orpheus,* which is a story about this guy who follows his lover back into hell. The world that he exists in isn't worth it anymore, so his main focus is to follow her. That's my own little fantasy version of what's going on in his mind, because of course he has never related what is going on in his mind. I imagine him almost losing his mind. And it didn't leave much for us.

⁂

In the face of their surviving parents' refusal to talk, children can imagine some very strange things.

Jan B. (50, f, 8)

My mother never talked about my father. She never said his name, she never showed pictures. We had this ritual every night around suppertime, and everybody was always there. We talked about school, but my image was that my father's dead body was *on* the dining-room table. And that we *ate* around the dead body. But we never spoke.

The one real vivid memory I have, and I don't know if I was eight and a half or nine, but *Lassie,* the TV show, was on, and that was one of those nights where Lassie got shot. I got up and went to the bathroom, and sobbed in a towel loudly, in the bathroom, in the towel, by myself. My mother was in the next room. She never came in. I was really in need. She never said anything to me until the next day. And then she said, "Why were you so upset about Lassie?" I didn't realize until many years later that my family was shamed out of our fears. My mother, by not sharing things, told me that feelings aren't okay.

She also never dated—thirty-two years old, a very attractive woman. So there was also a rule about men and sexuality, and it's all a piece of this that got buried with my father's casket. I'll be damned if I know why. And of course to this day she wouldn't touch any of this.

I felt like she might die. I remember listening to her footsteps at night to be sure she was there.

∽

Kristy's experience echoes others—her attachment to her late father, the pressure of hospital bills and money worries. But worse, Kristy also feared her mother might die. So at age thirteen she began making plans for how she would take care of her younger brother and herself. This sort of planning for future disaster seems logical to a bereaved child. To plan how we will cope in the face of imagined disaster can make us feel less helpless. It can give us a sense of power, whether the plans are realistic or not. In a way, Kristy's planning echoes Lauren Muller's sense of strength: both felt they had suffered the worst and could deal with almost anything.

Kristy (25, f, 13)

I totally looked up to my dad. I was always with my dad. I was angry that he left me with my mom, who I didn't relate to at all. She became so strict. She reverted to a kind of upbringing that I wasn't used to, which was old traditional Japanese upbringing. I totally resented that.

My mom went into a heavy depression. My stomach is hurting right now to talk about it. She was not present at all. And she used to have fantasies that she's now beginning to tell me. She'd have to lock the door upstairs because she'd see herself walking out of the window. She would scream in the middle of the night, or just let out wails. Cry. Get angry. But she never said, "I'm feeling very sad." Not a softness to it. It was very dramatic and strange, and I was terrified of it.

A couple times I had to call an ambulance because she had this inner-ear thing going on. She didn't want anybody else involved. I didn't know what to do, so I called the ambulance. The ambulance came, put Mom on the stretcher. Then they found out I was under sixteen years old, and I had to fill out a different form. I just felt completely disrespected. I was so terrified. And I had to take care of the paperwork.

I was prepared for Mom dying. I would find the letters that she was writing about how she thinks she has cancer, she thinks she's dying. I didn't know, was I *meant* to see it? I was ready to take care of the house. Ready to take care of my brother and get through. College was the most important thing.

✍

Alcohol abuse always complicates things.

Jim (61, m, 16, f, 18)

It was awful. I was completely isolated. I didn't like my father. I wasn't afraid of being left all alone. I was more afraid that he would come home drunk. There were a couple of good moments, when he was very good and kind. I remember a couple of times being with him and going out for breakfast sometimes, or something like that. He was sometimes effusive when he was drunk, and maudlin, and I just backed away from him. I didn't want to know much about him.

He felt really guilty. He'd been saying for the entire year that my mother was dying that he was going to take her around the world, one last time. Never got anything together whatsoever. And, he felt really, really awful. But he'd felt, he felt awful *all* his life. So, to me, it didn't seem that much of a change. He was depressed. I don't why he was so depressed. As I've gotten older, I've tried to guess at why he was so depressed. He self-medicated with alcohol. I cooked a lot from cans. I was pretty much on my own.

Tron Bykle, artist (51, f, 14)

My mother's boyfriend from her childhood all of a sudden was there. It was very chaotic, and our mother was no longer there for us, she only lived for going out on the town. And the horror was that there had been no substance abuse in our home. Now she would come home rather drunk—I mean, it was horrible, horrible.

One of the things that is really etched in my mind is one night she came home drunk, one, two o'clock, and I'd been lying in bed, waiting for her, worrying about her. Then I heard these sort of grunts and roars in the stairway leading to the fourth floor, and there were very steep stairs going up. I open the door, and here she comes in her black fur coat, with a red carnation in her mouth, crawling on all fours. I don't know why she came home, because she said she was going to go out and see him again. So I said, "No, you're absolutely not." And she said, "Oh yes I am." So I grabbed her literally in her fur coat and threw her on my bed and tied her to the bed with a clothesline, and found our bread knife and ran down to see if I could find this guy, because I was going to do him in. I ran all over the neighborhood trying to find him, and of course I didn't, and that was that. She was passed out when I came back and I untied her.

I felt shame. Nobody came up and said "Your mother is drinking and running around town," but everybody knew. I started to become a total—pardon the expression—arrogant asshole. My grades went. And what else did I do? Well, I started keeping relatively "bad company." Then there was "family counseling," where my godfather and some other people came in and one of my uncles just about knocked me senseless. He actually physically abused me because I had such an attitude.

Other Adults

Sometimes adults outside the family were helpful and sometimes they turned out to be harmful because of their own problems.

Lauren Muller, writer (34, f, 11)

I think it was the summer after my father died, a Christian minister friend of my father's and of the family did a pretty horrible thing. We would take walks and talk about God and death, that kind of thing. We were walking in the country when he unzipped his pants and pulled them down and asked me to touch him. I think I remember saying no. I remember driving home and not talking and then later calling him up and saying that we needed to talk. We went down to this big rock that hangs over the bluff in front of our house. I think I remember sitting cross-legged and saying I don't know what's going on, but I know it's not right and I'm going to tell my mother. And he started crying and asked me to forgive him, and I said that I did and then I went back to the house. He went home.

I remember telling my mother in my mother and father's bedroom and her saying she didn't understand. She was sort of saying, "I don't understand. Does he just want you to see what male anatomy is like? I just don't understand." Then she said, "I know he's a good man and you just have to think of this as mud on top of him." And I think I felt because I had talked to him and it never happened again that I had taken care of it. I would see him at church later. I think I felt that I had been very grown-up that I had handled it. And I don't think my memory is deceiving me. I think I had no more problems with him. But it had its effects later on.

It was much more of a violation than I had known about, and the combination of it happening right after my father's death, and this person who is called "father" in the church, who was a friend of my father's, who was, supposedly, the person taking care of us—all that combination of things affected me.

I also have a positive father figure from that time period. He was the seventh- and eighth-grade teacher at the school. I was reading M. Esther Harding, you know, women Jungians, Irene Claremont de Castillejo, and *Jonathan Livingston Seagull,* and so in between classes we would stop and talk about these books.

William (54, f, 14)

I'm extremely resentful to this day, and I'm very angry at those senior males. None of them, even my father's partner, and men that I thought that I was pretty close to, ever reached the slightest hand out to me. And when I discussed this with my mother a couple of years ago, she, with considerable anger in her voice, said they never offered to do anything for her either.

Soon after my father died, one of the priests from the school came and visited my mother and said there was a fund put up by other alums who had had the same experience. They simply paid the tuition and fees and books for me for the next three years. She never paid a cent for it, and in September or late August, the Jesuits would have us down there and they'd give her a gift certificate to a men's store to buy clothes for me for the start of the school year. They did a terrific thing.

My teacher from the fifth grade, a saint in my opinion, Mother White, sent me a sympathy card. That was the only expression of sympathy I directly received from anybody that was sent to me.

∞

"The only expression of sympathy . . . that was sent to me." That says a lot. When our world is falling apart and our families are thrown into chaos, it's nice to know that somebody cares about us as individuals.

It's never easy to know what to say to a bereaved person, but careless comments can make things much worse. Beto recalled an algebra teacher who wouldn't postpone a test because he didn't believe his mother died. Detta told a story about her gym teacher, who'd promised to flunk anyone who missed class. When Detta returned to class after her mother's funeral with a note from the dean, the teacher refused to look at the note and said, "I want you to tell me and the rest of the class why you weren't here." The teacher apologized later, but the damage had been done.

And then there are the more sensitive responses. Danny was happy to see his coaches at his mother's funeral, and Sandy's high school counselor helped get her through a difficult situation with her mother after her father died.

After all that Athena had dealt with, a teacher finally came through for her.

Athena (19, f, 17)

My senior year in school, they started this program with loss and grieving. I got this little paper: "Can you come down to this office?" I came down. She told me about the program. She said, "Yes. I have a list of names of people who have lost someone, had people who have died." I said, "How did you find out about me in the first place?" I guess teachers talk behind your back. She said, "Your counselor gave it to me." I was really mad because that's really personal, and I don't like people knowing.

Anyway, she said, "I want to make this group, and I want to know if you want to come." And I said, "Okay." So it was supposed to be about ten people. It ended up with one. Me. We only did it for a month. When I was getting ready to graduate, she said, "I really don't like leaving this open, and not working through it all." She was going by this book. I don't remember the name. I still have it at home.* She knew I had a therapist, and she said, "If you want to continue this, you can do it with your therapist."

So I told the therapist about the book, and he got the book. That's how we got into it. That book helped me a lot. The exercises helped me to work through our relationship. There were different exercises to go through—to talk about it, to deal with it, to learn, you know what I mean. It helped me see that there was a relationship with my dad that was incomplete, and I had to complete it to deal with what happened because when my dad died, I saw only bad things. I had only bad memories. Now I have good and bad.

∽

Walter Liggett and his sister were sent to live on a farm, out of the way of the murder trial of his father's killer. He remembers that period as an almost idyllic interlude, when he was well taken care of by the other adults in his life.

Walter Liggett, poet (70, f, 11)

During January, a month after the murder of my father, my sister and I went to live on the Wisconsin farm of a family our parents had known. We were there for nearly two months with their two daughters, who were about our age. I remember walking over a mile to school. There wasn't any school bus, so you just walked, and it was fifteen below zero. I knew that my father had been murdered and that there was a trial going on, but I sort of put all of that out of my mind. My mother wanted us out of the city, with all the publicity.

My memories are pretty abundant of the month we spent on the farm. I remember going to school, studying, doing the chores around the place. I had a bed right at the foot of the fireplace, so my job was

---

* *The Grief Recovery Handbook* by John W. James and Frank Cherry (New York: HarperPerennial, 1989).

to get up about six o'clock in the morning and start the fire. It would be really cold, down to zero. I'd sometimes dress under the covers. Then I'd get the fire going with the pile of wood shavings we used as kindling. We were fed well with good breakfasts, and we were given lunch to take to school. In March we went to live with my mother's family in Brooklyn.

Peer Group

Jeff B. (24, m, 18)

I think, because of my personality at the time, and the way I operated, my support came way more from my friends and a couple of close older adults, who at the time were part of my life in close-friendship types of ways.

At the time of my mom's death, I had just started seeing a girl, and we became very, very serious. Within a month, my mom died and I heard from a bunch of my friends and I didn't hear from her. After I went back to school and caught up with her, I said, "Whoa, you didn't call." And she said, "Right." Interestingly enough, and positively enough, her older brother had died a year and a half before I met her. So she was just dealing with that, and when we had talked about that, she said, "Would it have mattered if I would've called? What would you have wanted me to say? Nothing."

And we ended up talking a great deal about it. But initially her comment made so much sense to me. Like, "What the fuck can I say to you to make it okay? There's nothing. And do you really even need that to fill space? Why not let it be empty?" I mean, you can cut the pie a number of ways but it still sucked, and it still altered your life and your perception of things. So just let it *be* that.

At the time, I was always involved with a lot of different types of groups, types of groups that wouldn't associate with each other normally. I could pick and choose, which was valuable for me. I had one friend whose dad had died quickly of cancer. He was like a really goofy kid, so we would hang out and be at a party or something, and he would just say one thing to me, and that would be enough. Then sometimes I'd hang with people who didn't know how to deal with it. So their way of dealing with it was just like, "Do you wanna go to a movie?"

I think my relationship with my sister changed. I'm not sure if it was so much because of my mother's death or because of us getting older, and getting to that plateau where we weren't living together. She and I, at least my perception is, we are very, very close, in a distant way. And I think that helped her through that experience as well.

∞

Shannon, Jeff's sister, talks about how her relationships changed as well.

Shannon (24, m, 19)

I think probably for the first few months I was basically in a daze. You don't realize it then, but you realize it now. I went through things pretty regularly, but I don't remember a lot of it, except for always wondering when is this going to go away, when am I not going to feel like this anymore? Is there a period of time where it's not going to hurt this much and I'm not going to think about it as much? It doesn't happen that way.

The ins and outs of daily life didn't change that much, but my attitude started to change. I was still hanging out with friends from high school who were going to different colleges and universities around. Most of them were still living at home. And within two months or so, it was obvious that I was starting to break loose from that, and I don't think it was just the fact that we were at college. I had a couple of run-ins with people where they told me I was acting weird, and I would scream out, "Why the hell do you think I'm acting weird? You know my mom just died two months ago—of course I'm not going to be the same person I was a little while ago." I could feel that I was changing, that I was growing up, that something drastic had just happened. I couldn't go through my life being a little kid.

Doreen (36, m, 10)

I was in the fifth grade when I went back to school, and I remember the class members walking on eggshells around me for what seemed like a long time. There was a lot of whispering behind my back because I was this oddity. I was this child who didn't have a mother. I mean there were plenty of people in our community who didn't have fathers, but there wasn't anyone who didn't have a mama. And my mother had died. This was a big deal.

Marc (39, f, 10)

As for my friends, there's sort of this fear of death that kids have, and kind of a, ya know, a reverence about death? That it's both scary and somehow holy. So there was a kind of distance, because of that. But it didn't last too long. I mean, kids don't really think about things too hard. Or at least not other people's problems. So within a short time it was forgotten about, and things were back to normal with my friends.

∽

In Nan's experience, there were peers who knew exactly how she felt.

Nan (79, m, 13)

Well, do you know there were several kids in our classes in the same situation? I had this one close friend, her mother had passed away and so her aunt and uncle were raising her. So that wasn't uncommon back then. Like this friend of mine, her father passed away. They were the only Catholic family in my town. They were more supportive, I'll have to say, than anybody that I can remember.

∽

Eric Marcus wasn't supposed to know that his father killed himself, so he barely talked to anyone about it.

Eric Marcus, writer (36, f, 12)

I told almost no one that he died, because I wasn't supposed to know that he killed himself. It was kept secret, and I thought it was something horrible that he'd done. Not knowing exactly what he'd done, or the implications of it, I didn't know what to say to anybody. So I didn't say anything. It was my first year of junior high school, and a lot of my close friends were scattered, so I told virtually no one, other than my two best friends, that my father was even dead. I had one friend years later who said, "How's your father doing?" And I realized I had forgotten to tell him my father was dead. So I told him.

The First Year

One year—the first year after a parent dies—is an arbitrary demarcation. Yet it's a length of time often prescribed by culture and tradition that perhaps reflects the seasons of the heart. During the first year after a death, we live through the seasons. We live through the first holidays and birthdays, ours and our dead parent's. Spring flowers bloom and the mother who planted them is absent. Summer vacation comes and goes, with no father to take us to the beach. School starts again. We are different children, learning new things our dead parent will never know about, perhaps living somewhere he or she has never seen. Winter settles in, and spring follows. The first year becomes the second year. The second year becomes many years.

The full extent of grief is hardly ever felt in this first year, or indeed in childhood. The "experts," from psychologists to theologians to novelists to grown-up bereaved children, differ on whether a child is mature enough to fully experience grief or not. To us, neither view is true. Or both are. Children can grieve, and we almost all revisit our grief for many, many years, maybe the rest of our lives. But that is getting ahead of our story.

The grief of losing a parent is always a part of our lives. There is no arbitrary mourning period, after which things are all better and life goes on as usual. Yet we persist in talking about "getting over" grief, as if it's a disease, like chicken pox that leaves a few scars, and then we are good as new.

In the next chapter, we move on to what we call the "marked passage," the rest of childhood and then adolescence, when every new experience is filtered through the lens of loss.

5

Marked Passage

My father died suddenly when he was forty and I was twelve. For years after his death I was bitterly resentful of his abrupt departure: I tried to keep the memory of him, his voice, his face, the color of his hair, the way he moved, the clothes he wore, and noted the anniversary of his death each year as it came around.—Susan Kenney, *In Another Country*

We were told that her mother, who had been with child, died suddenly. I couldn't ever again bring myself to speak to her . . . she seemed such a shameful thing, a girl whose mother had died and left her alone in the world.
—Jamaica Kincaid, *Annie John*

[My father] was sitting in the living room, reading on the red couch so accustomed to his body that it obligingly hollowed to hold him more comfortably. After his death I used to curl up into this space and lie there with the cats, the warmth of his physical dent as reassuring as some ghostly hand in my hair.
—Lucy Grealy (f, 15), *Autobiography of a Face*

Our hearts, while affected by the conventions of the calendar, do not keep strict time with them. The first year with its initial upheavals passes, and still the rest of a child or adolescent's youth is marked by the early death of the parent. Anyone who experiences bereavement knows that, well beyond the first year, we carry with us the grief, the anger, and the impact of changed and changing circumstances.

In some sense, the path from childhood to adulthood is always a marked passage. The loss of innocence and the pain of adolescence affect us all. Every child sustains minor hurts. But some children contend with major injuries: sometimes personal events—divorce, illness, alcoholism; other times more global—war, poverty, racism. Among the serious injuries, the early death of a parent leaves one of the most lasting marks on a person's childhood history.

The structure of this chapter reflects the reality of our lives as orphaned children. The stories here revisit the themes of "The First Year"—sadness, anger, memories, the place of other adults in our lives, growing up—just as we revisit them in life. At various junctures—the first day of school, our first date, a surviving parent's second wedding, high school graduation—our dead parent, or the death of our parent, can come to mind. But it is not only on the special days that our parent's death is with us. It can visit us on the ordinary days, the days that make up our lives, the days that shape the people we are becoming.

In his novel *In the Lake of the Woods,* Tim O'Brien tells the story of John Whalen, a Vietnam veteran who has been an accomplished amateur magician since childhood. Whalen's father, an alcoholic, committed suicide when he was fourteen, and although Whalen's memories form a relatively small part of the book, his father's death figures large in his life. We witness Whalen's anger right after his father dies: "He wanted to take a hammer and crawl into the casket and kill his father for dying. But he was helpless. He didn't know where to start." Later, "John did the tricks in his mind. He'd lie in bed at night, imagining a big blue door, and after a time the door would open and his father would walk in, take off his hat, and sit in a rocking chair beside the bed. 'Well, I'm back,' his father would say, 'but don't tell your mom, she'd kill me.' He'd wink and grin. 'So what's new?' And then they'd talk for a while, quietly, catching up on things, like cutting a tie and restoring it whole."

For some, ongoing sadness, anger, or fear mark our childhood. That these emotions persist and sometimes overtake us after the first year can surprise and discourage us. Sometimes we spend days lost in memory or thoughts of how things would be different if our father or mother were still with us. Sometimes problems with the surviving parent take center stage and are felt all the more keenly because of the absence of the parent who we think would have understood us better. In this and myriad other ways, we idealize our dead parent. Some of us, like the character Whalen, have imaginary conversations with our lost parent. Some of us flounder looking for our role or place in the changed family. Still others of us try to become the absent parent. For a child or teenager, the death of a parent is not necessarily absorbed into reality in a day, a week, a year. It takes a long time to realize what hit us.

Sadness

Obviously, sadness doesn't go away after the official year of mourning. It persists, taking different forms: going underground, manifesting itself in fantasies of the parent's return, as uncontrollable sobs at every reminder of the loss, and in other ways.

And sometimes we see the sadness we experienced only in retrospect, years later, as a kind of repressed state. This is where the expression "buried grief" comes from.

Gloria Anzaldúa, poet and writer (52, f, 14)

For about four years, I expected my father to come walking back into the house. My image was that he would walk in the house, take off his shirt, you know, wash his face and wash his shoulders, and he would sit on the floor with his back against the sofa and turn on the TV. This kind of daydream of wishful thinking was based on what he would actually do. My idea was that someone else had been driving the truck and the face had been so smashed up that when they put it back together again, they thought it was my father. Because he was such a good man, God would bring him back to life. I was expecting a miracle.

∾

Irena Klepfisz's father died in Poland during the Warsaw Ghetto uprising, but she comforted herself with a similar kind of return fantasy, in this case based on some reality.

Irena Klepfisz, poet and writer (54, f, 2)

In the early fifties, there were constantly, in Jewish newspapers and in Israel, stories about people accidentally finding each other. Somebody you thought was dead would suddenly emerge, like husbands and wives who had separated and remarried. So in some ways I think I always had this fantasy that maybe my father didn't die and that he would show up one day. I was really a mess for a long time after I came here.

Ken Burns, filmmaker (41, m, 11)

Even three or four years later when I'd blow out candles at birthdays, my wish would be that my mother would come back. I think I just submerged the fact that she had died. My father never picked up my mother's ashes, and the funeral home went out of business. There was an unspoken knowledge in our family between the three of us—nobody mentioned it ever—that she didn't exist anymore. That was just the most painful part.

Walter Liggett, poet (70, f, 11)

I sort of kept the memory of my father's murder out for several years. I didn't really realize until later the effect it had on me. I was traumatized much more than I realized at the time, and there was no such thing as grief counseling or anything.

Sadness abates, changes form and content, becomes less pervasive. It does not go away, though. Seven years after her father died, Robin had an experience of overwhelming sorrow. It is a camp story, not unlike Doreen's story in "The First Year," yet surprising and disturbing in a way Doreen's story is not because it happened so long after the death. That nobody believed her or knew how to deal with it is not uncommon. Our culture doesn't give us tools to deal with the long time it takes to get used to the idea that someone we dearly loved is dead.

Robin (46, f, 8)

Once when I was away at camp, after my mother remarried and I was probably about fifteen years old, it actually hit me that I hadn't said good-bye to my father. And I was devastated. I mean I cried for a couple of days straight. It just seemed very strange at this camp that I should be grieving over this. I don't remember what set it off, and nobody at camp really knew how to deal with it, and I don't think anybody at camp actually believed me when I said that that's what I was crying about.

Barbara Smith, writer (49, m, 9)

Anything that reminds you that you don't have a mother makes you sad. It can be the simplest, slightest thing, and I think that the process of maturing and moving past the most visceral kinds of grief is that you can hear about things to do with having a mother and not just have the bottom fall out of your stomach.

Jim remembers that his grief affected his ability to form and maintain friendships. From his adult vantage point, he sees how his entangled feelings of anger and sadness kept him distant from people. In the telling, even so many years later, we hear his frustration at not being able to act the way he wanted to. His story demonstrates how sadness can get tied up with anger.

Jim (61, m, 16, f, 18)

I was deeply wounded. Depressed. In a lot of emotional pain. I never directed angry feelings towards my mother. I felt more guilty, I think, than anything else. After she died, I felt like, why didn't I make it up with her? I couldn't relate to people very well and I was sad a lot. One day, I would be friendly as hell to somebody. I'd be joking and everybody would like me. And the next day they'd see me and I'd be this incredibly sarcastic, bitter old man who they couldn't connect up to. I was a good guy and bad guy, really, almost a split personality. I was aware I was doing it. I couldn't control my anger. I wanted friends, desperately, but I couldn't keep them.

Anger

Anger after the first year takes on a slightly different cast than it had just after the loss. It becomes more of an ongoing presence in people's lives, not just the early acute reaction to loss expressed by some in the previous chapter.

Melissa (28, m, 9, f, 9)

My test scores were high before, but I couldn't remember my multiplication tables. No one said, "Well, these kids have been through a really tough time. Maybe they need to see a therapist." I didn't try very hard in school. I had a difficult time focusing, I was really fragmented, mentally, anyway. I would get really disappointed with myself, and, then, rather than try to get help, or because I tried to get help and it wasn't working out, I would just say, "Well, fuck it! Nobody else cares, then, fuck it." I didn't use the word "fuck" until junior high, but I got my first F on a test in junior high, and it was like, "Eh! That's not too hard."

Paul J. (28, f, 11)

I would say that I was a little angry at my father for dying. One way I dealt with it was to write poetry a little bit when I was younger. I don't tend to share it with anybody. I'd write it and put it in a drawer. So that was a constructive way that I dealt with it. But I also went through a period when I was known to be a very aggressive person, not extremely violent behavior, but I would tend to get in a lot of skirmishes on basketball courts.

༄

Lawrence talks about feeling let down by God, but he also was angry at family members. A lot of us shared Lawrence's experience. For whatever reason, people weren't talking to us. They weren't explaining anything. They weren't telling us stories. They were not helping us make sense of what had happened to us.

Lawrence (35, m, 2, f, 16)

I got angry at God, my mom, my dad, my family. I got angry a lot, especially as a kid, because a lot of things were never explained to me. My sister would talk about my mom all the time, but my dad never discussed any of it at all.

Barbara Smith, writer (49, m, 9)

I think both of us [she and her twin sister] were like little fireballs of anger. I was so angry, for the rest of my childhood, and sometimes that got channeled well and sometimes it just exploded and was *not* positive. I think that losing my mother made me furious. I think that losing our mother probably made each of us even shyer than we already were. Less trusting. Less confident. I felt like such an outsider. I felt like everybody else was normal, they have a mother, they have a father, and I'm an orphan. There was a level of envy that was just unquenchable. I mean there was nothing to do about that, because it was never going to be any different. And they were always going to have parents and I was never going to have a mother. And I would be angry at people who were around. I was furious. I felt that particularly around church. I despised church after she died, because for one thing, they had told us to pray and obviously that didn't work out. So I became an atheist at the age of nine. I realized that my mother didn't have a choice about it. When I would talk to myself I would think, "Why did this have to happen to me?"

Sometimes it's hard to separate feeling hurt from feeling angry, especially in Edward's case because of the circumstances of his father's death—having a stroke after getting into a fight at a party and being knocked down a flight of stairs.

Edward (30, f, 17)

I was taking a bath one night and shaving and looking in the mirror and my father's face sort of jumped out of mine. I wrote a poem about that, and I've rewritten it a couple of times since then. I remember resenting that, feeling like, "Look, if anyone's face should be on my shoulders, it's Mom's and not yours, because she was here, and she raised me and you didn't. It's not fair to be plastering your features on my skull like that, because you weren't here." So my anger manifested itself in that way to a certain extent.

Oh, I can remember crying. I remember playing a Cat Stevens record, something my dad used to play, and I had totally forgotten about it. I just started to sob because it really brought back a lot of stuff. It's difficult, I think, because in a lot of ways, part of me is really pissed off at him for having a stroke in such a stupid way, and I'm angry with him for what happened between him and my mom, although I only get my mom's side of the story, which makes it kind of awkward. So, on one hand, I'm angry with him, but then on the other hand, how can you be angry with someone who had a stroke and dies? I guess the anger prevents me sometimes from grieving, and then sometimes it will open up and I'll see another side of him that is obviously there and a wonderful thing.

Robin (46, f, 8)

I didn't take it personally like my father had abandoned me, but at times when I'd have questions that I really needed an answer to, or when my mother wasn't giving me the attention I needed, I would resent him for not being there.

Bob (58, f, 16)

You know, I might have been angry. I haven't been able to really identify that, but I've thought about it, over a period of time. There was probably some anger in that feeling of "I wish you were around."

Brown Miller, poet (51, m, 6)

I think when my anger and grief came out, a lot of it was directed at my father, some of that probably unfairly. I was also angry just at luck. Maybe because of my mother wetting the bed, and being taken out of the door on a stretcher, and seeing her in a coma, I really realized, even at that young age, that she was helpless to do anything. It wasn't like she abandoned me. She didn't mean to go.

∽

Doreen began a journal in junior high school, a few years after her mother died. During the interview, she shared her journal with us. In this portion, she's about thirteen and talking about her angry reaction to the possibility that her father might remarry. This teenaged journal is a memory artifact. It allows Doreen, and us, to get very close to the feeling of what it's like to be that young teen, facing the possibility of yet another change, trying to assume some control over it, and planning, however unrealistically, to do something about it.

Doreen (36, m, 10)

"If he married her, I would move out. I really do believe I would, because I hate her and her kids. I wouldn't be able to stand it. I don't like the idea of someone trying to take my mommy's place. Never. I would never stand for it. Because I believe I have as much say as Daddy or anyone else about this whole thing. If it happened, I would disown anyone and everyone involved. I'd better stop to cool down. But I mean it."

∽

As in Chapter 4, "The First Year," some people remember not feeling any anger at their parent for dying. We've included a few of their stories in this section as a reminder that anger is not a universal response to bereavement.

Michael (43, m, 9)

I felt a sense of loss. And I never felt that my mother abandoned us, or anger that she had left, or that somebody was to blame. I don't have any memories of having those kinds of feelings about it.

William (54, f, 14)

I don't remember being angry at my dad around this. I didn't really feel abandoned by him. I felt sorry for him. It was something he couldn't do anything about, you know. He didn't want to be sick.

Terry (38, m, 6)

Oh jeez, I've tried to get angry at my mother, because that's what you're supposed to do. I've been sad. I've been able to connect to the sadness for her and then for myself. But the anger was never really there so much. I'm not an angry person, even in a situation like this, as rational as it may seem to be angry for her leaving, I haven't connected up to that.

∽

Perhaps for some people, anger is not necessarily part of grief. Another way of looking at it, however, is that anger is a scary emotion, especially for a child. If children are too young to grieve fully, perhaps the angry stage of the grief process eludes them. Sometimes guilt might cause anger to go underground.

Paul B. (53, m, 11)

I never was able to feel that anger. And I've worked at it. I think it's there. It's just a sense that I have of wanting to blame her for going away, deserting me. I just can't connect with the emotion of anger. But I do have a sense that it was a punishment of some kind, to teach me to be more religious and a better little boy. In fact, something just came to my mind that I agonized over for years. Just before my mother went into the hospital, I wanted to go do something, and she didn't want me to go. And I said to her, "I hate you." It was a good relationship. This was one of those angry interchanges. To this day I can feel the guilt of that, and the association that that's probably the reason I got punished.

Fear

A number of our interviewees talked about how, after their parent died, fear marked their passage from childhood to adulthood. The idea of facing the rest of childhood without a beloved parent can be terrifying. So can the realization that you might be the only thing between your surviving parent's alcoholism and the disintegration of your family. And coming to terms with the ultimate unknown—death—at such an early age can provoke intense anxiety and fear.

Ken Burns, filmmaker (41, m, 11)

I think there was not enough affection. I think that there was not enough concern for where we were, and what we were feeling, and the things that we would go through. I remember once some researchers from the University of Michigan came and interviewed my father, years after the death. I was listening, through the heating grate, to what he was saying. I was surprised to hear him say that he had felt like if he could do it over again he would have gotten some counseling. It made me scared and nervous. Just the lack of control that all of this represented is what was terrifying to me. That mothers could die. That fathers couldn't be there, that fathers would be troubled.

Laurie (38, m, 13)

I was terrified that my father would die. I guarded him. When he would walk to the beer joint at night, I would stand by the window and watch for hours, waiting for him to come home because I was scared that somebody would jump out of the bushes and knock him on the head, and then maybe I would see him and I could call the hospital. I was totally paranoid.

Again, we turn to Doreen's journal, a record of these feelings at the moment they were happening. She was thirteen when she wrote this entry.

Doreen (36, m, 10)

"March 5th, and today I feel mixed up. I guess it's because I'm making a major step, to me. Deciding what high school to go to. And what to take. We talked about death in class yesterday. I could see that many kids in the class felt the same way I do. I've come to understand myself better, and now can accept the fact that I am scared of death, and always will be. Because that's the way I am. Another is that I'm scared to get old, scared of change. That will happen, when I go to high school, and again to college, by myself. I just can't picture myself alone, by myself, with no one. Probably my friends will go to other colleges. And I'm so scared."

Danny (30, m, 16)

I was a senior and basketball season was over, and track season started. I had to prepare myself because I had scholarships to college, but my grades weren't that good. I was preparing myself to go to college and to be on my own, but it was kind of scary. So I sort of resorted to smoking pot, which I think probably had a lot to do with my lack of goals. I never got to use those scholarships.

Lisa, after living with her father and losing contact with her old life, ran away from her father's house when she was sixteen. Eventually, she was able to reclaim some of her own life, and some contact with her family, but here she tells us of how scared she felt.

Lisa (28, m, 12)

I was petrified. I was lost. I was really nervous, all the time. And I didn't know how to interact with people at all. One friend of mine, who was my best friend, kept in touch. And, once in a while, I would see her, when I came to San Francisco to see my mother's mother. Except for my godmother, who was living in New York, and my mother's sister, who was living in San Francisco, I didn't see any of my mother's friends.

∞

Both literally and symbolically, not speaking seems like a reasonable response to the changing home circumstances Monica endured in the years following her mother's death. She moved from the protection of her mother's home in rural Mexico to the less-than-ideal conditions of her father's apartment in Los Angeles, and then back to Mexico, but to live with an abusive uncle.

Monica (30, m, 10)

I was practically mute for about three years. My brothers were very concerned about that. I would come home, turn the TV on, my brothers would be there, and if they bugged me, I would curse them out, but it was never like a conversation. My brothers thought that I missed Mexico, so they sent me back, but not to the same town, to live with an uncle. He was married, but after a while he got a divorce. It was just the two of us, and he thought that by me not talking he could molest me. I was mean like the devil, so he didn't succeed. I guess my mother not being around made me vulnerable. I had nobody to protect me.

Memories

Lost or found, lamented or celebrated, repressed or enhanced, our memories become a significant aspect of the years following the death of a loved one. Part of going on with life after our parents die is finding ways to keep memories alive without living in the past. Our memories can play tricks on us. They can also bring a parent to life in a new way. They can provide a source of comfort, and they can also be painful. But it's really hard when we search and find them missing.

Children who were quite young when their parent died have trouble remembering. That can be due in part to other people's reluctance to talk about the dead parent, either because they're trying to protect the child or because it's too painful for them to talk.

Diana O'Hehir, novelist and poet (72, m, 4)

I was in a position of someone whose mother has died when she was very very, very young. I was attempting to build up an image of what she could possibly have been like. People in Berkeley that had known her, I would always ask. And I would say it accreted, I acquired an image that she was smart and attractive and somewhat daring. One friend said she used to sit on the front porch and smoke. I just loved her for that, you know. We're talking 1922, now, and people didn't, at the time, sit on the front porch and smoke. I feel the lack of information about my mother—very, very much so.

I'm pretty sure my father was given to talking about memories. He talked about his own mother, who, interestingly enough, had died when he was four. But I find it very difficult to come up with any stories he told about my mother. Actually, I was afraid to ask my father. I know that his personality changed. He had a study upstairs. He went into his study and shut the door. Literally shut the door. It just was very obvious from his letters and memorabilia from before the accident and afterwards. He clearly had been very extroverted, outgoing, cheerful, funny, all these things. There are lots of evidences of it in things he wrote, a lot of papers that survive. He had started several novels and never ever went back to that kind of creative action. Afterwards, he wrote scholarly books.

Many of us got the message that it wasn't okay to ask questions. However children get this message, it doesn't take much for them to internalize it. Once that's done, it takes a lot to get them to talk again.

Brown Miller's experience shows how not talking can skew memory and keep fear and embarrassment alive for years.

Brown Miller, poet (51, m, 6)

My sister would say things like, "Mother was good at this, or liked to do this." Sometimes she would say things like, "Well, she used to yell a lot, but she was very loving, too." I was embarrassed in front of my father when he mentioned my mother. He mentioned her so seldom that I was afraid to ask him, "Well, what was Mommy like?" I never mentioned my mother to my father. The few times he did mention her, it was almost like, "Oh gosh! He's mentioned something that is not to be mentioned." And they were very quick little mentions, like, "She used to like to go fishing with me." He'd mention that, and then that would be it. All the way through my growing-up years, whenever my mother was mentioned, there was an awkward moment. I know that it wasn't healthy.

Ariel (27, f, 3)

I don't remember anything right after my father died. I think I blocked out a lot because I didn't start having memories again until the new daddy came into my life, about two and a half years later. I've always thought it was kind of strange that there's a whole segment of time I can't remember. I do remember thinking when I was younger that I was never afraid to die because I would get to see Daddy.

I just remembered something. There was a church where I think a friend of my dad's preached. I remember thinking that maybe my dad was in the basement of the church. I don't know why I thought that, but I remember there was a round part of the church which we were walking around on the outside— it must have been where the altar is—and there was that wood door on the ground that led to the basement, and I remember thinking maybe he was there. And then I remember later having a dream that was more like a nightmare, where that whole column went down into the earth, and it was all on fire.

My mother didn't talk much about my father's death until more recently. But she told me that I didn't really understand what was going on and kept saying, "My daddy dived." There's that image of going down, going under. My dad's name was Joe, and he was a doctor, so I used to think he made the aspirin they gave to children, St. Joseph's baby aspirin. I thought he had become a saint. I think I even told people that my daddy made that aspirin. It's hard to know exactly how that little three-and-a-half-year-old girl was actually affected by her father's death.

❧

When Kelly tried to draw a picture of her mother, she began with a totally blank page.

Kelly (43, m, birth)

The memory that I have is standing next to a red camellia bush, and being very short in relation to this camellia bush. I think that it was around that time that I began realizing that my grandparents were much older than the other parents, and I was asking questions about that. I remember asking my aunt, "Was Mama ever fat?" "No! Your mother was never fat." "Wasn't she fat when she was pregnant with me?" No answer.

I must have asked more questions like that, because one day my grandfather sat down in this red armchair in our living room, and he had me sit down in the pink armchair, and started telling me the story of when I was born. That I was born in the afternoon, and that my father went out to celebrate and when he came back my mother was dead. After my grandfather told me this story, I went in his bedroom, and there was a drawer where there were a lot of old photographs. I had looked through them before. There were some photographs of my mother and father in that collection. I never knew who the woman was. But instinctively, when he told me this, I knew that those pictures were her. I pulled out these pictures, and I can remember crawling under his bed with them and crying. I felt like it should be secret. How could I be crying about somebody that I never knew? How could I miss somebody that I never knew? But I remember doing that.

My grandmother wouldn't talk about her, period. My grandmother didn't approve of her because she was a divorced woman. My grandmother had no children of her own, she had raised my father and his brother, because their mother had died in childbirth. She had raised all these orphaned children. Two generations. And I was the girl, and I was hers. She just didn't deal with it in any other way than that.

I don't remember at what point my dad started talking about her, if it was in response to questions I asked, or if he just decided that now it was time. But he would start telling me stories of how they met, really created an archetype for me of Mother. Mother as a really incredibly generous person. That was sort of the picture he painted for me. According to my father, they were happy. According to my grandfather, they weren't happy.

One afternoon, my dad and grandfather decided to clean out the garage. Boxes and boxes, piled to the ceiling. And, at the very bottom of the pile of boxes was a big old trunk. When they opened the trunk, my dad called me over. He said, "These were your mother's things." They were forties-style movie-star dresses. And I was just the size then that I could wear them. My mother was real small, compared to me. My best friend and I dressed up in these dresses and paraded to the store to buy candy bars. I kept them for a long time. I don't know what ultimately happened to them, but I still have a belt. That was the first physical kind of contact with her. Oh it just seemed like a wonderful thing. I don't remember it making me sad. I felt really excited by it. It was the sort of sensual, concrete representation of her. She just had mythic proportion in my mind's eye by this time. It gave her physicality, a size and a shape and a color.

⁓

Kelly rejoices in the treasure of her mother's clothing, and Ariel tries to concretize her father, thinking maybe he was in the church basement, maybe he was the saint who made children's aspirin. The parent is gone, so we make attempts to evoke something of his or her physical presence. It's a way of discovering who the parent was, and a way of keeping memory alive.

People who were older when their parent died faced less of a struggle with the fact that they simply never knew their parent and more the challenge of what to do with the disappearance of memory due to the shock of trauma.

Addie (19, f, 16)

For a long time, I found myself not being able to remember what my father looked like and freaking out because I just couldn't remember him. And then, when I see my uncle, his identical twin, there is a big living memory right in front of me.

Janette (19, m, 12)

Just a couple of years ago, when I was seventeen or eighteen, I started remembering some things about my mother. I remember I was scared to put my mom's picture up in my room. Then one day I was just sitting. I had a dream about her. And things just started coming back to me. I started to remember what she used to do, what we used to do, and it helped me deal with it more clearly. Now, whenever things come up, we'll talk about how Mom did this or that. But there was a time when I kind of blocked everything out, where I don't remember her at all. I think I tried to block things out because she left me. It's like that whole image I had of her was shattered. I was mad at her. I mean, I know it wasn't in her hands, but I was mad that she left me, left me with kind of nothing. I was mad at God. I just didn't feel it was fair. So that's why I blocked it out.

Jeff B. (24, m, 18)

I think, yes, stories did help me to remember, or at least to visualize my own relationship with my mother. But it depended on timing. Sometimes I'm not sure if they were telling a story to have me react so they could feel okay about a situation, or they were telling stories because they were thinking "he probably needs one now to help him." I think sometimes it boils down to just simple delivery. Maybe I'm just way off the mark, but sometimes I definitely feel like this is really like an inside-out shirt. You put it on and then someone will say it's inside out, but it's still a shirt and you're still wearing it. That's what I view their stories as sometimes. You're giving me an inside-out shirt and asking me to wear it inside out. And you don't really want me to wear this shirt inside out, you want my listening to your story to turn the shirt right side out so you can wear it.

Shannon (24, m, 19)

The one thing that I always have trouble with is the fact that a lot of memories are from the time after she started to get sick. She was sick for like five years. So a lot of my memories are a little bit of that she's not as healthy, she's got more of a sunken face, she doesn't have a lot of energy, and things like that. And that's difficult. From what I can remember, she really tried hard not to be a downer all the time. I don't know if this is right or not, but I think she made a concerted effort to be as much of who she was before as she possibly could even though she knew she was dying and probably feeling really disgusting a lot of the time. I have to really push myself to think about anything before she got sick.

∽

Here Doreen shares another excerpt from her journal in junior high school, which she started in part as a way to keep her mother's memory alive.

Doreen (36, m, 10)

This entry is from the anniversary of my mom's death. It always is a weird day. "Today's the day, four years ago, Mommy died. I am not sorry because I don't know what's beyond life. I hope it's something beautiful." January 12 in all my journals is a lot like this. It's always an incomplete thought.

Terry (38, m, 6)

No one ever talked about her. I didn't remember her. So that wasn't going on except in my imagination. I think, in that kind of spiritual way, I always had the sense of awareness of her and trying to live up to her expectations and my expectations. It's kind of a confusing space. But I guess there was a kind of a sense that she was with me as I was with her even though she was no longer with us. I think I probably always idealized my mother. I mean I think I imagined her as this perfect person, beautiful, just the perfect mother-type person, which was easy because I didn't really remember her or she wasn't around to show me how imperfect she may be.

Barbara Smith, writer (49, m, 9)

I was too young to know what kind of woman my mother was. I think I've certainly romanticized her, because she died too early for me to see flaws. And because she wasn't our primary caretaker, I really didn't see flaws. I mean she was a person who was the source of all love and all fun. One of the things that my sister and I did after she died and I think of it with such sadness because it was such an effort to hold on to her—is that we started teaching ourselves to bake. It was an effort to keep some feeling of her alive.

William (54, f, 14)

I idealized my father very much. I realized, although I was fifteen, I still just had a child's view of him. He was some kind of a big person who knows it all and does it all or takes care of you. I had a very great fondness for him and appreciation of him. I think of him as a wonderful man. I tried to be him. I dropped the junior right away. I was called Billy. I became Bill; that's his name. I didn't try to be him exactly. I tried to be the kind of person he exemplified or had taught me, a very idealized and skimpy view of him. I didn't have much to go on. I learned by his example what it meant to be a gentleman, what I think of as what's expected of an alpha male in our society. How men conduct themselves. I think I learned that definitely from him, or from his friends. I realize now that aspects of that come from an earlier era, so I kind of have a foot in both, but, as a result of him, it's the way I act every day.

∽

Sometimes we can get trapped into obscuring the kind of person our parent really was by idealizing her or him. Jessica talks about the ongoing struggle between her idealized memory of her mother and who she actually was.

Jessica (24, m, 16)

I did idealize my mom. Most of the stories I got from family were these wonderful stories about what a beautiful woman she was, and she *was* really beautiful. I just felt like she was larger than life after she died. Her name, Lynda, means "beauty," and I really wanted to look just like her. She became this glory figure in my life, this wonderful ethereal guide and support in my dreams. And that was a role she was in for about five years, until my brother and I started talking about our family and our childhood a lot more, and he was telling me his bad memories.

Addie (19, f, 16)

I think I sort of idealized some aspects of my father, like his sense of emotional decorum. I forget sometimes how I used to get angry at him for certain things. Then I sort of remember and think, "Oh God, there were some awful things that I just hated, that got on my nerves." But I tend to definitely think, "Oh, good cook and just a great person to be around." He was a very popular, likable person, and I really wanted to be that and sort of in that way idealized him.

Robin remembers resenting any memories that contradicted her idealized version of who her father was. While so many interviewees lamented that people in their parents' lives did not share stories with them, there's also the danger of stories that don't fit the orphaned child's image and can cause added pain rather than comfort. Memory *is* a complicated and tricky thing, and it's important to realize that no one memory can ever be totally definitive. We might think about starting our stories with "The way I remember it is . . ." and ending them with "How do you remember it?"

Robin (46, f, 8)

My father's name always came up, so there was an awful lot of his spirit being kept alive. His being dead wasn't like he was gone forever. I remember the jokes that people said he used to tell and the stories about my father getting paid as a kid to talk on the soapbox for labor unions. And the stories about my father and his family, his mother and the boys sitting around and drinking at night when the boys would come home. His home was always the gathering center. Every now and then, something'll stir a memory of a joke that I used to hear. But when my mother and I were in Florida, we saw some relatives who had grown up with my father, too, and they thought he wasn't serious enough. They thought he could have been a genius, and instead he was a funny guy. And I really resented them saying my father could have been so much more if he had just been more serious, if he'd studied. I could never see how my father could be anything more than he was. He was wonderful.

Feeling Different

Strong feelings of being different, which figure so largely in "The First Year," don't necessarily go away in the years that follow. Almost everybody we interviewed talked about continuing to feel different. And, for the most part, of course, we felt different because we *were* different from our peers. Even if we had friends whose parents had died, we were part of a relatively small group—about 5 percent of the general population.

Suzanne Lipsett's self-consciousness was not unusual.

Suzanne Lipsett, writer (51, m, 4)

I have memories of feeling very self-conscious about having lost my mother, and people treating me in a weird way.

∽

Irena Klepfisz's story is affected by historical circumstances that made it more difficult for her not to feel different. After her father's death in the Warsaw Ghetto uprising, Irena's mother managed to retrieve her from a Polish Catholic orphanage where her parents had hidden her. Her mother, who was passing as a non-Jew, was working on the Aryan side. Irena talked of being born on her father's twenty-eighth birthday, April 17. Two years later, he turned thirty and she turned two, and then two days later, on April 19, the uprising started. He was killed the following day. Irena and her mother survived the war and later went to Sweden, where Irena felt very special since, in her words, "Children survivors were very precious and very rare." She remembers this as a lovely, protected period in her life. That soon all changed.

Irena Klepfisz, poet and writer (54, f, 2)

I did not really become self-conscious in a certain kind of way about my father until after we came to the States, and that was partly because he had become a kind of hero and public figure. I was eight when I came, it was my third country, I was on my fourth language. I was dislocated. I had lost a place that I really loved. I loved Sweden, I loved the house we were in, I loved the Jewish community we lived in. Suddenly, my mother, Rose, and I were living very isolated in a single room. I didn't like American kids, American kids didn't like me. In the Jewish community I was suddenly the daughter of a famous figure. I was very shy and self-conscious, and people were always pointing at me. I hated it all. I can't think of a single thing I liked then. It was so bad those first ten years. We started going to memorial meetings and Michal Klepfisz's picture would always be hanging there, which I found frightening and intimidating. It put me in a very weird position. Also, when I got here, there was an assumption that everybody had a mother and father; whereas, before we had been living among refugees, so the families were very broken up. I suddenly began to become self-conscious. In the Jewish community, he was a figure and I was his daughter, which made me different, and in the public school community I was different because I didn't have both parents. So it was almost a double kind of sudden shock.

Teresa also remembers feeling different and embarrassed because her father was dead. But she was also one of very few African-American children in her school. So her story demonstrates once again that a whole constellation of events go into making us who we are, and there are times when the parts are simply not adequate to define the whole.

Teresa (32, f, 8)

I was already a smart kid, and I was doing well in school, and I had lots of friends. But I do remember by about fifth grade just feeling completely isolated. I don't know to this day if that isolation was because I was depressed because of my dad, or if it was a race thing. There were never more than three black kids in class, and there were usually just two of us. I do remember feeling sort of tainted because my dad was dead. I remember feeling really embarrassed. I remember going through years when I didn't have anybody to eat lunch with. And it's sort of weird because I went on to become a really popular person, but I remember just feeling completely alone and being a loner, and at some point absorbing that as my identity. And I don't know if it was something different the kids were doing to me—it did feel like it sometimes, but I don't know if it was because of my dad. I don't think so.

✍

Joe's feelings of difference stemmed from living in a neighborhood and going to school with children from very different economic backgrounds, as well as from not having any parents. His single mother, who died, had been raising him.

Joe (28, m, 12)

I grew up in a semiaffluent neighborhood, and so there were two strikes immediately against me. We didn't have the money that my peers had, and now I didn't have the parents. So I kind of felt like a pariah. I think a lot of my close friends didn't even know that my mother had died. I didn't tell anyone. I already felt a little disconnected from a lot of my friends. I didn't want to have them ask questions. It was a way for me to think that they thought I was "normal." Very few of my teachers even knew because I never volunteered the information. I had one social science teacher, Mr. Phillips, that my sister had spoken with, and I think he knew, and I was pretty close with him. He was good to me and supportive.

The Surviving Parent

Our surviving parents—unless we had been completely orphaned— were the only parents we had. Some of them continued to "come up to the mark," as Doreen described her father in the previous chapter.

Others continued to be needy and unhelpful in the years that followed.

Some surviving parents purposefully didn't remarry because of the children. For some, this was a negative message: "Who would want someone with all these kids?" But for Horace Silver, Gloria Anzaldúa, and Doreen it was a more positive decision.

Horace Silver, musician (66, m, 9)

My dad never remarried, and he had plenty of opportunities. After my mother died, all the ladies were after him. They were on him. He went out with some of them, but he never married. He always told me and told some relatives, too, "Well, I never got married because I thought if I married somebody else, they may not treat my son right. I'll go out with some ladies, but I'm not going to get married to any of them."

Gloria Anzaldúa, poet and writer (52, f, 14)

We got Social Security, but it was minimal. So my mother had to go out in the fields and work full-time. There were a lot of money worries. At a certain point, I started working in the fields, too. At one point, after many years of being a farmworker, she became a nurse's aide in a nursing home in a nearby town. She'd come home really tired, and barely earned anything. She took care of us, but she would have a shift that started in the afternoon, and she'd get home at about eleven-thirty or midnight. My mother was attractive and still pretty young, and there were guys who wanted to go out with her. There was one guy who might even have married her, and I encouraged her to do that. My mother said, "You know, I'm not going to marry some *pelado*, because what if he beats up on you, or what if he doesn't treat you right?" So we came first with her.

Doreen (36, m, 10)

We'd go out to dinner once a week, which was great. My father wanted us to learn our manners and how to behave in more formal settings. We would keep our school clothes on on Friday nights, and we'd go out for dinner. That ritual went on for years. It was our time to be together, to talk about the week, what was going on. My father always still bowled on Thursday evenings. He was kind of a bon vivant, so it didn't take too long for him to get out of the grieving mode and be the happy widower. He was fairly young, in his early forties, had a good job, owned his own house. Oh God, they were lining up. But he never remarried. He always used us as an excuse, that no Other Woman was ever going to make it in our house, which is true because it would've been hard for that poor person. But his sister, who I saw recently, said, "He really wasn't the marrying kind of guy."

The issues of the surviving parent's grief, their withdrawal, or their ways of coping, continue beyond the first year. Some talked about ongoing difficulties, which were exacerbated in the years after the death.

Emilia (62, f, 12)

Life would have been different, because after the war, if he had lived, my father would have gotten a good job. Everybody made money after the war. They were rebuilding all these things, and I'm sure my father would have been able to do that because he had those skills. But that never happened. So my mother just took over. And, maybe, I wouldn't have moved to the big city if my father was still there. And, maybe if my father was still there, he would have had control over some of us. My sister probably wouldn't have had a child outside of wedlock, just like me, you know. I mean I think things would have been different. It's different, I guess, when you have a father. I looked up to my father. If my mother had some help from a man, or a husband, or my father, you know, things would have been different. My mother did her best. She worked hard. We would sell fish in the morning, and then in the afternoon she'd cook something and go from house to house. I carried the baby, and she carried the food. That wouldn't have happened if my father was there.

Sandy (46, f, 16)

There was a lot of tension in my house after my dad died, so I went to Family Services and said, "I need to see a counselor." They gave me to a middle-aged woman who was very nice, who listened to my story. And she said to me, "I've got to talk to your mom, and I've got to get her permission." When I approached my mom, she was very angry at me. She said, "I don't need a counselor!" She was in the generation that believed if you went for help it meant you were crazy, you weren't a good person, that kind of thing. The woman talked to me once more and said, "I'm not allowed to see you, but I just want you to know I think you did a very brave thing, and should be real proud of yourself." She just said to me, "Get away for college, or you'll just drown." I know that woman must have ached because she knew how badly I needed to talk it all out. I think I could've worked through years and years of pain had I been legally allowed to then with a competent person.

Anyway, to survive, I knew I had to escape the tension in my house. I had to experience the world that I'd never been allowed to experience. I'd been very, very sheltered. And, oddly enough, my dad's death helped me to get away to college, because it put us that much lower into poverty, so that I was eligible for financial aid. I could get a scholarship and I could go away to school. To grow up.

Lawrence (35, m, 2, f, 16)

My dad struggled with letting us go, taking us back, you know. I realized as a kid growing up that it was kind of odd. Everybody else had a mom and dad, and I didn't. It was hard to see the kids run up to their mom and dad when I didn't have a mom or dad to run up to. I was living with my sister again when my dad started getting sick—he died when I was about fifteen or sixteen—he moved in with us permanently. I loved him the best way I knew how. But as I got into my teens, I blamed my father for a lot of mistakes that I made because he wasn't there to correct me. I didn't get any information about what to expect as a man growing up. No one told me much about puberty, so I became a loner. I grew up with a lot of pain in the house.

Brown Miller, poet (51, m, 6)

My father was colder after my mother died. When I think about when she was alive, he was more affectionate. He played with me more, we went on family outings, and so, consciously or unconsciously, after she died, he did withdraw affection. And I, either consciously or unconsciously, felt it. He was sacrificing himself by making all this money, but, at the same time, failing to be affectionate. My father seemed like a rock, kind of a cold rock, but a very reliable rock. Sometimes, I felt that I could never get free of him. He was too solid. He was too there. But I remember after work and after dinner, he would go into the kitchen, turn off the light, and sit listening to this little tiny plastic radio for a long time, just in the dark room, with his head down and his hands over his eyes. I always wondered what he was doing. Years later, my sister said that that was his way of grieving.

Teresa (32, f, 8)

I do think that my mom was depressed. It's interesting because I've talked to white friends whose moms had kids and went through depressions, and their mothers just checked out. They went into hospitals, and other people took care of their children. With my mother that was not an option, I think, she considered, so she stayed and she did everything. She was one of those moms who would cook wonderful food, and she sewed all of our clothes, and she was really great. But she was angry, and she took a lot of that anger out on me.

∽

Even when a surviving parent takes good care, the bereaved child still sometimes feels inadequate and unacceptable.

Earlier in this chapter, Eric Marcus talked about the fact that when his father died, leaving his mother with three children, she had not yet dealt with the death of her own father when she was twelve. Kelly and Diana O'Hehir also bring up this generational theme. Here Jan B. speculates on why her mother may not have been able to handle her father's death.

Jan B. (50, f, 8)

My mother's mother died when she was twelve. What I was told about that by her sister was that my mother, who was the oldest, sat in a rocking chair alone, never spoke, and never cried. So the whole patterning of loss of a parent, and what happens to feelings in that process, got carried over. She never got mothered. And I don't believe anyone ever helped her process her feelings about her mother. And then when she was pregnant for the third time, her husband died. So I think that the history of parental loss is a very strong one in my family.

One of the other strong memories I have is coming home one night, and I was a teenager, late from a date. And I said to my mother, in a fit of anger, "Get off my back." And she wouldn't speak to me for three days. That message was real clear: if you express anger you get abandoned. The whole tone of our household was that you talk about the weather, you could talk about school, you could talk about everything, except for feelings.

Suzanne Lipsett, writer (51, m, 4)

My father was very protective, and very kindly, and probably an over-meticulous, overresponsible father. I guess he traveled a lot, so he would take me from Buffalo to Rochester for the weekend. Immediately when I'd get to Rochester to my father's twin sister's house, she'd take me to the beauty parlor and have my hair curled. It would frizz up for about an hour and then it would just drop straight, and she'd say, "My God, this girl, her hair won't even curl . . . the little glasses . . ." Every time my aunts would say, "This is Mitch's daughter," I'd think, "Oh, don't tell them. I'm too horrible. I'm not nice enough to be my dear father's daughter." Isn't that sad? He was a very loving father. He saved my life, no question. I remember he had me change my clothes a lot. I think he wanted people to see that he was really taking care of me. He took wonderful care of me. He fostered in me this feeling that I was very gifted and that whatever I wanted to do, he would pay for me to study it. But when I was a teenager, he was really worried about me. I did not find my direction until very late. Not until after he died.

Stepparents

Stepparents, especially stepmothers, take a bad rap in everything from fairy tales to movies. In the late twentieth century, divorce creates even more stepparent situations than death and complicates the lives of children whose parent dies. Lisa's story in the previous chapter told of the hardship of moving to her father and stepmother's house after her mother died. But not all the stepparent stories we heard were horror stories. They were mixed. Sometimes the stepparent provided some support and stability, sometimes even a great deal of love. Of course, the stepparent could never replace the lost parent, even for children who barely remembered their own dead parent and desperately wanted the stepparent to fill that role.

Ariel (27, f, 3)

When my second father came into my life, it was clear that he would not be my two older sisters' new father but that he would be that for my younger sister, who was still a baby. I came into his life really needing him. And he came from another marriage and had his own children who he wasn't with, and so it was really hard for him to accept that love from me without feeling really guilty. If somebody had said to me, and they probably did, "This is your new daddy . . ." I don't know when five- or six-year-olds hear that what they really think. "This is my new daddy? Okay, let's go!" Maybe you don't know that it's unusual to have a new daddy. So you expect everything that you had, but he had a whole other history that made it really hard to accept this needy six-year-old.

∽

Lauren Muller, Ariel's older sister, sees the logic in a new name and a new identity, and how the silence about their old life helped form that new life. But that silence rendered the old life with her father even more golden, more idyllic.

Lauren Muller, writer (34, f, 11)

One of the reasons we took on our stepfather's name and he adopted us is that my mother wanted there to be someone to take care of all of us if something happened to her. She couldn't imagine all four of us going to one person other than Tom. We moved to a new town. We had new names. We had a new family, and there was the sense that we didn't want Tom to have to compete with a ghost, although, of course, he *was* competing with a ghost. We didn't talk about that life, so it became more and more of a golden world to me. I understand why we didn't talk about it. It was a survival tactic. It was a way of moving forward, but it also meant that I had this completely new identity.

∽

Terry remembers that his stepmother brought some order into a chaotic family life. But Rose and Lawrence had opposite experiences.

Terry (38, m, 6)

The woman my dad would marry was living upstairs. Then she moved away to another place and then they got married. But we didn't go to their wedding, which didn't even dawn on me as being strange, because if your life has been strange enough at that point, what else is strange? She wasn't our mom. But I think over time she was a lot easier to relate to than my father was. She was a very said-what-was-on-her-mind type person, let you know exactly what was going on. I remember I used to come up with all sorts of fibs about things. And she'd just bellow out, "You know that's bullshit." She would put me on the spot, and I really appreciate that she was able to do that. There was a real normalizing effect that she had. Plus she structured our lives, and we bought a house. We did things that families do in many ways.

Rose (87, m, 13)

My father married again. I was nineteen. And I thought, "What's my father doing? He must be out of his mind." But I guess he was lonely.

She was a woman that came from the same shtetl, and somebody got them together. She told him he wouldn't have to worry about her children because she had money left from her husband. We had this big apartment, everybody living together. The oldest daughter, Tessie, was close to my age. One day Tessie came in wearing a fur coat, and my father was noticing that money was missing from his wallet. It wasn't Tessie who was taking it. It was her mother.

It got worse. I had a dear friend Dorothy, whose mother I would go to after my mother died. Dorothy's father had died when she was young, so she and I commiserated with one another. One time, Dorothy was at our house, and my father's new wife says to me, "Who told you to bring Dorothy here?" That apparently was the straw that broke the camel's back. My father took the tablecloth, pulled it off the table with all the dishes on it, and said to me, "C'mon. We're going." We left the house and never got back into it. My brother Jack went up to the roof, went down the fire escape when nobody was home, and took our clothes. But all my mother's silver, all the linens, we never got back. My father had this lucrative business, but I bet it was less than a week when he sold the store and left for Chicago. Then, within a short time, my brother Ernie and I joined him in Chicago. All I can say is that I cried all the way to Chicago. I left good friends and a boyfriend behind.

Lawrence (35, m, 2, f, 16)

My dad remarried when I was about eight, and we went into a Cinderella-like story. There was mistreatment there. My sister came in for the rescue again. Eventually, everything calmed down, after the stepmother and her two sons left.

Other Adults

We found a broad range of experience with other adults who were involved in the bereaved children or teenagers' lives, from the profoundly helpful to the horrific.

Melissa (28, m, 9, f, 9)

My grandmother had a lot of control over us. My father's family may have wanted to be more supportive, but my grandmother didn't allow it. Any letters that came from my father's children she sent back, or just took. My brother and I would go and stay with the teachers who became our foster family on weekends and for summers and stuff. They wanted to adopt us, but my grandmother didn't want us to be adopted. There were good things about my grandmother's house, too. She had books, and she had a love of learning that the other couple didn't have.

My brother and I, with the help of my sister, tried to run away from my grandmother because her drinking was so bad. And we were practically laughed out of the social services department. They showed us pictures of bruised and bloody children and said basically, "Come back when you look like that." It was awful. And then, insult to injury, the caseworker knew my grandmother. He called her.

Doreen (36, m, 10)

Basically, we were an emotional family, and nobody held too much in. Feelings got out very easily. We weren't saving anything. My mother's mother was a big support for us. She was ten minutes, walking, from our house, and she was always there for us. We had a lot of support—so much support you wanted to get them out sometimes. We had a typical African-American family in that sense. The structure was all there. But any time that anything went wrong, I'd cry that if my mother were here this wouldn't have happened. She became a saint.

∽

Marc's story once again points out how difficult it can be to talk with children and teenagers about death. His story shows also how hard it is to just break through the wall that bereft children often build up around them, but how important it probably is that adults try. When we asked Marc what could have helped him, he replied, "A slow but persistent building up of trust."

Marc (39, f, 10)

I remember that my mother was concerned that I wasn't learning about sex, and she didn't feel very comfortable about talking to me. So she asked me if I would like to talk with a doctor, which was only slightly less embarrassing than talking to my mother. I remember trying to convince the pediatrician that I knew everything there was to know, and he, of course, didn't believe me. But he also didn't tell me anything. In some ways, I respect him for that. I basically just picked up what I needed to know about sex on the streets, from talking to friends and reading books or whatever. I remember that my uncle and his son, who was around twenty, made a few attempts to try to follow me in a way, which I felt a little uncomfortable about, and responded a little bit to, but not a lot. So it was sort of a halfhearted giving and a halfhearted taking I guess. No one really talked to me about the death, but I think that would have been a very uncomfortable conversation, very hard to do. I don't think people really wanted to deal with it too much.

Laurie (38, m, 13)

My mother's older sister, my aunt Mary, who lived in Baton Rouge, would come up to Memphis maybe once a year. I was really close with her. She was a creative person, and she just didn't think like the rest of them. She was my surrogate mother, and she encouraged me in all my creative ways. She saved every letter I ever wrote her, every picture I drew. Also, our neighbors were all women, and I spent a lot of evenings in the summer sitting on the front porch in these big white rocking chairs, talking with them and listening to the tree frogs. So I knew how to reach out. I had a teacher who was definitely somebody that I really admired, and I felt like she was very kind and compassionate. She was kind of a symbol of culture and some kind of life outside of the craziness that I knew. I was lucky to go to a school that was just filled with women whose whole lives were teaching. They loved their kids, and you go back and they still remember you.

Paul J. (28, f, 11)

When I moved back to Philadelphia with my mother and sister, I had a man named Joe A. who sort of filled a paternal role for me, and then a different friend also named Joe who ended up being my best man when I got married, who filled a sort of big-brother role. Both of them filled in gaps of what I needed. Joe A. helped with the sports and helped me integrate into the neighborhood. He was one of the leaders of the neighborhood, one of the more respected figures, at least around the playground and all. And his liking and acceptance of me, and working with me, helped me be accepted. The other Joe was my boss at the store I worked at when I was fourteen. His parents suffered a messy divorce when he was young. His mother was around my mother's age, and I could identify with him a lot, and emotionally he was more of a support. He also taught me how to fight by beating me up. So I sort of had those two people filling in, and we've remained close.

Barbara Smith, writer (49, m, 9)

Our grandmother was a very austere individual and incredibly strict, and we got very little from her emotionally. I don't think my mother's death had anything to do with how she treated us. I think she was sadder after our mother died, and probably had less patience. See, our mother was like a mitigating influence, because she was incredibly loving, gentle, just a really nice person. I feel like I'm so lucky because my aunt, the person who stepped in, was somebody who I just loved to pieces already. She was much more flexible than our grandmother, and she doted on us. As we got to be teenagers, a decision was made that we would move upstairs because we were having such conflicts with my grandmother. We were given our own keys. I will never forget her saying, "Now, when you come in, after school, you can do your homework, and you can watch TV or whatever, and I'll be home at six."

∽

No matter how many adults we have around us, including our surviving parents, many of us look for substitutes for the dead parent well into our adulthood. This search can be frustrating, but it can also add a certain richness to our lives.

Diana O'Hehir, novelist and poet (72, m, 4)

What I was looking for was somebody who would love *me*. I fastened on any older woman who came my way and, quite successfully, made this series of people into that—a woman who would listen to me and love me. In Berkeley in those days, the standard sort of help you had in the house was known as "the college girl." The college girl lived upstairs, in the attic, and worked much too much, for far too little money. There was a series of such young women, and I did fasten on each one of them. They were like six or seven years older than I, but enough older for me to make them fit this role. Certainly, I was inventing absolutely a perfect mother, a perfect person who would answer all of my needs.

Peers

Several people said that as they have grown older they've found themselves feeling a special bond with other people whose parents died when they were children. But during the transitional time of marked passage those bonds didn't often form.

Jessica (24, m, 16)

My boyfriend moved out of town. And some friends I lost by virtue of their parents not wanting them to associate with me because I came from a poor white family to begin with, and then I didn't have a mother, so I obviously didn't have a good influence. And there were a couple of friends who I grew away from, because I don't think they understood the intensity of the grief. It became such a trial and such an effort to be my friend. I wasn't willing to deal with anybody else's problems. In return, they weren't very helpful. That's something I think is too hard for people that age to deal with—somebody else's grief, or pain, or needs.

Rob (44, f, 15)

I had some friends who were sort of afraid to talk to me because they really liked my father. This is a paradox; the kids in the neighborhood really liked him. And they sort of had a sense of loss, too. So they really didn't abandon me, and I would talk about it with them. I would certainly talk about it with the girls I was with. That was a real good attention-getting device, a really good way to get sympathy. I didn't feel like people ran out on me. But I did feel like I was in my own little world, and it was really tough to feel like I was connected to other people.

Rich (36, m 14)

It was a total transitional time. I was starting high school in the fall. It was like I was a new person. People didn't know my past. People didn't know my mother. People didn't know that I had a mother. I started to become popular. I got involved in all sorts of activities. In general, I tried not to think too much about her. The people around me gave me signals that she's gone and you don't think about her and I think I sort of adopted that to some extent as well.

Siblings

Older siblings sometimes helped to ease the passage.

Edward (30, f, 17)

It's kind of a mystery that my brother and I hold between us that is a bond as well. But I don't know that either one of us has figured it out. My mom is obviously not male, and my brother and I obviously both are, and this male role model that we had sort of had his problems. It was something that my brother and I shared that my mom wasn't part of because we would fly back to visit my dad after my parents divorced. We used to joke about him sometimes, things like, well, you know, "I'm not gonna be a loser like Dad," or whatever. I don't quite know how to articulate it, but it has become a sort of strange thing that my brother and I toss back and forth a little bit. I think, perhaps, between us we were trying to construct a role model that wasn't my dad. That had elements of my dad in it, because my dad did a lot of incredible things and was just amazing in so many different ways, I think, but there was a real tragic flaw in his character, I guess.

Brown Miller, poet (51, m, 6)

I became a little closer to the sister who was six years older, quite a bit closer, actually. I turned to her a lot for real personal, intimate kind of family contact, the kind that you would have from a mother, because the housekeeper and the friends were nice, and they performed a kind of practical function, but she was the surrogate mother.

Lawrence (35, m, 2, f, 16)

My oldest sister took over because my dad wasn't ready for all of us. She was also married and had two kids, with one on the way at that time. She had all of us and a husband who beat her up. At first, we stayed with my dad, and my sister would come through from time to time, but then it got bad with him because he started having a drinking problem. I feel he was able, but he gave up. So my sister ended up taking over.

In the first chapter of the book, "Something Died in My Heart," Leslie tells of sitting at her father's desk shortly after he died and beginning to write down stories so that her brother Marc would someday remember the same father she knew. While she may not have succeeded completely, it's clear from this part of Marc's story that she was a good influence in his life.

Marc (39, f, 10)

When I was about thirteen, my sister became a kind of a mentor for me. She would suggest books for me to read, or activities to do, or just gave me guidance. Before then, we had been friendly in a sibling way, but I was a much younger boy. We'd had fun and been close, but we were very different. She was seven years older and a girl, after all.

Early Independence

The taking on of adult roles is an important theme in many of these stories. Some people remember being asked, almost forced, to help with things beyond their understanding or years. For others, it was an expectation they had of themselves. The adult roles we took on were emotional, financial, and physical—from comforting our bereaved parent to keeping house. Some of us learned in this way to assume responsibility. We all became mature beyond our years.

Bob (58, f, 16)

You closed on it, you remembered, you buried them, you had a headstone, and you'd go there once or twice a year and say a prayer. When my mother died four years later, it was the same kind of behavior pattern. I was on my own. There was a sense of freedom, and that kind of a freedom also brings a bit of guilt. Why am I feeling so free? Am I still an okay guy by thinking this? But there was, at that time, no route to take for solving this. You worked through it yourself in those days.

Deborah H. (45, m, 16)

There were some things I avoided doing that I would have been pushed to do if I had a mother there. And there were some things that I did earlier on my own because she wasn't there to do them. A funny mix. Like not making a dentist's appointment for four years because my mom always did that, and it was one of the things that my dad didn't sort of pick up. He'd say to me, "You're old enough to make your own dental appointments—make them." I didn't want to go, so I didn't make them. Before she died, I would be happy to come home from school and not have her there telling me what to do or how to do it. It's every sixteen-year-old's fantasy, I think. The fact that the fantasy came true was complicatedly horrifying. There were a lot of nights when I went to bed and I felt an excruciating pain about the loss of her, too.

Madlaine (84, m, 1)

You know, I don't think that my mother's death was that traumatic for me because I had all these other people around. In fact, I was given probably more leeway than a lot of other people. They never did not talk about something at the dining-room table because I was a child. They talked about politics, and they talked about Nazi Germany, and they talked about what was happening in the world. And they probably talked about who was having an affair or something. I simply listened, and I learned a lot. I was not excluded from any of the conversations. Nor was I included. Children that I played with didn't know where babies came from, but I did because it was talked about in the family without excluding me.

Kelly (43, m, birth)

Eleven or twelve, that is the age where, at least among my friends, we were starting to move away from our parents, starting to become more independent. And I had the advantage there. I had almost complete independence. No one paid much attention to where I was after school. I became sort of a free spirit in that time, the one without those kinds of restraints that mothers represented. I think there's a part of me that really cherishes being on my own, and I know I can take care of myself. That was probably born at that time. When my grandmother died, that was very hard, but, oh, in a year or so after that, my life really sort of turned outside the home and into the hills around my house. And that would've never happened with my grandmother around. My grandmother was my model for mother, and my grandmother certainly would've never talked about Tampax with me. What was it I was needing a mother for anyway, you know?

Rob (44, f, 15)

Indirectly, in terms of the dynamics of the family, I took my father's role. His father was evidently a real tyrant. I never met him, and I've just heard some stories. But he used to beat up my grandmother. And my father witnessed all that. So, consequently, he was always very protective of my mother. If I criticized her, or did anything, he would jump all over me, he would really overreact. My sister used to act up. I remember one time, I was about eighteen, she was acting up, and she was just crying. We were on vacation and she was ruining our vacation. I took his role, what he would have done. I smacked her across the face. Really hard, which I regret. I don't think it was a good thing to do. Then there are probably other subtler things, in terms of the anxiety, trying to control things, being irritable, being impatient.

Gloria Anzaldúa, poet and writer (52, f, 14)

My mom would look up to me; she would ask me, "Should we buy this and this or should we do this and that?" Kind of like the things that my father had the say-so in before, I now had the say-so in. But then, that say-so would get contradicted by my brothers, who felt that the older of the brothers, because he was the male, should, you know, have the say-so.

Eric Marcus, writer (36, f, 12)

I always treated my brother as a very much younger brother, and he's really only two and a half years younger. One of the difficulties was that I suddenly tried to be parental with him. I'm sure he resented it. What he needed was a brother, what I needed was a brother, and we both needed parents. My mother is now a therapist, and in her therapy realized that what she had done in a classic way was to parentify one of her children. And I was the one.

I couldn't believe there were kids who didn't know what their parents' finances were. I knew everything. It was a real partnership with my mother. A few years later, after my grandmother died, my mother had a little bit of money, we went out and bought a house. And I say *we* went out and bought a house because I thought of it as *us* going out to buy a house. I remember better than she how much the mortgage was on the house, what the percentage rate was. I very, very much felt like an equal partner, and I was included in all the decision-making. My mother looked very young and I looked grown-up. We traveled to Europe together when I was fifteen, and people thought we were a couple. I didn't like that at all. I know she didn't realize what she was doing or how negatively that would ultimately affect our relationship, but it was what she did, and I was very willing.

I also excused my mother a lot. I had had a very hard time being critical of her because she was a thirty-nine-year-old woman left with three young children and with little in the way of family support. Then her mother died three years after my father died. It's a lot for one person. And her father died when she was twelve, and she was an only child. She hadn't yet dealt with the death of her own father.

Ken Burns, filmmaker (41, m, 11)

We had a lot of responsibilities, and it was a very strange, a very difficult time, fraught with lots of tension and psychological anger. My father certainly ran the family, but he would often be very discouraged and depressed and silent. He began to go out on field trips again. When he left, I guess I was about sixteen and Ric was probably fifteen. He left us alone for three or four months to go to France. I ran the house, paid the mortgage, the electric bill. I had a joint checking account with my father and was utterly responsible.

Laurie (38, m, 13)

I feel I learned how to parent myself. Sometimes I even had to sign my own report card. I had to cook. I couldn't get completely blasted doing drugs because I knew there was no one who would bring me back. So there was always this kind of internal parent saying, "You're the only one paying attention here." I really bonded with my father and was very protective of him because he was all that I had. He was a mail carrier, and his route was the wealthy section of Memphis, so every year he would get invited to come to this picnic with the mayor and people like that. It was a big deal. I remember one year noticing that my dad had this big hole in the back of his pants, and he was walking around talking to the mayor and all these other people. I didn't know how to tell him, so I just kind of stood behind him and walked behind him so no one would see the big hole in his pants. At some point, I pulled him aside and I said, "You've got a big hole in your pants." That's the metaphor of my childhood. I was always covering up the big hole in my father's pants in one way or another.

Martin Yan, chef, writer, TV personality (43, f, 3)

When you don't have a father, you have to learn to be very independent. In school, I was basically always very active and very independent, and I had a lot of buddies. I was very much the one to always say things, and I was never afraid. When I left China, to go to Hong Kong, I really didn't have any fear because I was still pretty young. One of my father's former business partners had a Chinese restaurant in Hong Kong. I helped out in the restaurant. I actually lived there. When the restaurant closed, I would put the board on top of the booth and would just sleep.

Marked Passage

Sadness, anger, and fear may mark the years following the premature loss of a parent. Some children learn how to cope through the use of cherished memories and with the help of adults and sometimes older siblings. Others are not so lucky. Their memories are blocked, and their support systems break down. But no matter the degree of the sorrow and the pain, there seems to be a positive by-product of this childhood tragedy: early independence. That was a theme that remained constant in most of the stories. Even those who deeply mourned their dead parent feel that they grew up earlier than their peers and often with a sense of real exhilaration. Despite an occasional mention of guilt for having any kind of positive feeling related to their loss, most of our interviewees reported a sense of confidence and satisfaction at their ability to take care of themselves. Yet as they crossed the actual bridge into adulthood, establishing more secure adult identities, they were presented with fuller and deeper opportunities to grieve the loss that will affect them in small or large ways for the rest of their lives. We now turn to how these people, orphaned young, have negotiated their adult years.

6

The Floating Bridge

What's buried, airtight, in tomb or peat bog or brain, is out of time, preserved forever; old guilts, old enmities, old terrors. All myths intact, the image in the child's eye unchanged. If these things are dug up, restored to time, some will disintegrate from light and air. Others will serve the truth, or what of it can be reconstructed from potsherds, tools, bones, and scraps of cloth.—Signe Hammer, (m, 9), *By Her Own Hand*

It would be time to dance soon. She could hear the drums. Everything was prepared. . . . She picked up the round, smooth abalone earrings made by her mother. . . . As she put them through her ears, she missed her mother freshly, as though she'd just died; and, again, she realized her mother would not see her dance as a woman today. But her Spirit will, she reminded herself. Remember, she promised she'd return for my first dance as a woman and the birth of my first child.—Alma Luz Villanueva, "The Edge of Darkness" from *Weeping Woman, La Llorona & Other Stories*

I am puzzled but pleased by this dream. There was my father, dead two dozen years, in a new flannel shirt and gray trousers, sitting in the kitchen. . . . My father spoke softly to me, serenely, as if he had been away and was soon to leave again, allowing us only this small conversation in an unrecognizable kitchen.—Barry Gifford (f, 12), *The Phantom Father*

Making sense of death is never easy, especially for a child or an adolescent. What is the meaning of life? Of death? What does it mean to lose a beloved person, and never fully recover that loss? These are some of the hardest questions human beings ever confront. To face them at five, or eight, or thirteen seems almost incomprehensible. And although some psychologists believe that children, even at very young ages, can mourn, others view mourning as a process that cannot be fully engaged until the period of adolescence has ended and the person has started to build an adult identity. While an adult can grieve from a place of relatively secure identity, the argument goes, children and adolescents who are in the process of forming that identity cannot totally grieve. So as the bereft child enters adulthood, he or she is presented with a second and more full opportunity to grieve.

The passage from adolescence to adulthood is difficult in the best of situations, but when a parent has died, the child confronts an additional challenge. It is as if somehow part of the natural bridge—the walkway between childhood and adulthood—has been destroyed. A child whose parent has died must come to terms with the reality of final loss and permanent absence. She or he must face that there is no possibility of return, no last visit or smart words of advice, no chance of reconciling a troubled relationship. The partial grieving that began as sadness, and sometimes anger and fear, can now flower into full mourning.

The metaphor of a floating bridge may help to describe some of this grief process. The earliest floating bridge consisted of boats tied together to enable a river crossing after a more traditional bridge had been destroyed by a violent storm or by an enemy in wartime. Bereft children, becoming adults, can build a bridge to take the place of the one that was destroyed. As we come of age, we can reconnect with the dead parent by revisiting memories and stories, and so grieve, releasing our pain and going on—making the loss conscious, making the death make sense, and our lives with it.

This floating bridge can also serve us during later rites of passage, when we enter into intimate adult relationships, bear and raise children, start new jobs and careers, confront middle age, or come to terms with old age. As we reinvent ourselves at each stage of our lives, we may decide to reconstruct the bridge, using fragments of our lost parents to help us cross over. The spirit lingers. The love persists. And memories of past hurts can evolve into points of understanding.

In several recently published memoirs, writers who lost their parents in childhood speak of how they have come to terms with their early loss, how they have found ways to reconnect with the dead parent.

In *Being Red,* the memoir of his years in the Communist Party, novelist Howard Fast refers back to his mother's death when he was eight and a half. He describes his childhood slipping away as his mind chose "forgetfulness and sanity" over "memory and madness." He did not reembrace memories of his mother until he was past thirty. For a long time, then, he survived by forgetting, but the survival entailed a kind of shutting down. What if he had stayed forever in what he labels "infantile amnesia"? Perhaps his life would not be nearly so rich.

Novelist William Styron in his 1992 memoir *Darkness Visible: A Memoir of Madness,* explains how he saved himself from a depression so relentless it was pushing him toward suicide. While he acknowledges the genetic origins of depression, he believes the loss of his mother when he was thirteen was "an even more significant factor" in his self-destructive despair. He then reports how hearing a passage of music she used to sing helped pull him back to a place where he could ask for and receive the help he needed to survive.

French professor Alice Kaplan's father died just before her eighth birthday. When she goes to interview a fascist intellectual who wrote against the war crime trials, she has an imaginary conversation with her father, one of the lawyers who prosecuted Nazi war criminals at Nuremberg. Her father "advises" her, "'Take it slow, just let him talk." Kaplan's memoir *French Lessons* focuses on how she used the French language as a place to hide when "life got too messy." But, in concentrating on the work of the fascist novelist Céline, she drives close to the heart of her father's work and life, giving herself the opportunity to visit and talk with the ghost of her dead father.

Fast, Styron, and Kaplan all revisit the dead parent, sometimes to mourn and remember, other times for advice and salvation. They reconnect and renew the bond severed so long ago.

In this chapter, we look at how a group of our interviewees, now grown-up, reflect on their early loss as adults. We concentrate here on how remembering helps the grieving, and how grieving helps soothe

the pain. Mourning need not be debilitating. Yet the pain of loss never completely goes away. It can and does recur at various times in life. It can, in fact, lead back and forth over the floating bridge, to new experiences of sadness, to new insight and new levels of resolution.

Coming of Age

Coming of age. In the United States we generally consider this period as the years between eighteen or nineteen and twenty-five. As we leave adolescence, each of us faces the challenge of creating an integrated, adult identity. How do you get to be a grown-up when one of your parents is forever gone, and cannot guide you—can't teach you how to drive, give you advice about work, comfort you as you experience your first serious broken heart, help you through college. The list, as they say, goes on. But coming of age gives us the opportunity to return to our original pain with a more full sense of who we are in the world, so we can grieve more deeply and more fully.

Athena's father died of AIDS, which he contracted through his drug addiction. She was very angry with him, but through the process of grieving she's been able to recall the bond she had with him in earlier, healthier days. She marks his passing and her coming of age with a stunning tattoo that incorporates his initials in its design. She has found a ritual that allows her to both grieve the loss of her father and celebrate their love for each other.

Athena (19, f, 17)

My dad used to have a little "M" on his arm. His name was Mario. He was going to get his whole name. I asked him, "Dad, how come you just have an 'M'?" And he said, "Well, because"—it was hand done—"because it hurt so much." So what I did was to go a step further. He died in March, and I got a tattoo on Father's Day, in June. I felt like I did it. I went through the pain. My tattoo is a memorial to my father. I got his full initials, *M.G.*, and an arrowhead with the coin that has an Indian's face on it. I'm Mexican, but I found out that I have Apache blood, so it's really special. I felt that when I did it, I did something my dad didn't do. You know. Go all the way. I feel like if he were still alive, he'd like it. I was really afraid of what people were going to think, because it was my senior year and I actually had people come up and ask me, "Why did you get that?" I'd just tell them, "You don't know what it's about." And when they'd ask again, I'd say, "It's because my dad died." And then they didn't say anything. It made me feel better. You know, I've realized that my dad and I had a bond. We were both really sensitive. I felt it even when I was young, but I didn't know what it was. I think when he did the drugs all of that got blocked.

∽

Both Shannon and Lisa mourn the loss of their mothers, who they're sure would have provided a special kind of friendship had they survived. Both of them have found ways to keep their mothers alive.

Shannon (24, m, 19)

We were friends when I was in high school, and I can see us having called each other every day for the last five years. I mean I can see us having a really excellent relationship. And that makes me feel a big loss. One thing that I've had to deal with is that I hold on to things, whether it's possessions or people. That's, I think, very much to do with my mom. The things that I have are very, very important to me because a lot of them were hers. Why do I need a shell? I don't need a shell, but it was hers. And I need those things around me. I need the pictures so I can remember how she looked before she got sick.

Lisa (28, m, 12)

I sometimes look at my life, and I think how it would've been if my mom were alive. It saddens me a lot because I know she would be living in the city, and I know we would be great friends. I know she'd be there for me, I know she'd be proud of me. Four semesters now, I've been on the dean's list, I've been doing *so well*. You know, all I have of my mother is an album. At first, it hurt a lot, because everybody was taking my mother's things. Then I thought, "Well, they can have all that because nobody could have what I had. I'm her daughter. She was my mother. She was an incredible woman. I don't need the material objects. The pictures are different because in the pictures I can see her."

∾

Like Lisa, Joe feels a great loss in not having his mother see his accomplishments as he has come of age, but the memory of her love for life helps him cope. He, too, feels his mother is inside him, alive that way.

Joe (28, m, 12)

I want to show my mother how well I've done. I think she would be proud. Sometimes I miss not being able to call her to say I got an A. I'll call my sister instead, or my brother, or my friends, to say that I scored thirty points in a basketball game or that I got a job interview. Sometimes I think, "Do I really need to call him for that?" It's almost like I overcompensate. My mother was very responsive. She would probably cry to hear that I got into law school. A sibling or a friend can be supportive and they can say "That's great," but there's that certain sense of satisfaction in a mother's voice. In that one phrase or statement they make, there is love, and pride, and just joy, and all that. From a friend, you don't get that sense of pride, the feeling of going back to Mama and making her proud. That's something that's definitely lacking. But, you know, certain things help. There are ways that she comes through me. She could laugh at the lowest, most discouraging of situations, and I try to find humor in everything. That's her living through me.

∾

Ariel and Melissa have been working on regaining some kind of connection with their lost parents as they come to know themselves as young adults. They talk about how their work at self-understanding fuses with their exploration of the lives of their dead parents. We need to know what we lost before we can mourn that loss.

Ariel (27, f, 3)

I remember in college, I think it must have been the first year, walking home from working in a deli shop and looking at my hands, realizing I was 50 percent Joe Parsons. I think part of wanting to know who my father is is part of trying to find out who *I* am. And so it's as if a part of me is a mystery, and to be able to fill in those parts with any information I can get is important to me. But I also think that if I want to know him, I only need to know myself.

I need also to talk to that three-year-old whose father died. I need to pay attention to her. I need to nurture her and be gentle to her. Recently, I've wanted to meet three-year-olds because I want to know how much they know. I'll ask their mothers, "How attached are they? How much are they conscious of their daddy?" A lot of it is wanting to figure out what happened to me. All I've got is sort of this part of me inside that represents him, and I want to fill that in and know more about it, because it's kind of a mystery. I look for an image that might describe something to me because the language of a three-year-old is so limited.

I horseback ride now, and horses are something that have always represented my father. I've always loved horses and collected toy horses as a child. It's part of that whole sort of Camelot image. The myth and magic of that time are all wound together. I love the smells of the barn, my whole body relaxes, and it feels like coming home. It means trusting a much more instinctual part of myself. Just a couple of weeks ago, I was helping my riding instructor with a really large horse, and he was so big that I could crouch down underneath him and be in the relationship of a child to a horse. I could look out from underneath at his nose and his whiskers. Being close to his smell and hugging him was all about that kind of sensory access to memory. Seeing these tall men in dark hats and dark boots gets my heart beating faster. It's all nonverbal.

∾

Melissa talks about learning how to mourn her loss through therapy. With her father killing her mother, and then himself, she was angry at both parents; with her father, for the obvious reasons, and with her mother, for not recognizing the danger. As she deals with that anger, she can also experience her grief.

Melissa (28, m, 9, f, 9)

I had a nervous breakdown in my mid-twenties, when I first started to work on the loss of my parents. My dad I saw mostly in work shirts and jeans. My mother was not there. Now, having done the work, I can see her in school clothes, or working around the house. Mostly, I see her face and her hair. Before I would see her hair, but not her face. Or I would see her from the back and not from the front at all. The first step to remembering her was just to get me to be able to be present. And vision in general was kind of hazy. I wouldn't see very much. It was very tunnel.

I guess remembering my mother's face is probably the biggest example of an unaddressed grief. I wasn't able to start rebuilding her face until I could develop a person inside, a me that I could hold on to, that wasn't going to disappear, that wasn't going to become something else or something fearful. Then I could actually start to work on the grief part. As I got stronger with myself, I knew I existed, that I have a personality. Once I was able to work through that, I could get to the rage. I would mourn for my mother, then get to the rage. And then back to the beginning again. I still see myself building the iron horse, building the railroad track that's going to get me places that I'm going to be later. Sometimes it's not working, sometimes it's really hard. But I'm building the track.

∽

Connecting with other people who had lost their parents early on helped Eric Marcus. Therapy also gave him some answers.

Eric Marcus, writer (36, f, 12)

It was at college where I first met other people who had been through similar experiences. I connected with them, not knowing that they'd lost a parent, and then learned that they had. One friend's father committed suicide and another's father died when she was very young. I had a hard time connecting with people unless they had been through some sort of painful experience. In my early twenties, I became so unhappy that I felt compelled to see a therapist because I couldn't understand why I was so miserable. And, of course, it was related to my father's death and never having really experienced it fully.

∽

Marc also talks about the hard passage from adolescence to adulthood. He and Daniel Meyers explain that their coming to manhood required extra perseverance because their fathers weren't around to guide them.

Marc (39, f, 10)

When I was twenty, I went through a very difficult period of my life. I was finally coming to grips with the end of adolescence, coming to grips with whatever strategies I had employed to get through it, just struggling with it, and that's when I think I felt some anger because I had to invent myself, since there was nobody there to guide me or help me. I had to come to grips with making an adult out of myself, which was wrapped around my sense of my father, because a lot of it had to do also with my sense of manhood. Also, there was partly a cop-out of blaming any problems in my head on the fact that I didn't have a father. I was very unhappy, and depressed, but not just depressed, I was also pretty wigged out, and thinking too much and too self-absorbed, some of which is normal at that age, but the degree to which I was doing it was pretty out there. So I had to accept responsibility for myself, and put everything into perspective. Basically, I had to just sort of grab hold of myself and find some direction.

Daniel Meyers, filmmaker (34, f, 18)

Oedipus killed his father to become an adult. We didn't have to do that at eighteen if our fathers died. So now, how do we go off into the world, become a mensch, become an adult, become a human being? What is it in our parent that we want to have as an example and what is a disexample? I know that in my father's lifetime he gave me an enormous gift, and he continues to live in me after his death. But one of my big regrets is that I never knew him when I was an adult. I would like to have seen what kind of relationship we'd have had, what kind of connection, what kind of guidance and appreciation I'd have gotten from him. But fate gave me the push at the age of eighteen to do a lot on my own, which probably matured me much quicker than if he had stayed alive. Things would be different. I would have been happy if he had stayed alive. I would have preferred for him to still be around. But, ironically, every life has its lesson. Mine was that I had to do it more on my own.

~

Danny describes his premature coming-of-age experience as a mixed bag. He was a teenager when his mother died and only twenty-five when his father died.

Danny (30, m, 16)

Taking care of my little brother, I think, accelerated the process into manhood. It gave me a sense of responsibility at an early age. But sometimes I feel hopeless. I wish I had someone to go to for advice. Both my parents were good at that. It's hard not having anyone to share certain experiences. I feel like I might have more drive if they were here.

~

Like Danny, Kenyetta, a teen when her father was stabbed to death, talks of taking care of a younger sibling. Taking on this mentoring role helps her develop her adult identity. At the same time, sharing stories about her father with her brother facilitates her own grief process.

Kenyetta (20, f, 18)

My little brother comes over on the weekend sometimes. He goes to school across the street from our house, so I pick him up from school. I take him out, and we spend time together. We have a good relationship. I talk to him about our father. I tell him about when Daddy came to my graduation. I share a lot of stories with him, but I mostly like him to talk to me, and share his stories, because he was right there when it happened. He saw it. So I like him to get in touch with his feelings, to talk to me about them. Sometimes he remembers places and points them out: "My daddy took me here. I went there one time with my daddy." I want my little brother to know that, no matter what, he can come talk to me.

✑

Several people told us how literature has helped them deal with their grief during their late teens and twenties.

Beto (52, m, 14)

For a long time, I felt really bad about being relieved that my mother died even though she was in so much pain. I was very morose, depressed, brooding. In college I loved the Romantic poets, especially Shelley and Keats, and I got into existentialism. It took a while, but the guilt finally began to leave in my late twenties. I needed to play that process out. Not to blame myself.

Lauren Muller, writer (34, f, 11)

My senior year in college, I did my honors thesis on Flannery O'Connor. Working on that paper was very intense for me. I was possessed and driven by it, driven nearly crazy, I think. I would just spend days working on a paragraph. The paper turned out well. I got highest honors for it. It wasn't until a few years later that I realized, of course, I was writing about my father's death, because it was a violent death, unexpected, sudden. You know how in Flannery O'Connor's stories just out of the blue these things will happen? She would see grace in the unexpected. I was looking at the idea of the wound as blessing.

Addie (19, f, 16)

I wrote a whole series of papers on the elegy, the AIDS elegy. But I'm really finding myself very academically interested in loss itself and sort of what happens, and the interaction between making art and loss. I think that's sort of a positive interest that came out of my father's death.

✑

Part of coming of age is recognizing that our parents aren't necessarily the heroes or saints of our childhood recollections. As we grow up, we begin to adjust the picture.

Edward (30, f, 17)

As I got older, I started to question this whole business of my father taking my brother and me to the bar at the Ramada Inn. The oddness of that didn't strike me until I was a lot older. I remember thinking about that all of a sudden, how it was a real weird thing to do. By that time, I had started to question my father's actions. I was old enough to realize that people aren't perfect.

Paul J. (28, f, 11)

By dying, my father became a martyr. If he had been alive, I might have rebelled against his ideas, but instead he became this godlike figure for a while, which was something to go towards. Then, I guess, in my late teens, I began to get a more realistic view. It was a slow process, but maybe from seventeen to twenty-one, as I became a man myself, I began to realize his flaws. When I was young, I managed to overlook them, but then I saw them and realized he was human like everybody else. I think it actually gave me more confidence. I realized then that this wasn't a figure I could never live up to but somebody that I could probably surpass, not to belittle him, but it wasn't an unreachable goal now.

I have to say, even to this day, I have put off dealing with my grief. At some point, I probably will have to, but I'm not sure when that point will be. One thing that sort of complicates my understanding of my father is that when he died he was going through a great transformation. His personality was changing. His focus on life had completely changed. He was back in school trying to get his degree. He was sort of working towards the things he didn't get when he was younger, and trying to improve his economic status basically. So it's hard for me to imagine what he'd be like today because I didn't have a fix on him.

Lauren's Muller's father was a handsome country doctor devoted to his community. Irena Klepfisz's father was a leader in the Warsaw Ghetto uprising. To a certain extent, the larger-than-life myths surrounding their fathers have been a burden. As they came of age, Lauren and Irena had to balance the heroic public images with more realistic private ones. Part of how they have dealt with the loss is by facing the fact that they'll never really know the full picture, that something will always be missing.

Lauren Muller, writer (34, f, 11)

In some ways, my father remains a mysterious mythological figure. And I know that in the past, I'd say five to ten years, I've been trying to debunk the myth. My mother went through a stage where she was angry at my father for going steeplechasing when he had four young children and a wife. She thought he had no right to sort of take his life into his hands, to desert us. Her anger helped to puncture the myth a little bit. There have been some ways in which I've wanted to get out from under the myth because it's so large. It's sort of feeling that I didn't have a chance to ever rebel against him the way this culture thinks you need to do. He wasn't perfect, and if he had lived, we might have learned more what those imperfections were and have had a chance to work them out. You just don't know.

Irena Klepfisz, poet and writer (54, f, 2)

My mother actually didn't talk a lot about my father, so I don't know very much about him. It's very hard for her to speak about the war, but she's always been, I think, very praising of my father when she does talk. Sometimes I've been almost afraid to ask, because my picture of my father is so untainted. I've asked a number of people, and he seemed to have been extremely well liked. That's great when you're maybe seventeen, but by the time you're thirty-five or forty, you know that that's not very real. Not having any memories of my father has been hard. I kept writing, and I kept thinking I could try to remember something. I wrote about him, and about his death, obsessively for years in my late teens and twenties. It was very intense and very frustrating. It wasn't, I think, until I was able to let go of that and move on to other things that I think my writing turned in some way. I finally came to terms with it. In some ways, I'm just never going to know.

Other Rites of Passage

Coming of age is the first adult rite of passage, but we often think of our dead parents during later transitional times. The passage from adolescence to adulthood requires hard, steady work, but other rites of passage also demand that we assess who we have become and where we stand in relation to the world around us. At those times, we may find ourselves thinking of our dead parent, wishing he or she were with us. Michael reflects on other typical rites of passage: college graduation and marriage.

Michael (43, m, 9)

I think of my mother at all of those transitional times. Like when you get married. I know I did this as I was younger; I remember thinking, well, I hope she's seeing this. I hope she's watching. It does make it easier to accept it because it's a positive. She's not burning in hell or judging me. I don't know how much of this just relates to the fact that the family maybe isn't that close, or whatever, but I've always kind of just done things on my own. When I graduated from college, I didn't even go to graduation. I just got the diploma sent to me. I know it's probably because I lost my mother when I was so young. I don't have this need to share things with parental people. Not having known her as an adult probably affects that a great deal. It's sort of a form of independence. I mean, I say this with a little bit of regret. I think it might be nice for people who have parents to want to share every transitional thing in their life. But, on the other hand, I don't feel I miss it.

Deborah H. explains how she uses floating-bridge periods in her life to release some of her sadness and grief.

Deborah H. (45, m, 16)

I use the tools of bringing up memory as a way to bring myself to the still ongoing need to express the grief and the sadness. So when I'm at an anniversary period of time, I will read what she wrote about me in my baby book. Or I will look at old photographs. Or I will read old letters or any of the stuff that I've saved, that I have to ignite the memories and bring her to me and feel my sadness and my grief and my loss. But I also, you know, integrate this experience in my life.

∽

Some of the people we interviewed talked about a unique rite of passage among adults who were orphaned young: living beyond the age at which their parent died. A particular sadness comes up at that time, especially if the parent died relatively young. We mourn for everything the dead parent missed out on. And there is also sometimes a superstitious fear of not living beyond the magic number.

Irena Klepfisz, poet and writer (54, f, 2)

The whole first third of my life was all framed around sort of trying to get past certain things. At one point, I had two things facing me. One was my twenty-fifth birthday and my friend who committed suicide. She had been orphaned by the Holocaust. She had been a poet and had gone on to graduate school. It was very hard for me to move past her point in graduate school, and it was very hard for me to move past her age. And the other one was my *thirtieth* birthday, the age my father was when he was killed. So it was as if I were bracing myself for years. I don't think I really had a sense of the present in my own life until after that. I was in very, very bad shape when I turned twenty-nine and was facing my thirtieth birthday. After thirty, I sort of started getting my life together, and thinking I had a life and that I was going to survive. Up until then, I don't think I believed I would live beyond thirty.

Eric Marcus, writer (36, f, 12)

I've always been nervous about the number forty-four. Always. I've feared that I'd wind up committing suicide, because of what happened to my father, and feared that I would wind up mentally ill. It will be interesting to get past forty-four. I'm assuming I will, barring any catastrophic circumstances. It does make me nervous that my mother's father and my own father died at forty-four. It's shocking to me now when I meet people or have friends who turn forty-four, it's not so old, it's relatively young.

Paul J. (28, f, 11)

My father's and my birthday are within five days of each other, and his birthday has no effect on me emotionally, nor does his death day. But people always wonder why I'm depressed on my birthday. And I think it's not because of his death, but more that he didn't accomplish what he wanted and then he was trying to make up for it when he was thirty-one. Similarly, I judge myself, and I see every birthday as another reminder that I'm getting sort of closer to that, and I haven't gone where I wanted to be. So every birthday is sort of a letdown. Most people consider me very successful. But I look at that and think, "I'm not where I wanted to be." And that thirty-one bridge, I guess, it's staring me in the eyes. My father tried so hard to make up for what he hadn't done, and then he died before he could accomplish what he had set out to do.

For Kelly, whose mother died giving birth to her, there was no possibility of having any of her own memories. She has found comfort piecing together the woman her mother might have been. The process began when Kelly reached the age her mother was when she died.

Kelly (43, m, birth)

After my oldest sister and I had reestablished contact through a Christmas card she had sent me, I was particularly interested in her memories as a child because I had maybe five vignettes from my dad. There was total silence. No response from her. And then, sort of out of the blue one day, I got a letter from my sister's aunt, who grew up in the same little town in Kansas that my mother had grown up in. At the request of my sister, she shared some memories of my mother. She was a few years younger than my mother and, I think, had really probably looked up to her as kind of a glamorous figure in that little town. I had become a mother myself by that point, and, after corresponding with her a little bit, I made an arrangement to go down and meet her in San Diego. I was thirty-three, and that was the age my mother was when she died.

I started to see her human side, which had never come out in any of my dad's stories. He had romanticized her with all these stories of amazing acts of generosity that really impressed me as a child. But there was nothing about leaving her kids at the hairdresser for a couple months at a time, or things like that. Another thing this aunt told me was that my mother had lost *her* mother young. All of this was almost like opening a trunk and finding my mother's dresses. And now I had somebody who could wear the dresses. I really had a physical picture of who my mother was.

Suzanne Lipsett, writer (51, m, 4)

When I was twelve, I had had a horrible temper tantrum. And they gave me a portrait of my mother, which I kept on my piano in my room. It's a very formal portrait and it's very blank in some ways. When I was thirty-four, the age my mother was when she died, and had my first son, my father dug up this big envelope of photographs, which really show my mother as a living being. I don't know what kind of a person she was, and that's a major frustration to me. I scour these photographs, but she was young. I don't know what kind of person she would have matured into at fifty-two.

Barbara Smith, writer (49, m, 9)

My mother died at age thirty-four, and when I was thirty-four, I thought, "Oh my goodness, I'm the same age as my mother was when she died, and it's so young, it's so young." Now that I'm experiencing menopause, I thought, "Oh my goodness, my mother never even went through this." It's just amazing to look back down the years and to think about what she didn't have.

Waves of Grief

Fresh mourners talk about how grief comes in waves. It's almost physical. It could be compared to the intensity of labor contractions, with their intervals of relative calm. But, unlike giving birth, grieving never completely ends. You go on with your life. You may even lead a full, rich life, but in the middle of an ordinary day, when you might be happily at work or play, some song will come on the radio, some man or woman will walk past you on the street, and you'll feel that old ache. You ride with it and then move on through your day. The period of time between each wave varies. It might last months, but you can also go for years before grief hits again. Sometimes the wave is fierce, and sometimes it gently washes over you. Sometimes you see it coming and sometimes you're taken by surprise. With each wave, you look at your loss from a new angle, one that incorporates knowledge accrued from the last time you met up with your sorrow.

Daniel Meyers, filmmaker (34, f, 18)

I went back to America because I had this dream that my father was dying. I think I started grieving right away. I grieved before he died. I grieved in the months before I knew he was going to die. I cried a lot and thought a lot about it. But I think I only had a certain level of maturity. Much of it I couldn't deal with, and over the years I have just been pulling layer after layer after layer off of it. I feel like I'm close to the end, close to the core of this thing that has so many layers in it. To sort of being at peace with my father's death. There have been cycles, probably a number of moments where things were amped up, and I've been dealing with it more than others. I think it's been a long, long process. Making the film I want to make about him will be important. I don't think I was ready a year or two or three or four years ago.

Jeff B. (24, m, 18)

It's always interesting to get the vibe from yourself, when you know that your grieving cycle is coming around. Either it's a time of year that brings it around, or just something that strikes, a series, like a flood of memories or something. And you go through different phases, some where you think about it but you don't talk about it, and you go through phases where you're not sure if you're really thinking too much about it, but you're okay with talking about it. Sometimes you're not okay with talking about it.

∽

As we age, our childhood memories intensify, so the memory of the dead parent may seem even more present.

Nan (79, m, 13)

At different intervals, the older I would get, the more my mother would come to my mind. In the earlier years, you just sort of pass it off. But it seemed like the older I got, the more she entered my mind. It was a long time before I even bothered to go to her grave or anything. And now I don't let her birthday go by.

Diana O'Hehir, novelist and poet (72, m, 4)

My mother's death certainly affects my life still. I have periods of depression. And it's only fairly recently I recognized that these are related to her death. I said to myself, "My god! You're seventy-two years old and you're not over this? You never will be. You never will be. I mean this is just part of your makeup." Now, I'm not manic-depressive, and they're not serious depressions, but, you know, it's just that there are times when I feel sad. For no particular reason that I know of. And then I say, "Oh, oh that's what it is." I just simply feel sad.

∽

David Joseph deals with both the grief from his mother's death and his depression stemming from the years of her physically abusing him.

He, too, experiences the ebb and flow. The effects of the abuse seem even more powerful than his grief.

David Joseph, poet (40, m, 14)

When people die, I've found that the memory of them persists, and part of them never quite leaves you. So you never quite get over the grief—it just changes over the years. For many years, I have struggled with feelings of depression and grief. I have just struggled with feelings of mental pain. I've found that, as I get older and continue to struggle with things, it changes, but the pain is like a physical pain, like something that becomes hard at different times, very hard to endure. At different times it's harder than others. But you know, because of the abuse, the thought has occurred to me that if my mother had not died, or that if I had had the power to resurrect her, I probably would have killed her again.

Irena Klepfisz, poet and writer (54, f, 2)

In many ways, this interview comes sort of at an interesting point in my life. I've always thought throughout my life at various moments that I finished with that part of the past. And each time it really feels very final; it feels like I'm purged. It really doesn't feel like I'm in denial; I think I actually am finished, except that it comes up again.

∽

When we feel our grief reemerging, it doesn't mean we are being self-indulgent or allowing our grief to overwhelm us. It just means that we are human beings contending with a deep loss.

Rich (36, m, 14)

I initially started therapy because of feelings about my relationship with my ex-lover falling apart. And immediately it started focusing on issues relating to my family and my mother. I've done little bits of exploration and work on that, and then I retreat from it, dramatically, for long periods of time. It's just sort of rising to the surface again. I would say to my therapist, "I thought I was done with this. I thought this was over. You know I made this trip. I thought it was over." The truth is, it's not over.

∽

Peggi became involved in this book first as the transcriber. Later, she asked to be interviewed. Eventually, she found a way to talk to her new daughter-in-law who, like Peggi, lost her father when she was a teenager. She also discovered the paradoxical nature of feeling pain, the way in which it can be a comfort and a release.

Peggi (56, f, 19)

My memories of my father got stimulated by doing the transcriptions, so I don't know if some of these images, especially as the years have gone by, have been as vivid as they've become over the past couple of months. At first, doing the transcribing was painful and distressing. But now it's become a pleasure and a comfort. I enjoy hearing each new person's story. It's been therapeutic and enriching. Other people around me have lost parents in childhood. The woman my son just married was seventeen when her father died. Having done these transcripts, it was easier for me to talk with her about that. I even used some of your questions.

Death Revisited

To revisit a parent's death at the time of a subsequent loss is a common experience. It's as if death is a place marked out by memory and pain. When a loved one dies, we go back to earlier losses. This experience is related to the natural grieving cycle, but it's also different. This time it's not just the loss of a parent that we're returning to, but the whole territory of death itself—what it means and how it feels.

Sometimes the end of a relationship can feel like a kind of death. Deborah H. talks about grieving her mother when her lover left her, and again when her brother died.

Deborah H. (45, m, 16)

When I broke up with my lover thirteen years ago—we had been to-gether five years—it was pretty much an abandonment scene with a person I trusted and loved. I got left because she fell in love with someone else, and I did grieve and rage about that loss, but it was re-ally fundamentally more, I think, about my mother than it was about losing the relationship. Although there was content to it, and that was an important relationship for me, the real core inside emotions that I felt were, at the time, "This is worse than losing my mother." What I was saying was that I'm feeling it now. I'm feeling both of them now. I was more capable of grieving at that age than I was at sixteen, so it came out stronger.

When my brother died, there was another level of resolution. Jon died with warning; we knew he was going to die; I felt very resolved when he died. It was very sad, but it was much more resolved than my mother's death, so I felt a piece of resolution about her death in the process of doing resolution work about Jon that I couldn't really do until that other death. I think every loss experience that I will ever have in my life will have some of my mom in it, and hopefully it will include some more of the transformational part, some more of the deeper healing from the original loss.

Sandy (46, f, 16)

My mom always wanted me to go to the cemetery where my father was buried. I could light the *Yahrzeit* (memorial) candles, but I couldn't go to the cemetery. When my mother died, it had been six-teen years since I had been there. So I went. First I saw my father's grave. I hadn't been in his presence for all those years. It was a sad but peaceful moment. I greeted him, "Hi, Dad." I experienced an over-whelmingly strong and oddly happy feeling. It felt good to be re-united. I think I finally understood my grief. It was my mother's moment. She was the one who had just died, but it really was my fa-ther's. Then this wonderful image crossed my mind of my mother crawling over and snuggling up to my father and pulling the blanket up next to him.

Jeffery K. (22, m, 8, f, 18)

I kind of went into my own little world again. When my father first passed away, it made me realize, *again,* and this'll sound probably funny, that my mother had passed away. I was a year older than my brother was when my mom passed away. I just realized what my brother went through. It was kind of like, I don't know, like a lesson you learn. Maybe it was their way of, or God's way, of pushing us into the world, or something. I don't know.

Teresa (32, f, 8)

Sam, my youngest brother—the baby my mother was pregnant with when my dad passed away—died last January 17, on my father's birthday, and my grandmother died in October. I delivered two eulogies last year. There is this sort of undertow of sadness, which I had felt free of for a very long time, but I have it all over again now. When Sam died, we had to pick out the casket and my sister had to go buy the suit, and I did the eulogy. I don't remember any of that stuff from my father because we were kept out of it. There are a lot of things that I can't remember about how I felt as soon as my dad died: Did I cry? How did I respond? I don't know. The enormity of the loss didn't really become apparent until I was older and there were other losses.

I used to be an editorial assistant at a large newspaper. And one of the editors there was a very dear friend of mine. He was one of these older men–mentor people. Well, he died of AIDS about three years ago. He didn't really remind me of my father, but it just got to be that every time I thought about him, it would be on the same plane as my father and my brother and my grandmother. I'm wondering if part of my grief for him is really displaced grief for my father. His death in some way tapped a lot of that grief that I felt for my father. It was a trigger that I needed in a way. I think, whether you like it or not, something's going to happen in your life that will bring this stuff up.

Kristy (25, f, 13)

My boyfriend died three years ago in a car accident on April 12, and my dad's memorial is on the seventh. When George died, a lot of *Dad's* stuff came up. A lot of getting angry at my father. I was able to say, "Goddamn it! Why did you leave me then? Why didn't you talk to me? Why didn't you prepare me?" A lot of that intermeshed with my stuff with George. Now I had another issue of major abandonment in my life, and I decided I was not going to go through years of torture. I was going to be as expressive as I could about it. Through George's death, all of this old stuff from my dad came up. That's when I felt a lot of anger. Growing up, I don't think I wanted to feel angry, but it was there, nudging me.

Barbara Smith, writer (49, m, 9)

Whenever someone dies, I always go back to my mother's death. Those feelings always come up. Again. That is, when somebody who's close to me dies. Because that was the first time I ever experienced anything like that, it was the most brutal. And it can't help but have a ripple effect.

Coming to Terms

Coming to terms with loss can mean many things. It can mean accepting that the pain never completely disappears. It can mean learning that in order to remember the good we have to remember the bad. It can mean using our memories and the strength we find in dealing with them to take care of ourselves.

Marc (39, f, 10)

There's still a search for my father. I'll probably always feel that there's something a little missing, no matter how much I come to terms with the fact of his death and his life. I think there's always a sense of trying to find him, and somehow that if I found him, it would answer a lot of questions, which is obviously false, but there's a certain emotional truth to it. That search for my father has sort of led me to other searches and other understandings, and so in some ways it's a very positive thing, but it also is a very negative thing in that it leaves kind of this empty feeling. I feel more of a lack of memories than their presence, and, therefore, a real loss. There's something missing. There's a piece missing from my life, and no matter how hard I look for it, I can't find it, and the older I get, the further away I am from finding it.

William (54, f, 14)

When I got to therapy, it changed my life—my internal life and my emotional life. My external life didn't change so much. Maybe the way I relate to people improved. But the getting at it eventually was so relieving and finalizing and completing that it really patched my heart up and made a tremendous difference. So it had a transforming effect that was directly related to my dealing with my dad's death however many years later. Dealing with his death changed my life— emotionally, spiritually, in many ways. Anything I want to say to my dad, I say to him now. So I don't have any unfulfilled desires around that. Fulfilling that desire though, actually talking to him, took me many years to do. I realized that mostly I just wanted to tell him I loved him, and how sad I was, how sorry I was for him that that happened to him, that he was sick, and how it had come out and things like that. I did have my conversation. I got to say what I wanted to say.

Rob had to face the fact of his father's abusive behavior toward him before he could come to terms with his loss.

Rob (44, f, 15)

It was like my father was this wonderful man. Then, years later, I was with a consultant, working on an abuse case. We were talking. She said, "Your father used to hit you?" I said, "Yeah, he used to spank me real hard once in a while." She said something like "And that was okay then, right?" I said, "No. It wasn't." This was about twelve, thirteen years ago. That started changing the whole way I looked at it.

I guess, when I really allow myself to feel, it's terribly sad that I do have those memories. It's so sad to feel what I lost. It's easier to feel the anger. I get more out of feeling the sadness, though. I benefit more from it because the anger sometimes doesn't go anywhere. The sadness is a real release, not only honoring what happened, being in touch with that, but also being able to say good-bye.

How do we think about people who die? Are we supposed to just get amnesia and forget them? No. Are we supposed to honor their memory? Are we supposed to not talk about it? How does one come to terms with what happened? It's not by forgetting. It's not by not talking about it. I only delayed dealing with my grief with excessive drug use. It made it more complicated because I was trying to figure out things while I was on LSD, which you can't really do very well. Now I go back to my father's grave, and it's a very unique kind of experience. I'll be there all alone. I'll be talking out loud, when nobody's around, and I feel like he's answering me back, at times.

As a therapist, I use sand trays with my clients. With one-on-one talk therapy, you can tend to intellectualize things. In sand-tray therapy, you really can get to the feelings. You have thousands of figures to choose from, and you play with them in the sand. You position them. I've spent a lot of time in the sand tray with my father's grave. I used to feel like I can't go there. It's too scary, it's too numbing. But now I feel this is a place where I learn a lot and get a lot of wisdom. I used to feel that I couldn't keep going back there, because it's wrong, you're supposed to move on. Now I want to go back there and see what I can learn.

Monica (30, m, 10)

I feed myself with memories of my mother. Many times I find myself behind my shop, fixing things, and I think about her, and it's just a wonderful feeling. Instead of a sadness, I learned through the years that memories of her have become a good influence for me as a woman. But there's still a lot of pain. When she died, part of me died, and I have not gained it back. I have a friend who is the first person, besides my brother, who I can talk to about my mom. Once I found myself crying, telling him that sometimes I want to die. He said to me, "Monica, if you die, your mom dies. You're the only one who keeps her alive." I thought about that. The goodness that she taught me when I was a kid, I'm passing on to my son. It keeps her alive.

I have a lot of my mother's needlework. I have the best of her, her handiwork, the release of all of her pressures and loneliness. Her colors were very bright. I decided that when I have the money, I'm going to make a metal box for her things, so they won't be destroyed in a fire. A metal box that I can open and close and look at, like a book. Also, I have this portrait of her that someone painted from a black and white photograph. I feel comfortable walking in the house. I see her picture, and I smile. It looks just like her, except that she had green eyes, and in the painting her eyes are dark. I guess the artist didn't think dark people might have light eyes. Someday, when I'm ready to really look at her, I'm going to have the eyes redone.

Rich (36, m, 14)

I'm just now starting to deal with some of the issues surrounding who my mom was and her death and all the intervening years and all the rest of this stuff with my family. And to me, in a lot of ways, there's a lot of unfinished work for me, both in terms of grief and in terms of coming to some sort of peace with my sense of who she was. I think that her death is at the center of what I'm going through right now.

The trip I took back East two years ago was motivated by wanting to have some sort of reconciliation with my family and also to embark upon some sort of journey towards closure regarding my mother's death. That whole trip was sort of magical. Various things occurred then that were really important—going to my mother's grave, talking to her and crying, and grieving, to some extent, as I'd never done. Having this conversation with my sister, which was painful, but I think it was all in some ways motivated by my mother's death. It was an odyssey.

∞

Ken Burns has begun to come to terms with his mother's death only very recently. Part of this process was precipitated by a painful divorce, which can be like death revisited. When his mother died, his father never went to pick up her ashes.

Ken Burns, filmmaker (41, m, 11)

As in the movie *Shadowlands* [the movie Jan spoke of in the intro-
duction, which profoundly affected her as well], my mother was
brought into our house, in a wheelchair, and her bed was put in the
living room. I must have been eight or nine. Before she came back
from the hospital, I had been looking out the window for hours,
waiting for her to come home, just as in the film. Years later I sat bolt
upright in bed the moment she died. When I saw *Shadowlands*, the
moment it was over, I walked outside. I was with two women, friends
of mine. We were in the living room looking at it one night, and I
was just stunned. But I closed down. I mean I couldn't really cry. It
was just too close to the bone. And I remember walking outside,
looking up at the sky, and I just said, "Mom." It was freezing, it was
February a year ago, and I said, "Mom," and a shooting star streaked
across the sky. And I just sank down to my knees. I came in, trem-
bling, and told my friends, and then we all cried again.

My therapist asked me if I had ever celebrated or recognized the
day of my mother's death—April 28. And I realized there was this
phenomenon that had gone on for twenty-eight years. I would be
aware of the impending date, and then I would be aware that I missed
it. It was kind of magical thinking—keeping her alive. So eventually,
in 1993, my brother and I went to Ann Arbor on the date that it had
happened, and we had a little ceremony at her church, and did a lot
of crying, and then went out and discovered her remains at this un-
marked grave site, miles from the town where she was eventually
buried when my father did not pick up the ashes. We ordered a
plaque. We came back in the summer for an intimate ceremony, and
I brought my kids and my father. When we brought my father to the
grave site, he was initially reluctant to deal with it, as though it were
our problem. But he told us, quite poignantly, about her last days, stuff
we didn't know. My brother and I cried.

Over the sink in my kitchen is a photograph of the gravestone. I
look at it every day. I don't always see it, but it's there. It's funny,
though . . . my memory's slippery. It's like trying to grab at soap in the
bathtub, it sort of gets away. I was trying to think of the details that
my father told us that day on the grave about her last day, but all I can
remember is the quality or the color of the emotion.

My therapist asked me to write a letter to my mother when I realized a couple of years ago that she was dead. There was some real anger in that letter. I pulled it out the other day. It was surrounded completely by love, but there was a sense of "Why did you leave me?" I told her that I understood that she was now dead and that I hadn't really acknowledged it until now. I tried to tell her how I used to blow out my birthday candles and wish for her back. That I felt my brother had accepted it, but that I had not. And that I was trying to learn how to do that. I felt in some ways that pain had also compromised another relationship with nearly equal importance to me. I feel that I continue to experience tremendous pain probably because I haven't really fully grieved.

It's interesting that we build these floating bridges in wartime. There's this temporary sense of emergency, to get over them, to improvise something, and they're tenuous and they disappear afterwards. It's no accident that my first film is a history of the bridge. We respond as beings to a log that has fallen across a little steam, no more than a foot wide. Every kid wants to walk across it because it connects one thing to another. It's the metaphor of heaven and earth, of trying to communicate with the dead. It's about waking the dead, this floating bridge.

∽

Ken Burns now sees his documentary filmmaking as a vehicle that reconnects him with his mother. Until recently, all of this operated on a more subconscious level. The grief work he is now engaged in has made the process more apparent to him. Others have also used their art forms to open up their grieving.

Brown Miller, poet (51, m, 6)

I think part of the reason I wrote so many poems about my mother, about her death, and all of that, is that I never grieved properly at the time, and didn't have anybody to talk to when I was little. I feel that some of the most useful grieving is in the constructing of my poems. It was very therapeutic just to put these words together. It really was almost like creating this parent. I did idealize certain aspects of her, yet it was balanced. In my poetry, I never make her into some perfect mother. But I *was* talking to her, through these poems. Lashing one pontoon to another.

∽

Jim has also used writing as a tool and a source of comfort.

Jim (61, m, 16, f, 18)

My mother's death affects my life in every way. I just think it's there, everywhere, something I carry all the time. I'm still working out that early wounding stuff, I think. I worked through a lot of bad poetry, a lot of depressing sort of poetry, actually managed to throw most of that away, or lose it. I worked through it somehow, and then I became more, not completely positive, but with at least a balance of positive and negative stuff. When I'm writing my poems, I'm lost in space. And I feel that time doesn't exist. For long periods of time, I can feel totally relaxed. Poetry is playtime, time out. Recently, I've been learning a lot more about the poetry, mostly because I'm teaching it so much. Maybe that's a transformational process, the combination of poetry and teaching.

Mary Montgomery, writer (61, f, 3)

In my children's books, I think I am dealing with feelings that I had as a child and never expressed. They weren't dealt with or taken seriously. And I take writing for kids very seriously. What I really think happened to me is that my feelings were never taken into account. I kept everything from my mother, not wanting to give her one more thing to worry about. I've also written for adults. One book is called *Beyond Sorrow,* and another is *A Time to Mourn.*

∽

One of the paradoxes of grieving and acknowledging a loss is that it can help us feel closer to our dead loved ones. Many of the people we interviewed talked about how they feel the mother or father they lost in childhood lives on. They acknowledge the presence of their parents in their lives in their waking moments and in their dreams.

Daniel Meyers, filmmaker (34, f, 18)

There were times when I sort of struggled with "Do I want to be like him this way or that way or how?" And now I'm really so much more at peace with it. He just is a part of me. I am a part of him. We're not born out of a pile of mud someplace, we're born out of all our positive and negative influences. There's lots of things I've learned about life that I do not want to emulate from him, but there are more that I do want to emulate, and he just lives on. My understanding of death is that somebody lives on in what they've done in their life and who they've affected in their life, in positive or negative ways, they live on in others. My father is alive. He's like the silent partner, he's the character in our lives. He is regularly in my thoughts and dreams.

Addie (19, f, 16)

I remember having a dream, I guess, a year or so after my father died. It was at some kind of gathering for me, a party or a wedding or something. I was sort of scanning the room, and I saw his face and I just kept going. And then when I woke up, I thought, "Oh God, why didn't I go to him and talk to him and this was a great opportunity that I missed." And then I realized that it's kind of nice to just stand there and see his face and recognize that it's there and just know that he's there.

Eric Marcus, writer (36, f, 12)

I had a dream about my father several years ago, the most vivid dream I've ever had. In the dream, I had come home one afternoon to the house that my mother bought after her mother died. I was in my thirties. I heard someone upstairs and I walked up and there was my father shaving in the bathroom. He was a young man, very much my contemporary. I said hello and sat down on the edge of the tub. I don't remember exactly what it was anymore that we talked about, but I woke up and I thought, "We had a visit." I am not spiritual. I don't believe in any of that stuff. But I woke up with such a good, warm feeling, that we'd had a conversation. We had visited. And it was okay.

Horace Silver, musician (66, m, 9)

You can send your dead ones your love and you'll, no doubt, which I do, have dreams about them, which is their way of telling you that they love you still. When you're sick or depressed, they come to you in a dream to try to cheer you up. I believe in eternal life, life after death, so I believe my mother has come many times to visit us. My son lives with me here, and I believe she comes and visits us very often. I feel sometimes that there's a spirit in the house. I get a little kind of sensation that there's somebody else here. I can't see her or hear her, but sometimes I feel like she might be around. I know she's not oblivious to what I'm doing. I know she's keeping tabs on me, wherever she is. And she knows how my career is progressing. I believe in spirit.

Lisa (28, m, 12)

Every once in a while I still dream about my mother. In the last one I had a communication with her. I think we were talking, I was having some problem, and she was helping me out. With all that I've been through—losing her, the abuse in my father's house—if I didn't have the firm ground to work with that my mother gave me, I would be a different person today. She was very loving, and so were my grandparents. She taught me to respect elders, and myself. If I didn't have that, I don't know where I'd be. The happy childhood she gave me provided solid ground. I'll always mourn my mother. Even today there are certain songs I'll hear, and I just start crying. You can't make yourself not feel sad. You can't change what happened. But I feel my mother in me. My hands are like hers.

Deborah H. (45, m, 16)

When I was in my twenties, I was on a backpacking trip with my best friend, and we had hiked all day and we'd made a dinner and we were just lying on the rocks watching the sky. And I literally had a vision and saw my mother. She came to me, probably sparked by cloud formations. I really saw her coming towards me and carrying a baby. I felt her inside me. I felt her talk to me, and I was really bowled over.

There were several other incidents like that. The January before my little brother died—the anniversary of her death is in January—my other brother and I went for a long walk in Muir Woods, and we were just walking along and talking about my mom. And all of a sudden there was this deer in front of us with these eyes. It was my mom. And my brother does not have a spiritual bone in his body. But he whispered, "I feel Mom." I said, "I do too." It was just a very kind of strong feeling. Once, when I was in a car accident, I felt sheltered by her somehow. I feel that there's a way that her presence in the world gives me a sense of safety.

Kristy (25, f, 13)

Dad is present with my art, and he has a solid part in my body or my psyche. It's definitely a wonderful base. There's a solidity about it. There's a part of me that feels like Dad understands, especially when I feel like I'm in a place where I feel like an alien from another planet and I need someone to say, "But I know you're connected with me. You need to do it this way." Dad is there. There's actually a physical sensation. When I think about my dad, there's a tingling that happens in this side of my arm. I don't know if you'd call it a presence, or a reminder feeling of my dad or my boyfriend who died. Whether it's real or not, it doesn't matter to me. It comforts me. I don't tell a lot of people about this, because I could easily be labeled, but I let myself pretend or feel like they're in a room with me. "Great! You're here. Thanks for visiting me in whatever form you're in." There's something very comforting about that. They seem eternal to me.

Dad was always joking about spirits. I remember going to the cemetery with him to put flowers on a grave for his father and his uncle. It's the same cemetery he's buried at. I loved going to the cemetery with Dad. We'd go and buy flowers, and I'd just run all over the graveyards. I remember once I jumped out of the car, and I was running to get some water for the flowers, and Dad says I have to respect the spirits and the ghosts underneath the ground because they're all having a party and we don't want to disturb them. I remember tiptoeing around. So there was always awareness of respecting the other world. His view, I think, has allowed me to open up to places that I may not have been able to explore.

Kenyetta (20, f, 18)

My sister has conversations with my father all the time. She will call me and say, "You know, Daddy told me not to go there and I should have listened to him because something happened." She'll wake up, and she'll see a shadow of him. She hears him in dreams, or when she is awake. It doesn't matter, any time of the day, all times of the night, it doesn't matter. She's really in touch with him. I think about him, and I want to be in touch with him, too, but it's nothing I have done yet. I'm scared to have a conversation with him. I'm scared I won't get an answer. I won't get what I'm looking for. I'm just in touch with him within my heart. I listen to the music he liked. And when I listen to it, I'll go into a deep thinking about him. I eat the food he liked. I cook the things he liked. That's how I stay connected to him.

Cultural Responses

Many cultures have established ways of helping mourners work through their pain long after the funeral is over: ancestor worship in Asian and African traditions; All Souls Day in European Catholic cultures and the practice of marking the anniversary of the death with a memorial mass; the Jewish tradition of *Yahrzeit* (anniversary of the death). In the contemporary United States, most of our families have unfortunately abandoned these traditions. Yet there seems to be a natural yearning to communicate with the dead, which probably accounts for perennial ghost stories in cultures that have been emptied of the traditions that honor ancestor spirits. And it probably explains a spate of movies about ghosts.

Robin (46, f, 8)

I think part of my going to temple was influenced by my father, because it's something he would have done. Also, I wanted his name to be mentioned at his *Yahrzeit*.

Ken Burns, filmmaker (41, m, 11)

I think we need to deal with death. I mean death was a part of nineteenth-century life and eighteenth-century life. But now it's so removed. We forget to tell people things are done. We forget to say that things are resolved. We forget to say parents are dead. We need to attend to the children. The biggest thing I wish my father had done was make me realize my mother was dead. The central understanding of anthropology is rituals, rites of passage, of marriage, of birth, of fertility. Of death. We had none of that in our family, or just about. There was no finality. Nothing close. So I've had to do it myself.

The Chinese have the ghosts of the ancestors present. Edward Sapir, the linguist, would say we have a spurious culture, not a genuine one, because we lack that ability to have a firmament, a set of ancestors. That's why we like baseball, because there's ancestry. A .300 hitter today means the same as it did to our father, to our grandfather, and to our great-grandfather. My longtime collaborator Geoff Ward and I wrote in *Baseball,* "It's a haunted game, in which every player is measured by the ghosts of all who have gone before."

Kelly (43, m, birth)

Anytime my mother arises in my life, it seems like a transformational experience. When I turned forty, I felt as if my mother was leaving my life. I felt very sad. On my birthday, which was the day that she died, I remember sort of saying good-bye to her. But now I feel like it was sort of a transition in our relationship, more of "You're on your own now." How is this relationship really possible between these two dimensions? What is it? I don't know what it is to describe it. But I feel like she's still a source of energy very much available to me. I guess maybe I'm creating my own energy strand now to weave with hers, and together we're building something.

I've just come back from the Molucca Islands in eastern Indonesia. The people are either Muslim or Christian, but they have an animist foundation that is rooted in a tradition of honoring the ancestors. The ancestors are seen as carrying the message to the supreme beings, to the gods. They're not to be confused with gods, and, in fact, they inhabit a lower world. They travel by boat, and they carry our prayers and our thoughts to the gods, who live in the higher world. That made sense to me. It seemed very sensible to me. It explained how I feel about my relationship with my mother. It felt so comfortable to be in a culture that took that in such a matter-of-fact way. When someone dies, they make an ancestor statue, and so they have this little gallery of statues for people in their families who have died, or they save the skull, and the children play with their grandparents' skulls.

I filmed one dance for a coronation ceremony. One man went into a trance and was possessed by the ancestor spirit. Later I learned that by doing this dance they were honoring the traditions of their ancestors. And I thought, "We don't have anything like this, we have no way to connect with our ancestors, we have no way to honor that connection with them." Our grieving process is sort of meant to get over it and to put it behind us.

✍

The Day of the Dead, a traditional Mexican holiday, has been institutionalized over the last twenty years in the city of San Francisco, as a result of the work of a group of Chicano artists. The tradition has now spread across the country. Several years ago, a large Day of the Dead exhibit was installed in Grand Central Station in New York.

Wendy (27, f, 16)

Towards the end of last year, I was kind of depressed, just out of my mind. I couldn't get a grasp on life or myself. I was thinking about my father and wanting to go off and find him, leave the planet and go find him. But last November, during El Día de los Muertos, which is the Day of the Dead, a Mexican holiday, I put together a group of my friends to march in the procession. The Day of the Dead is all about remembering relatives or people that you've lost, and just giving praise to them for a day. You make offerings to their souls to come back and join you for the day so you can be with them. So that's what I did. The whole day was for my father. We all made big masks, and we marched in the procession in the Mission District. I also did stuff at home, preparing for my father to visit. This ritual of just bringing my father into my home centered me a lot. Trying to figure out my purpose, trying to figure out what is happening to me, trying to deal, trying to cope with being alone is all very hard. I have no family, really, so I had to do something for myself. What's great about the Day of the Dead is that you're not alone. It's a group effort. It's not just me who is longing for someone who is gone. It really helped me feel connected to my father.

Gloria Anzaldúa, poet and writer (52, f, 14)

The Day of the Dead altars provide a place for the dead parent to reside. Somehow or other, it's protected, it's safe, it's sacred. And you can have a particle of his clothing—sometimes I use my father's glasses—or a photograph, and you can meditate at the site of an altar. You can have a dialogue with this ancestor. I think that my father who's dead is always with me. I have little altars everywhere. El Día de los Muertos is very much a ceremony with me, but also the other kinds of deaths, you know, the identity changes, like the dying of the old identity and the birth of a new. When I finish a piece of work, it's like a little death.

I'm working on a book and one of the essays focuses on the *nepantla*—in-between ground, the middle ground, the spaces in between—and I talk about the process of creating art and changing identity. So death and my relationship to death and dying is in all my work. The concept that I'm trying to articulate in art is the in-between place, the bridge. A bridge between consensual reality and the spirit world, the supernatural world, or the world of the imagination and the world of fiction. Even though it's a word that originally meant the space between two places, I have taken it into some other realms, to be a kind of a gateway, a passageway, a bridge, a door to this kind of reconfiguring your identity. You're negotiating, living between all these different realities. It is a journey, it is leaving one thing behind in order to enter that thing over there. I always think of crossing over to these other planes, these other levels of reality, of which death is one. So I think my father is always with me and I think of him very often. And I think my memories are a gift. But until I became an artist and a writer, they weren't a gift, they were burdens. I think somehow what the artist does is to transfigure sad memories in some way into something more positive, so I'm lucky that I'm a writer.

Always

The pain of a deep loss never really goes away. But if we're lucky, we can transform it into something positive. Below, two of our youngest interviewees, Athena and Janette, express that wisdom and are echoed by two of their older counterparts, Tron and Sandy.

Athena (19, f, 17)

You know, at the end of the grief book that we used in my support group in high school, there was this chapter "Letting Go." I didn't understand that at all. What are you supposed to forget? Let go of what? I still don't understand that. I guess it's about letting go of the grief, but I think I'll always want to talk about my dad.

Janette (19, m, 12)

When my mother died, they put me in these groups at school to deal with her death. But I would just sit there. I wasn't ready to deal with it, I guess. When they would say things to me, it would just make me feel worse about myself. I had to do it within myself, to help myself. A person should take as long as she wants to deal with it. Even now, I still cry. You know, it's always going to be in you, but you take it and learn from it and use it in a positive way.

Tron Bykle, artist (51, f, 14)

I haven't done any particular ritual for my father, and I think that since we don't have a way of releasing the pain, it's always a part of you. Sometimes you can get rid of a little part, but it's always going to be there. That's where the loss is. But you know, I was talking to my kid's friend, who lost his father about the same age that I did, and I told him that he has to honor the memory of his father, because that's all he has left, and in that sense his father is still with him. And that the joy of having known him for as long as he knew him will help. I told him that he could use that as an energy to get over this immediate loss. And to honor that memory.

Sandy (46, f, 16)

The periods of time that you can forget the pain keep getting longer, but death is always there. Although it's on the back burner, your life is forever altered. On the other hand, it's not good to *mourn* forever. You're entitled to a little joy in life. It's good for you, it's not bad for you. And it doesn't mean you loved the person any less. I finally learned to laugh and to smile, so many years later. If anything, I do greater honor to my father that I'm a whole person rather than an emotionally diseased person. There will always be things worth living for. And you owe it to the person you loved to make sure that there still *are* things worth living for.

The Floating Bridge

We honor our dead parents by living full, rich lives. And when the affection for the dead parent is strong, some people remember songs their parents sang to them, dishes they cooked for them, or poems they read to them. Others call on the ancestor strength and power recognized by many cultures. We might name this power "spirit" or "ghost." For those of us whose training or belief system does not acknowledge spirits, our homage to our dead parents is reflected in ways we've fashioned and worked our identity so it can receive the memory of the lost parent. All of us are always constructing our floating bridges, finding ways to reconnect with what we lost, building for ourselves a way through each passage. We fashion these bridges out of love and memory, stories and dreams, songs and sometimes even ceremonies.

We know a man whose father died over twenty-five years ago, when he was nine years old. On Father's Day, shortly after his sister was diagnosed with cancer—the disease that killed their father—he brought flowers to their father's grave and stayed there for three hours with his sadness and his fear. Bringing flowers to the grave can help us make the crossing during times of crisis and change. In writing this book, as our daughters leave home, we are bringing flowers to the graves of our parents, telling them of our pride and listening for their advice.

This chapter has explored how the people we interviewed have lived with their grief, how they continue to hold it in their hands, examining it from different angles. Not necessarily dwelling on it or obsessing over it, but confronting it. This chapter also leads the way to the second half of the book, where we allow our interviewees to tell the stories of how they have loved, worked, and pondered the world about them. How they have survived their loss and, in most cases, flourished.

7

The Arms of Love

It was at that moment that I felt I did not want to belong to anyone, that since the one person I would have consented to own me had never lived to do so, I did not want to belong to anyone; I did not want anyone to belong to me.
—Jamaica Kincaid, *The Autobiography of My Mother*

Most of the time when I think of him at all it is with muted sorrow that he has not been here to see how I've grown up, married a good man, had these beautiful and clever children, bought a nice house in Vermont; see how well I've done all these years without him.—Susan Kenney, *In Another Country*

I believe that the very feel of our baby's skin, the sound of his cry in the night, the depth of his gaze as he stared mildly up at us with infancy's utter lack of self-awareness—these flesh-and-blood experiences worked on us. . . . Within my soul, ripped places began to knit together.—Suzanne Lipsett (m, 4), *Surviving a Writer's Life*

The bookshelves, television programs, and advice columns of this country in the late twentieth century are chock-full of sound bites, ideas, cures, and laments about love. We talk about building intimacy, we analyze the demise of the family, rue the divorce rate and the rising number of single mothers. As a nation, we search for love, find it, lose it, find it again. As orphaned children all grown up, why should we deal any more or less with intimacy than our brothers and sisters in the general population? Sometimes we don't. Yet our bereavement irrevocably shapes our love relationships.

In telling the stories that comprise this chapter, almost all the interviewees talked about their fears. Some fear the loss of loved ones through death, some abandonment, some through never being able to connect intimately. Hand in hand with fear, for some, goes crippling worry, or worry lurking in the background, overtaking us at odd times. Knowing, as a child, that a parent can die makes it impossible to ignore the fact that anyone can disappear at any time. That makes some of us worry about our loved ones, and sometimes treasure them and life more deeply. Some people's response in love relationships is to feel needy or not deserving of love, or both. Others describe holding back, feeling reluctant to form intimate connections. Or they talk about being incapable of forging intimate connections.

But the stories in this chapter do not offer any simple formula. It's not always true that because we lost our first big love now we cannot commit or ever love again. In some stories, in some lives, the impulse to connect is strengthened by the parent's death. For some, the healing touch of a spouse or lover nurtures the now-grown orphan. Sometimes children become the gift that begins to knit the ripped places together, as Suzanne Lipsett says. Some people spoke of finding connection in close friendships. Often those who have experienced the worst can value the best.

This is not a chapter about cause and effect. There is no prescription for finding love and happiness with friends, family, and children simply by dealing with one's parent's death once and for all. If anything, these stories show that a parent's death may pop up in unusual and unexpected ways, when one is happily in love or lamenting a loss, when one is welcoming a new baby or raising a child, when one is connecting with friends or having difficulty forging deep connections.

There are gifts in these stories, and the stories are gifts. The gifts are both in the details of the individual's lives, the testaments to life and love persevering, and in the ways that each of us reading this book can connect the stories to our own lives. Then there is the simple human comfort of knowing that someone else out there has felt the same despair, or sorrow, or joy we have.

Fear and Worry

We worry and fear loss and abandonment. Practically everyone we interviewed for this book—from the nineteen-year-olds to the eighty-somethings—talked about it. It comes up over and over again in relationships to lovers and spouses, friends, and children. Bad things can, do, and will happen, whether we are prepared for them or not. Subsequent losses can be that much harder to deal with because every loss potentially invokes the first one. Rich discovered that when his lover, a man he'd been living with for nearly a decade, and he broke up.

Rich (36, m, 14)

I think experiencing my mother's death makes me feel frightened a lot, frightened of loss. It makes me cynical—good things, good people, being good doesn't save you. It becomes a compulsion that I constantly let the people who are important in my life know how important they are to me because I feel that I didn't do that sufficiently with my mother. I crave getting close to people, but I fear it. I crave intimacy, and I don't have a whole lot of it right now. It's my big fear that my ex-lover's going to leave me. There are ways that I behave as if it's exactly the way it was except that he and I don't live together. I cling to the comfort of that relationship and have not been brave enough to sort of risk things with people.

ఞ

Deborah H.'s worry over losing loved ones has consumed her over the years. Her first attempts to deal with it involved hooking up with people whose loss wouldn't mean that much to her. It's a simple mathematical equation many of us have tried: if we don't become too attached or become attached to people we really don't like or who aren't suitable for us, then their eventual—and in our minds, inevitable—loss won't be so painful. Of course, that equation works in two directions. If we involve ourselves in relationships like this, the likelihood that these people will leave us is greater. After all these years, Deborah says, she doesn't expect the worry to go away. But she has learned to forge more solid relationships and to cope with the ever-present anxiety.

Deborah H. (45, m, 16)

I think that the place where I was most affected—and the place where my not having had the support, the comfort, the ability to grieve— was in relation to intimacy. I chose for a very long time to be with people who I fell in love with, whatever that means, but I didn't really like them. There was always a mechanism for keeping me safe and keeping them at a distance, so that my potential loss of them would be less searing.

I think that my mother's death was the beginning of my feeling if somebody was five minutes late I was sure they'd never show up, they were dead in a gutter somewhere, all of which is still very much with me. My partner and daughter were away recently for four days. I was having a great time being single and hanging out. I guess it was because the house was empty, I just burst into tears and thought, "What is this about?" And I realized that I was having an undercurrent fantasy of them dying in a plane crash coming back from Chicago. I wasn't even consciously thinking about this story, but I play those tapes constantly. They're readily available to me.

My coping strategy now is that anybody that I'm really close to can come home in the middle of the night; they can do whatever they want to. I just need not to be left somewhere worrying they're mauled or whatever. Only when I hear their voice again will I stop doing that. And believe me, they pay heavily when they break that rule. So they usually don't break it.

I fully feel that what this lifetime is about for me is to deal with issues of loss and grief and how it affects everything, so everything from this loss is deeply embedded in all of my relationships. I think that it's so much more conscious now and a part of what I deal with in a direct way that I finally am able to be in a relationship that I've been in for eleven years and know that there's still intimacy and loss issues in there, but it finally has not crippled my being able to be intimate.

∽

Many of us fear that people we love will be killed. Two men, both middle-aged, rational human beings, told virtually identical stories about worrying. On occasions when their wives were late, both have literally jumped in their cars and gone driving along the highway they expected their wives to take, looking for the accident. Rob, a psychotherapist, experiences the same kind of overwhelming "What if she dies?" fantasy that Deborah does. His solution is to face the fantasy, without dwelling on it, while at the same time acknowledging the devastation his father's death and its aftermath wreaked in his life.

Rob (44, f, 15)

From running this bereavement group for six years, I've seen something that's real common, with mostly everybody. I get into these really prolonged kind of morbid fantasies of what's going to happen? Okay, what if my wife dies? What's the funeral going to be like? What am I going to be doing? Am I going to be able to work? Then I go, what am I doing? Why am I doing this? And I realize why. It's in an effort to try to prepare for the unpreparable. And you *can't*. But because the loss of my father was so devastating, it's like I try to do anything I can *not* to fear that it's going to happen again. I think it's normal. I've heard so many people's stories. But that doesn't mean that you need to dwell on them. That's what I think, too, because it's not going to do any good.

My dad's death affected my relationships very deeply, like with my wife, who is a strong person. We've essentially grown up together. I married when I was twenty-one. I would do things to try to get her to reject me. Say mean things. I'd never be violent with her, but I'd throw things and break things. I think the closer I felt to her, the more threatening it became, in a sense, and the more scared I got that, well, what if she leaves? What's going to happen then? That sense of abandonment, that raw kind of feeling, every once in a while I have this, and I allow it to happen. I try not to run from it.

Part of it was the fear that I would have to go through this the same way again like I did with my father. It was so convoluted and so long, and the feelings were blocked for so long. Now I realize that I don't have to do that. If I lose somebody, it's going to hurt like hell, but it's going to be different. I'm not going to be numb forever about it. I'm not going to be totally confused about it. I'm not going be stuck in some space I'm not going to be able to move from.

Jan B. (50, f, 8)

I don't think, actually, that I really talked about my father's death until I was in my thirties. I went to the convent. I consciously thought to myself, "One of the reasons I'm going to the convent is so that I don't have to go through what my mother did, so I don't have to have a husband die." That wasn't a primary motivation, but I consciously figured that. I didn't do those normal dating patterns. Having my father die so young, men got very idealized in my life, and then I was always falling in love with them. And then I was acting out. Then I was into serial monogamy. I would have a relationship with a man, and then I would end that and have another person. I think death was very much a factor in that. I wouldn't really let myself fall in love with someone and leave the convent because of death. And then I fell in love with a man who was Irish and totally charming, and that's when I left.

It fell apart the following year, when he decided he didn't want to marry me. Then I became clinically depressed. I was thirty-four when that happened, and then I did stuff about my father's death. His leaving me got me to do all the unfinished grief business. I was seeing a psychologist. We focused on my relationship and then did a whole big piece on my dad's death, and I think that's when I really started as an adult. That triggered it.

Three years after that, I met my husband, and I am always afraid he's going to die. That's very strong in me. He's a jazz musician, and plays at night, and if he doesn't come home about the time I expect him, I panic. By the time I married, I was forty-two, ten years beyond my mother's widowhood. So for all those years, I think I was protecting myself. I'm not so afraid of emotional abandonment, that he's going to leave me for another woman, but that he will die.

∽

The fear of abandonment is an overarching theme among those bereaved young. It may take the form of consciously choosing relationships that lead to abandonment since it seems bound to happen anyway. It may take the form of abandoning a relationship before one is abandoned, or of distancing oneself or holding back—maybe subconsciously, but habitually—in almost all relationships—not only with lovers, but with children, and with friends.

Ken Burns talks about his pervasive fear of loss and how it leads to circling behavior: fearing loss, attempting to make things better; craving control; destroying possibilities; experiencing the feared loss. The fear informs behavior and almost inevitably leads back to loss. And then there's "never being able to be at a place where I could rest and feel relaxed." This theme arose over and over again in our interviews: from finding our place in the world to making intimate relationships. Burns articulates it most directly, but others certainly talked about feeling it. It goes back to the question of "The First Year" and "Marked Passage": who are we in the world now that we're orphaned?

Ken Burns, filmmaker (41, m, 11)

Without a doubt, my mother's death has affected my ability to form intimate relationships. It's the fear of loss, which then paralyzes the possibility, it's the control, that is attempting to make everything right, that makes it harder and harder. There are other reasons that have to do with that sense of just the absolute pain of never being able to be at a place where I could rest and feel relaxed, which you have to do in order to maintain an intimate relationship. I mean I have unbelievably close relationships with friends, particularly women. But intimate relationships become just incredibly fraught, because they have the possibility of acquiring the feeling of that fear of loss, which is why my divorce is so incredibly hard.

Kristy (25, f, 13)

When I get so close to a man, when I'm very much in love and very much connected, I just feel like this person's going to die any moment. It's just there. I usually appreciate the moment I have with him. The part that's hard is saying good-bye. I hate saying good-bye. Good-bye doesn't mean death. I just have to repeat that in my mind, and I can learn to just say "Bye!"

I had been seeing the first man I completely, really connected and was really in love with for about three years. Being in an intimate relationship brought a lot of Dad issues up. He was very wonderful about being there and hearing what I had to say. And I'd actually see Dad through him. The last six months we were beginning to part and start thinking of seeing other people, and then he got killed, suddenly, in a car accident. I remember laughing and crying about it. I made a decision in myself, if I have any control over what I create in my life, I don't need to learn whatever lesson I'm needing to learn this way anymore. I don't have to learn about issues of abandonment, release, attachment, or whatever, through having a close person die like that. I laugh just because I feel this is like the ultimate, universal joke on me, or something. It seems so unbelievable.

At the time of the interview, Tim and Jane were expecting their first child. For Jane, the emphasis was on worrying about her unborn child and the hurdles to follow. Worry, she says, is a near constant in her life about things, and people, she cares about.

Jane (30, f, 17)

When I got pregnant, at first it was, okay, let's just get through the first three months, because that's the scary time. And now it's, we just have to see if it has to come out and be alive and well. Then I think, "Oh God, then I'll have to go through the SIDS part, I'll have to worry about that." But that's a constant thing with me about everyone that's important to me.

Tim's fears seem to be rooted in the past.

Tim (35, f, 17)

I think we went into marriage knowing that we wanted to have a kid. I thought a lot about it, and it's made me change some things. My dad at one point in his life was 320 pounds. When he graduated from high school he was 150 pounds, which is exactly what I weighed when I graduated from high school. It definitely has an influence on me—

eating healthy and trying to maintain my weight, and I quit smoking. My dad dying of a heart attack at fifty-two has made me much more aware of taking care of myself and being there for my family. I would like to live past fifty-two.

Holding Back

Holding back, for many people, involved fear of making a commitment.

Tim (35, f, 17)

I was so picky, or I just made it not work. I think there were opportunities; there were people I went out with who I could've gotten close to, but I just didn't, partially because I was afraid to get close to somebody. I'm not sure that it was my dad dying, or just that I wasn't very good at relationships. I didn't get married until I was thirty. I had a hard time making a commitment. I went out with Jane for three years or four years before making that commitment, and I was a little afraid of it. I mean I didn't want to get too close to anybody because of things that had happened, people dying on you.

Kenyetta (20, f, 18)

I'm actually going through a relationship now and it's hard for me to feel secure, which has a lot to do with my father. My boyfriend doesn't understand because I really haven't opened myself up to him, to let him know that yet, but it's hard, and I'm experiencing it right now because all the people I love I lose, and I'm just afraid of getting that close, and something happening. I feel I'm enduring so much, and I just don't want nobody to play with my heart.

∽

Gloria Anzaldúa talks about various losses, how they relate to her father's death, and how sometimes it is simply too difficult to take emotional risks. She acknowledges her pain and the patterns she's followed to try to prevent further pain. She challenges the notion that simple acknowledgment of loss allows us to progress beyond fear or holding back. She also considers the additional risks of trying to make connections outside the mainstream of society, in this case, in a homosexual context.

Gloria Anzaldúa, poet and writer (52, f, 14)

I had a very intense love for my pets. I had five dogs; the first one died as a puppy. I brought the puppy in, covered it with some plastic, and he suffocated. Then I had four more dogs that died of various things. One was poisoned. One was stolen. Another two were run over. I'd teach them tricks, and I loved them. Losing those five and my father, I kind of swore to myself that I was never going to have any more pets because they would leave me, and I think, unconsciously, I also told myself that I would never have such intense, intimate relationships, because the person would leave me.

My father's death just brought up all those feelings of "Something's wrong with you, and your punishment is losing this man that you love." And so that was my experience of first being abandoned by a man, which I later experienced a couple of other times. One was with a lover, and the other one was with a best friend. With the lover, I broke it off with him before he could break it off with me, but I thought it was going to end. And with the friend I was completely devastated. It was like my father dying all over again.

I had some very strong, intense friendships with three different people. Two of them I am not in contact with anymore, and it was really hard to live through those breakups, because it so brought back this feeling of once they're gone, they're gone forever and ever, and the pain of losing somebody that you love. The first two were women friends, queer friends—and this third one is a queer male. Somehow or other when we became friends again after this intense separation, I have kept my distance. And he's noticed and commented on it.

I haven't told him all of this stuff about my father. I think I told him about the dogs and I told him about my other two friends, that when I get very close to somebody and then lose them, that it's devastating and that I don't want to risk it again. But I think someday I'm going to explain to him about my father. I noticed that I have friends who are so brave, you know, that they'll jump from one intimate relationship to the other. I think, "God, those people are really risk-taking," and, "Will I ever be at the point where I can totally open myself up to another person in that way or will I always have a reserve?"

I can articulate the fact that I'm cowardly about intimate relationships. But to articulate that and to jump into a very intimate relationship with no boundaries are two different things. I think you have to acknowledge it to yourself before you can break this kind of pattern. But it's not enough to acknowledge it to yourself, you have to do it, and I don't think I'm that brave. I have suffered a series of wounds, of which my father was one. And they are so longtime in healing and I have been so traumatized that I feel like part of the time I'm living with this posttraumatic syndrome, a survivor of some of the wounds I think I probably haven't even started to articulate.

I think it affected me with both straight and gay relationships and that it gets a little scarier with gay relationships because there's a way that gender differences are not as defined between two women as between a man and a woman. And even if it's between a man and a woman, if they're both queer, there's a kind of understanding of homosexuality as opposed to heterosexuality. It's scarier in some ways when I'm intimate with women, or I'm intimate with queer men, queer people, because the walls aren't as externally set up by society.

୬

Terry struggles to feel that he deserves a good relationship. He is trying to break the pattern of staying in relationships in which he doesn't feel love or closeness simply because the other person shows some affection for him. These battles are echoed over and over again. Even as children, and certainly as adults, our heads know we didn't cause our parents' deaths, that their loss is not a punishment for being bad or undeserving. Yet the feelings linger in our hearts and inevitably affect our relationships.

Terry (38, m, 6)

I think for a long time I didn't believe that I could have a good relationship where I really liked and wanted to be with someone and they could possibly want and like to be with me. It's given me a sense of distance from people in many ways. I thought that that perfect world, or that ideal situation, wasn't really possible. And I relate that to my life and relationship to my mother and that perfect life, that life with my mother and a family, is never going to happen because she is dead. It's a battle, but I'm trying to stick with my belief that I *can* have a relationship that is real, fulfilling, and satisfying.

Rich (36, m, 14)

That fear that people are going to leave me is still present very much to this day. I also grew up in a family where after my mother died nobody ever talked about anything. So the subtext was you don't reveal the deep parts of yourself. I guess there's always been a part of me that believed that if people really knew me they would go away and they wouldn't like me and they wouldn't value me. I have real ambivalent, confusing feelings. Either people will leave or abandon me or I will leave or I will make them leave. I don't know. It seems like it's inevitable that's going to happen. It's been in much more recent years that I've very clearly connected it with my mother dying.

Jim (61, m, 16, f, 18)

I was very conflicted because I found myself doing the same thing in relationships that I did with my mother, which is trying to punish them for not being enough, not being there enough, or not being good enough, or having already abandoned me, because they weren't good enough, or something. I was very aware that I better get out of the relationship before they left me. So I was always looking for something that was going wrong. I wasn't aggressive or angry about it. I was just kind of sullen. And when something went wrong, I ran for it. So a lot of my relationships were not very good. I was afraid, I think, to invest too much.

∽

Walter Liggett put emotional relationships, including friendships, on the back burner. He concentrated on his intellectual life, and on superficial relationships, not realizing until recently the effect of his father's death, and what that did to his ability to connect to people. Walter's story points to the news that it is never too late to begin to explore the effects of our early traumas on our lives, and that figuring them out and coping with them is probably a lifelong process.

Walter Liggett, poet (70, f, 11)

When I was young, I was intellectually mature, but I had this feeling of superiority towards others because I was so intellectual. The death never affected my capacity to learn or study. But emotionally I was isolated. I hadn't been able to make friends. I think for a time my father's death did affect my ability to form intimate relationships. I finally started getting close to friends in the fifties when I joined the Unitarian Church. Until then, I had more superficial friends, so you could say it affected me in that way for nearly twenty years. But I still didn't yet realize how traumatic my father's death had been for me. It wasn't until the last ten years that I really began to reflect on the effect all of that had on me. I didn't get married until I was in my forties.

Jamie (45, m, 19)

I think I've been holding people at bay for most of my adult life. That and a couple of other things finally sent me back into therapy. If I get attached to somebody, they'll be gone. I think there is a definite connection in my mother's death and my not having married, settled into a relationship. I think that I prevented a loss, prevented a lot of people from getting close enough even to know me well enough, to have that kind of relationship. I think I also chose people where it was just so difficult to start with that it wasn't going to get too far.

I'm sure it has to do with my mother's death. Maybe it's that supposedly the true love of your life is the closest thing to the person who brought you into the world, and you feel like you got wounded by that loss. Or it's the lack of a role model at a certain point. Or a combination of both.

∽

Daniel Meyers looks at connection from another angle. He has known and felt intimacy in his life. He wants it, yet he struggles, and part of that struggle, he speculates, he learned from his father.

Daniel Meyers, filmmaker (34, f, 18))

Every friend or lover that I've had over the years has met my father through me. And I have some issues about intimate relationships. Actually, the physical has been no problem; the emotional-intimate side has not been, at least I don't think it's been a problem. I love intimacy. I had it with my father, I had it with my mother, I have it with my grandparents. The problem is more the commitment. In some ways, I'm like him. He was monogamous, but he could easily not have been. Easily. And I know that. He was a sensualist, and everything in the world was a fascinating and interesting celebration of life, and I feel that way, too. I think my father did give me mixed messages along those lines. He adored women and he would sometimes stop me on the street when a beautiful woman walked by, and he'd say, "My God, they're all so beautiful." And he'd tell me some of the stories of his romantic exploits before he met my mother. He would talk forever about how wonderful women were, how beautiful, how marvelous, how soulful, how sensual, how they were the earth, how they are the greatest creation of nature. He would also say, "Daniel, I would like to see some grandchildren."

I don't like superficiality, I don't like casual stuff, I like things to be real and intimate. That's very easy in work partnerships. It's very easy in friendships. I find it gets more complicated in the romantic relationships, because most women want a monogamous relationship, and I don't think that, in some ways, I am a monogamous person. On the other hand, the two most important models in my life for relationships were my mother and father, who had a twenty-one-year, monogamous, all things considered, very good relationship, and my mother's parents, who have been together for more than sixty years, and they have, all things considered, an amazingly good relationship. As a child, I knew that one day I would meet my perfect soul mate, just like my mother and father did. One day, I would have that and live happily ever after. I'd have the kids and the house and a few dogs, and I just knew that. Well, over the years, things have gotten more complicated.

ℒ℁

Eric Marcus, in his attempt to create peace, created distance. His story once again points out how many different factors, besides the death of a parent, enter into our lives to make us who we are. Marcus talks about his expectations of bad things happening. He uses the word "terror" when talking about his fear of abandonment. This is a strong word, but reflective of many people's stories.

Eric Marcus, writer (36, f, 12)

My parents' relationship and the craziness of our household growing up left me with a strong desire to live in a home that was peaceful. In my first serious live-in relationship, which I was so happy to find, I was determined that we would not have words. To me it was a badge of achievement. We generally didn't argue. I later realized that that's not necessarily an admirable goal in a relationship, that relationship does involve conflict. But in my experience conflict usually led to horrible and physical fighting. I had no example of how people can have words and resolve things. And that ultimately proved incapacitating in my relationship. My partner in that relationship also came from a crazy household. I think we both respected each other's emotions to the point that made it impossible for me, and, I think, for him after we'd been together long enough, to carry on in our relationship. Less my dad's death and more who he was affected my relationships. I hate to feel like a living cliché, but abandonment has always been a big problem for me. This terror of being left. Or being alone. The irony is, in that long-term relationship, I was the one who left, as much as I feared always that I would be left.

I have this expectation in life that something terrible is going to happen, especially when things are going well, as they were before my father died. I've only discovered this very recently in talking at great length in therapy. When things are going well, I get depressed. Especially in a relationship, there's this ominous cloud and I have a sense that something terrible is going to happen. And my therapist said, "Well, something once did." It was such a shock to hear him say that, because I realized, of course, of course.

∽

In the interview, William recounts how he has realized only in the past few years that his parents' relationship was the center of their family. When that ended with his father's death, his family life ended. He learned to cut himself off and hold back.

William (54, f, 14)

I realized that part of my heart had been closed, that the women I'd been married to and loved I had loved indeed quite fully, as much as I was capable of, having the door shut at fifteen. But there was a kind of wall there, or a level below which I had no emotional contact, or was totally suppressed, so those individuals never had access to part of my heart. That half hour I cried in my room right after my dad died—I didn't cry again from then until I was breaking up with my first wife. Later, I spent some time with a wonderful teacher working on trying to open my heart up, and eventually that wall was breached. A part of my heart, or a part of my loving nature, was opened up at that time. I realized that it had not been available to the women in my life before that time. I think my dad dying affected my ability to let anyone in, not just women. My relationship with women was affected by my relationship with my mother and feeling abandoned by her after my dad died.

Looking for the Dead Parent

Is it a truism that we look for our parents in our love relationships? And how does losing that parent to death make a difference? Several people told us that their therapists pointed out relationships between a partner they were having difficulty with and a dead parent.

Perhaps it is not too far-fetched to see the child, who thinks that if he or she is very good, gives others what they want, then he or she will get something back, maybe the love of the dead parent.

Lawrence (35, m, 2, f, 16)

I saw a psychiatrist who broke it down for me why I didn't see my path and why I was having problems with friends. "You've gone through major losses in your life. So everyone you come in contact with you try to hold on to, and when it doesn't happen, then you go into this affect of rejection because you lost your mom, your dad, your sister, then your wife, your daughter, and your brothers and sisters." And it didn't open up until she said that. I mean I couldn't really put the puzzle together from my mom to why I'm feeling this way, so down, so lost in life, with no motivation. But when she said that to me, it just opened me up to face things. As a kid, the pain kept compounding itself. I didn't know or understand these losses until I got into a relationship where I couldn't understand the breakup or the rejection. I found myself giving and giving while other people were just taking and taking. I realized that I was looking for my mom and dad in those relationships. My past was with me. It was living with me daily. That was very hard for me. But I started seeing the pattern and getting more positive.

 confused

Mariam, whose father was quite a bit older, grew up in a traditional Iranian household, with separate quarters for men and women. She virtually did not know her father and she wonders how that has influenced her attraction to powerful men.

Mariam (39, f, 13)

I don't know if it's my father's death or just the way he was. I'm always looking for real powerful men. But at the same time, I need the affection from them. And it's kind of like I need both things at the same time, which is a problem. I don't know if it's my father or my father's death, but I'm kind of afraid of being emotionally dependent on somebody and losing them. I don't know if it's because I wasn't that emotionally attached to my father. I think it's mostly to do with my early relationship with boyfriends, that I lost them and I got hurt. I mean most of the time I think it's better not to have any.

confused

Note that in Mary J.'s story it is not necessarily the fact of her father's death, but the circumstances of her life with her father the alcoholic that affected her romantic choices.

Mary J. (early 40s, f, 18)

My therapist said she felt that a lot of the ways that I reacted to problems in my life and to men in my life had to do with the instability in my life as a youngster. And how it affected my sense of self-esteem, like the fact that I married a man who was an alcoholic, and even though I loved him dearly, I chose a set of circumstances that were familiar to me. So I don't think my life choices were really good, and I think part of that was affected by the instability when I was younger.

∽

Brown Miller freely admits to looking for a substitute mother.

Brown Miller, poet (51, m, 6)

I got married so young, seventeen, the first time, and I think I was looking for some kind of a substitute mother, which was bad. It was an attempt at an intimate relationship that was inadequate, and that's why the marriage didn't last. It was sort of a superficial reaching out for a substitute mother that didn't work. It's almost like the need was too great, or the need was great enough to make me jump at a relationship that wasn't really a good one.

Tron Bykle, artist (51, f, 14)

As time went on, I realized that I never got to know that guy [his father]. I had an idealized memory of him which prompted me into a lot of exploratory sexual activities. I've sort of come to a number of realizations about the associations that I make with the male authority figure, and it's not a big issue anymore. But in my teens and twenties it definitely was. When I was eighteen, I hitchhiked all over Europe. On my way back to Norway, I met this guy outside of Heidelberg, and we made incredible contact, so we went to Amsterdam and Paris. He was American and had been visiting his daughter. In the spring, I decided to come to America. I cared quite a lot for this guy. I thought, "Can you love the man?" I thought, "Well, why not?" But after about four or five months, I realized that to be in this relationship I had to totally subjugate myself as a son to a father. So I left.

∽

Life and love do not lend themselves to simple equations.

Lauren Muller, writer (34, f, 11)

Something interesting is that every single person I have fallen in love with or have had a crush on has been a visual artist. Is this my father, who fell in love with my mother the artist? Is this me falling in love with my mother the artist? I'm often attracted to people who have a sort of strong sexuality, and that's probably true about my father. My father was very faithful to my mom. I'm sure of that. I think he probably had a very visible sexual energy, and it seems that I kind of have been drawn to those sorts of people. But they often are people who don't tend to be loyal. So am I getting involved with someone who won't really commit because I don't trust the commitment would last anyway?

∽

Kristy talks about her delight in finding her father in her boyfriends.

Kristy (25, f, 13)

The first man I slept with, I remember thinking, "Oh! He plays acoustic bass, like Dad." I saw my dad through him, too. Sometimes I'd actually see my father's face. I'd be attracted to men that had similar characteristics. I would see my dad's eyes. I'd see my dad's hair. I loved it because it was like "Oh! Here you are."

Ariel (27, f, 3)

Freud would probably love this, but I really like men's necks. I think they're the sexy part on men. And it's the same part that I remember about my father.

Attempts to Cope

In the stories that follow, people continue to talk about their attempts to cope with intimate relationships in the face of loss. One way is to give and give in an effort to win love. Another is to attempt to fix or heal oneself by fixing an even more damaged lover. A third is to build walls, tear them down, and then build them up again in the face of new loss.

Janette (19, m, 12)

When my mom died, it just seemed like everybody that I cared about would leave my life. Everything would just push me farther away. It's like I had built this wall or whatever, but I let it down, kind of broke it down, and I learned to care about people more. I started to break down the wall because of my boyfriend, but after three years he hurt me, so I'm rebuilding the wall. My close friends all went away to school, and that hurt, also. Maybe what I need to do now is define myself more.

A lot of times I think that because of my mother dying and because she always smothered me, I need someone, not to smother me, but at least show me that they care. Sometimes I think I ask for too much, but I think it's because I've always been left in the dark with everything.

Diana O'Hehir, novelist and poet (72, m, 4)

I was in love with anybody who came along and said to me, "Oh boy, you're terrific." Anybody. Anybody. The insecurity, of course, was partly a result of all the bouncing around in very young childhood. I think of it more as a result of my stepmother cutting me down, which she did absolutely consistently. Then suddenly, when I went to college, I blossomed. Instead of an ugly duckling I became a swan. All kinds of people said, "Oh you're fabulous!" So I was in love with a whole series of them. I mean all that was necessary was approval. So that was the first set of people I was in love with.

I certainly sensed I couldn't relate to men properly. The husband

I'm with now* is a father figure, and, reliable, and loving, and good and funny and secure and stable. I did not feel abandoned by him, the way I did by my second husband. He is a completely reliable, loving person. My second husband was a mirror image of me. His father died when he was four. We started having very hard times very quickly. We'd been married about eight years when we first had a big death threat, and I was quite aware at the time that I felt abandoned because I was reliving the time when my mother died. I sort of looked at him and said, "Oh my god! If I can save his soul, I will save mine." I was going to make him happy, love him, I would convince him that life was wonderful and life was worthwhile. I was going to be his adorable wife and all of that stuff. I know that's the way my mind works. The past would be all right. I suppose I thought it would be reciprocal. The desire was to rescue him and thereby rescue my past. And he was terribly damaged. It was a very bad relationship.

We were married a long, long time, pretty close to thirty years. And we separated three times, before we finally separated. A basic problem was that he was totally insatiable. Nothing would ever reassure him that he was safe. Nothing would reassure him that I wasn't going to desert him. Anytime we did anything and anything went wrong, it was my fault because he had chosen me because I was going to rescue his life. I was going to change everything. The world was going to be different if he was with me. And then along with this, I was suddenly saying "Hey! I'm bored." And I started writing, and teaching, and getting recognition.

The implication in this last sentence, of course, is that once Diana O'Hehir started to find herself in her writing she was able to separate from the man she was going to fix, who was then, in turn, going to fix her. O'Hehir was seventy-two at the time of our interview, and her attempts to connect and cope have continued over long, productive years. If we are looking for quick, easy fixes, O'Hehir's story is probably the bad news. Yet, if we look at her story, and the stories of other older people in this chapter, and if we look at life as a learning,

---

*This husband is also her first husband, whom she divorced and then reconnected with after thirty-nine years.

growing experience, a process rather than a goal, then it's the good news.

Women of O'Hehir's age, orphaned or not, were pretty much taught that the way to self-fulfillment is through a relationship. Ariel is from a different time, and her impulse to take care of herself may be reflective of that, as well as of her father dying, especially since her mother had so little money after he died. Connected relationships seem to lie somewhere in between.

Ariel (27, f, 3)

One of the challenges I find in an intimate relationship is that I want to have all my shit together before I ever enter into the relationship. And I am finding that perhaps those are two things that can travel together, that they're one and the same and they feed each other. I think, perhaps, wanting to have my career and a strong financial standing first might be because I want to know that in the event he should ever die, desert me, any of those things, I'm okay. I think it's emotional as well as financial. I think it has a lot to do with my dad dying, my mother not having any money, and having to be resourceful. As a woman, that's something that isn't always necessarily expected. And I think I'm tenacious about it.

Children

We asked the people in this book to consider whether their parents' deaths had any effect on whether or not they choose to have children.

Jeff B. (24, m, 18)

The older I get, the more I appreciate the effort my mother put forth to be the kind of parent that she was. I think about having my own children, and I could see myself being a rickety old father who wants to spend an hour with the boyfriend for the evening. I laugh about it, because I realize how much freedom I was given. Maybe that was trust and maybe that was just a realization that kids are going to do whatever they want to do. And if you talk to them about the ways to deal with freedom, it ends up being a little more effective. The other way that I think about her in relation to children is that I'm just frustrated that she won't have a chance to see my kids.

Shannon (24, m, 19)

I'm real bummed that my kids won't be able to meet my mother. I'm very concerned, although I don't think about it very often, about how she got cancer when she was thirty-three, and I'm almost twenty-five. Do I want to have kids? What are my chances of having children and then having them go through the same thing I went through? That scares me. I'm not in a situation where I'm even thinking about children yet, and I know that when I do finally sit down and say "Okay, I want to have a kid," my mom's death is going to be a major, major issue in that decision.

Jessica (24, m, 16)

The feeling like love's being taken away is still a major issue for me, and I imagine it will be for a long time to come. I don't think I will ever get over it. I think that having a family of my own might alleviate some of the fear and pain of being left behind. Maybe I want to have a family so badly because then maybe I'll feel more resolved about it.

Lauren Muller, writer (34, f, 11)

I thought about my father's death when I had my abortion. Of course, because it's death, but also because it seems that having a child would be a way of passing on part of my father and keeping my father alive, keeping a connection with him. I think I've even thought of naming a child somehow in relation to him.

∽

Another group of the people we talked with do not have children and have decided not to. Most of the people who have passed the age when they would consider doing so talked about their conscious choice. Although we haven't included all the stories here, some people, particularly women like Patricia who grew up in large families and saw their mothers' struggles, decided early on not to have children, and stuck with the decision even though they reconsidered it at various stages of their lives. Others, like William, who was fifty-three at the time of our interview, talked about never imagining himself having children even before his father died.

Detta (47, m, 17)

I think I had decided not to have children when I was a child. My parents' divorce may have affected that decision because I was only thirteen then. But seeing how hard it was for her to raise kids on her own probably had much more of an effect on it than her dying young. I think part of it is I feel like there was some part of me that was arrested at that age. I know I'm not seventeen anymore, but my mental age still doesn't feel like someone who's old enough to have kids depend on me. I was in tears this morning dropping the cat off at the vet. I don't think that I could deal with children. I would be so afraid. I can't imagine what it would be like to have to offer a kid up to a doctor and leave him overnight.

Robin (46, f, 8)

I was afraid to establish a relationship with men because I was afraid they would leave me. I don't think I was really cognizant of that for a long time, that being afraid to love someone too much. It's one of the reasons I wouldn't have children. I don't think I was as afraid of being abandoned as I was that I would bring into the world a child who would be abandoned.

Eric Marcus, writer (36, f, 12)

I'm gay, and having children within the context of a gay relationship is more complex. You can't just have them, you really have to think about it. And I'm very glad that I'm not going to have children. I often half-jokingly say, "It stops with me. There won't be another, I'm not going to pass on any genes." And, as I get older, that makes me feel sad. I wouldn't want to hurt any child in the way my father did, whether by choice or because I died. That was so terrible. But by the same token, I am very glad to be alive, and I'm assuming any child I had would be, too. I love my two nephews and my niece. I get to be a good uncle.

∽

Many of those who chose to have children have experienced a wholeness, or healing, through their children, as Suzanne Lipsett wrote about in *Surviving a Writer's Life.*

Suzanne Lipsett, writer (51, m, 4)

With my first baby, there was a sense of knowing what to do in my hands that had come from being handled by a woman who was confident in her motherhood, and joyful. Somehow just the feeling of the hands on my body as a baby had been latent all this time and it had come out in joy. It felt like a reconnection of torn fibers between myself and my mother. I did feel very strongly that a healing had occurred. Maybe not the total healing, but a change of direction. When I was diagnosed with cancer, I considered the possibility that my children could forget me to the degree that I forgot my mother. I had an existential fear that was not to be believed, and that was the impulse for writing *Surviving a Writer's Life.*

Marc (39, f, 10)

For no good reason, the instant my son was born, when he popped out, something about him just made me think of my father, something about looking at him reminded me dramatically of my father. It was just like seeing my father there, in some form. It was a very unusual experience, but it was very undeniable.

My son is now at an age that I never was when I had a father. It's not that I don't know how to parent him because of that, because I really don't parent my children the same way I was parented anyway. Also, at that age I didn't expect to be parented. You're starting to feel you're not a kid anymore, and you kind of shy away from any overt parenting—which my son is doing now. All that seems normal. You don't want to be parented, you don't want your father in your business, and, in my case, he wasn't. Okay, you don't want it, you don't expect it, but you *need* it. So it's something I have to watch out for, and something I have to deal with. I've felt that I was frightened by life as an adolescent. Again this could be copping out, but I've always felt if I had a father there kicking my butt a little bit, I might have done things differently at that age. And it's sort of made me make sure I'm there for my kids, and not just being a gentle, father-knows-best kind of guy, but also making sure they're not wasting their time or being stuck somewhere, making sure that when they are afraid of something they go in there anyway.

But I will say my father gave me a sense of being loved, a sense of being safe and protected and important and cared about. I think that's the biggest gift a parent can give their child.

Doreen (36, m, 10)

When my daughter was born, I thought about my mom. It was the first time in many years that missing her really kind of came back. I remember calling my aunt and asking her what she remembered, because I wanted to know what my mother was feeling when I was born. My aunt said to me, "Do you really want to know?" And I said, "Yeah, I do. I understand that she was a human being. I just want to know." And my aunt said, "Well, to tell you the truth, she must've cried for a couple of days because you weren't a boy." I came home from the hospital with no name. So my sisters named me Doreen after the Mickey Mouse show. But it was great, because, in a way, that whole story colored my feelings about the gender of my children. I really tried to let go of wanting one thing or the other, because you've got no control over it anyway, so why want something you can't make happen?

As I'm parenting my own children, I understand more about my mother. I am not doing things the way my mother did them. But there are some things where I can feel her presence, in a sense. I can't put my finger on it, because I can't bring back the memory exactly, but I do feel that sometimes when I react to my daughter, I hear my mother. Sometimes with my son, also, but with my daughter in particular. That first sharp thing that crops up, that's Mommy. Yeah, I hear her. And, yeah, she's still there.

I'm approaching the age my mother was when she died, and that's scary, so I want to spend as much time with my children as possible. That's part of why I'm home-schooling them. I had children because I really wanted to be part of their lives while they were children, because I know when they grow up they have their own lives. I don't have them for long, so, the idea of sending them off to school, for the prime-time hours, five days a week, wasn't okay. I really want my children to remember me well, and to know who I was. I want a total family life, that we incorporate into each other's space more than not.

When I was really young, I felt so lost that my mother was gone. I felt strongly that the getting away was going to be the answer for me. I knew I couldn't be dependent in the way that I felt I had been dependent prior to her death. I would not allow myself to become dependent in a relationship for a long time. Yet here I am home with my kids, and I have allowed myself to become dependent again, but it has taken a long time to come that full circle, to allow that to happen, to surrender to taking care of my children and really deciding that was more important than my stuff about being independent.

Peggi (56, f, 19)

I was one of those mothers that was always looking to see if the baby was breathing. And always worried about where they were, and coming home, coming home late, and stuff like that. Again that's one of those things that you don't know whether you would have been that way if you had not lost your father so young. Worries like that about them still cross my mind, although it's easier now to put a damper on it. After my kids got to the age I was when my father died, I thought, now their life is really different from mine because they have both of their parents still alive. After that age, I thought of them as more separate from me, as launched, sort of.

Jim (61, m, 16, f, 18)

I got married, but I wasn't in love. I didn't know what love was. When we had our daughter, I was almost thirty. Then we stayed together until my daughter was about a year old. The marriage was not working; it was just one stormy fight after another. So I left. I wanted to leave before my daughter, this little one-year-old child, got terribly attached to me. All I remember thinking was, it's better if I'd leave before she becomes a really conscious person and knows who I am. I thought I could just pass it off, slough it off. So I went to Alaska and tried to make some money commercially fishing. I dreamt I was on a cruise ship, and I was standing on the upper deck and I saw my daughter fall from the upper deck of a cruise ship into the water. My one-year-old daughter who I thought I was not thinking about at all. And I jumped into the water to save her, and I came up with her. When I woke up from that dream, I realized I had to go back and make a relationship with her. And probably that's the first experience of love I ever really had. My relationship with my daughter is the first time I really knew what love was.

∾

For many of the people we talked with, the fact that their children don't know their grandparents is a continuing sorrow.

Rose (87, m, 13)

When Enid, my first daughter, was born, and then when Karen was born, I thought, "If my mother could have been here." Every occasion, I would always think, "If she could only have seen this."

∾

Lawrence hopes to mitigate his sense of loss by teaching his daughter about family.

Lawrence (35, m, 2, f, 16)

When my own daughter was born, I thought about my mom, my dad, and my oldest sister, who were all dead by then. I thought about what my mom would say to her granddaughter. What my dad would say. What my sister would say, especially that. I'm trying to get my daughter to know her cousin who's around the same age as she is. I try to explain to her about my parents and my sister when she asks about my family.

&

In "Ground Zero" and "The First Year," some people shared stories about how religious and cultural traditions provided some measure of relief and comfort in their initial grieving. For some people, raising children in the religious tradition and with the values they were raised with provides a sense of continuity with the dead grandparent.

David Z. (52, f, 13)

I had an extraordinary event take place with both my kids when they were bat-mitzvahed. It was really almost mystical and spiritual. I'm very logical, and I was quite surprised by all of this. I really believed my father was there to witness their bat mitzvahs. When they were reading from the Torah, I felt his presence very strongly. In the Jewish religion, when someone close dies, you're supposed to go to the temple for eleven months and say Kaddish, which is really a sanctification of God, not a prayer for the dead. But that's what it traditionally is, a prayer for the dead. I remember having everybody stare at me when I would rise to say the Kaddish. I envisioned them saying "Oh poor David." I remember for a year straight the fear and the hate of going to the temple, because when they said "Will the mourners please rise?" I would be there, this kid, whereas most people who were standing up were in their fifties or sixties or seventies. And I always remember the poor-boy syndrome. Yet when these bat mitzvahs were taking place, I stood there very proud to say this prayer. That was the first real feeling that something about my father was connecting with me, other than the guilt of killing him off. And it happened twice, with both my daughters.

Sandy (46, f, 16)

The first Friday night, after Michael arrived, and again after Rebecca arrived, when I lit Shabbes candles, and I held my children, I think I probably felt more at peace with the loss of my parents because, for once, they would have been so proud. The loss that they didn't get to know these children is a terrible, terrible loss to me. I know how much they would have adored these kids. How much it would have meant to them that I was passing on the tradition that meant so much to them. I always felt like I could never do right with my parents, but for once I was doing something right. I like the Jewish notion of immortality that you live on in your good deeds and love and memory. I was carrying on their memory. My parents gave me such good values, and I want to honor them by perpetuating what they valued. Equality. Being fair. Caring for those less fortunate. Being honest. Education. Not being materialistic. I want to pass those on to my kids. It strengthens my parents' immortality.

With my own children, when I get angry, I say, in particular to the older one, "You know sometimes I get angry at you, and we exchange harsh words. But I want you to know, always, always, that I love you, and I know that you love me. And yes, I still get angry at you. But I love you with all my heart." If a car should hit me today, I want my children to know how much I love them.

My dad's job kept him trapped in many ways. He never got to know his kids. He was always at work. My son recently did a poster at school where the kids included three wishes, and his first wish was, "I wish my daddy could come home earlier." It just hurt so badly, because his dad also works incredibly long hours. I want so desperately for my children to know their father in a way that I didn't know mine. A lot of times my daughter will say to me, "I love Daddy." And I'll say to her, "Make sure you tell him that. That would make him so happy."

For Kelly, who never knew her mother, having children meant, first and most obvious, that she didn't die in childbirth like her mother did. And having children meant learning what and who a mother is.

Kelly (43, m, birth)

I guess I really didn't know what a mother was for until I became one. I remember drawing pictures of Mary and Jesus over and over again. Later, as I started to explore my own art, I started looking at the

Madonna imagery that I was sort of obsessed with when I was a child as being about the mother-child relationship. I remember my dad, who lost his mother when he was six, telling me that he often wished for his mother, that his mother would understand him. But I certainly did construct an imaginary mother figure that had mythic, unattainable proportions. When it came time for me to assume my role as mother, the mythic picture that I had built up of a mother was not something I could really attain in my real everyday life. I didn't really know why it was so important to have a mother. So when I was a mother myself, it was quite a shock to me—all the things a mother was supposed to do. I was completely unprepared for the intensity and the level of demand, physically and emotionally. That's when my mother surfaced in my life in a really concrete way. When my daughter was born, we went to the place where my husband and I were married, a campground on the California coast, and we had a naming ceremony for her. That place became a really holy place for me. I left this mask that I had made. That was my offering to my mother to introduce the next generation to her.

Finding Connections

Having come this far in the chapter, we know that by no means are all of our interviewees lovelorn, friendless, unhappy people who feel disconnected from themselves and the people in their lives. Although fears of abandonment and keeping distance in relationships still affect many of us, when we do connect, it can be at very deep levels.

Suzanne Lipsett, writer (51, m, 4)

I read this article in the Sunday *Image* magazine that said a child who loses someone very young can go one of two ways. Either they never make relationships again or they never break relationships again. I have all my friends from camp. I've had great friendships. By and large, I am a pathologically loyal friend, to the poor people's regret sometimes. Maybe they're thinking, "Get her out of my life already!"

So many ratty things have happened to me. I was brutally raped in this bathroom at Cal at my job. I was bereft. My father was very kind when I told him. Five years later, two men broke into my apartment.

I was living with my eventual husband, Tom. I had been beaten up and kicked in the face and all other places and beaten with the part of a bone that was lying around the house, the leg bone of a cow. Tom picked me up at the hospital. He took me to a friend's house. They put a mattress in the middle of the floor with a beautiful blanket and pillows, and all my friends sat around this circle and we drank and talked about it. And then Tom said—and this was just at the beginning of our relationship, "Tell me everything they did to you. Everything," intuitively not turning away, not looking away. "What happened here? What happened here?"

That was mothering. He saved my life by looking right into my eyes. I guess what I'm saying is that the maternal presence matters; I don't think it matters if it's a mother or father. My father was very nurturing to me emotionally. My husband is very nurturing emotionally. He is very kind and he's a fabulous nurse. If he was the one with cancer, I would probably have run away a million times. He takes care of me. In the morning, now, since I've had my third recurrence, he brings me coffee, he does the kids, he makes the lunches, he drags them to school, and I read, like a teenager. He's just wonderful, so maybe that's the answer, he's my mother. He can do emotional healing. I feel like my father saved my life and laid the groundwork for me because he truly loved me, and then when these things happened and I had no inner support, no idea what to do, Tom saved me.

༉

It's interesting to read Laurie's story about her lover next to Lipsett's story about Tom. Not only can we tell our painful stories; we can hear those of others. And both are healing.

Laurie (38, m, 13)

Regarding close relationships, I love intimacy, and I've always been able to have one-on-one things. My partner Carmen lost both of her parents in a car crash. And she said that I was the only person who wanted to hear her pain. I wasn't afraid to ask her the details. She's told me some things that no one's ever wanted to hear. I can hear it because I've had so much death around me. I can talk about it and it doesn't creep me out.

∽

At different times in our lives, most of us have experienced the push and pull of fear and holding back. At other times, even though we're the same people, we reach out, seek relationships, and connect. Rich, whose story about overall fear and cynicism appears in the very beginning of this chapter, and who talks again in "Holding Back" about his fear of revealing too much of himself, also experiences connections so intense they make him cry.

Rich (36, m, 14)

On one level, my mother's death very much affected my ability positively and my desire to establish intimate relationships. I think it made me appreciate others. When I think about my close friends in my life, it practically makes me want to cry just because I value them so much. And I do think that has something to do with her dying. I also think it has something to do with being gay, in the sense or way in which gay people make family with friends. From the time that I was in high school through recent years, I've tended not to have a large body of social friends, but a few very intimate friends that mean a lot to me and that I value more than practically anything in the world, and that I never want to let go.

Patricia (48, f, 13)

I think marrying Robbie probably is a transformational experience for me. Everything in the world said to me, "Don't do it." I was very willing not to. I remember the night he asked me. He came home after he was out to dinner with a friend, and he said, "Would you like to marry me?" And I said, "Uh-huh," and rolled over and went to sleep, and he woke me up again. This went on a couple of times, and he said, "Well, hon?" And I said, "Well, it's not an issue." It was pretty clear that my life with him would be almost exactly like my life had been before I married him, that marriage would merely enhance it. I wouldn't have to have children; I wouldn't be controlled; I wouldn't have to be any of the things that I didn't trust in this world. I haven't had to change into Mrs. Homemaker or Mrs. Nice Wife. I would maintain myself as I did before. And I think what I felt then was an incredible amount of trust. If anything, I have probably let him help me more than anybody I know. There's a vulnerability there that I have with him that I don't have with anybody else.

⤙

Martin Yan, who grew up virtually without a family, finds fulfillment in his connection with his wife and her family.

Martin Yan, chef, writer, TV personality (43, f, 3)

I feel very fortunate. My wife is a very gentle, very kind, very unique person. She never complains. All these years that we have been together, we never fight. Every time I raise my voice, she says, "Psst, no fight." It takes two to fight. Also, she never, never bad-mouths any individual. And this virtue is very, very rare. Also, she is very close to her family. So, after I got to know her, I learned a lot from her. Because of that, in the past fifteen, twenty years, I am getting a little more human.

⤙

When Barbara W. met the man who became her husband, she found herself able to connect to him with her heart, despite what her mind was telling her.

Barbara W. (34, m, 18, f, 19)

My husband was probably the first person I fell in love with after my parents died, and I can remember saying, you know, "Oh God! I think I'm falling in love, and I don't want to be connected with anyone, and I'm not going to put myself in this position." I can remember specifically saying, "I am not going to fall in love with anyone. Don't, don't even consider this. I'm not going to be a part of this. So just stay back." He was like, fine, whatever. I think of how stormy I was. I couldn't have fallen in love with a kinder, gentler person. I mean he totally let me do my own thing, be the person I wanted to, never pushed anything on me. And it was probably the healthiest thing I could have fallen into.

∽

For Addie, one of the connections is telling stories about her father to her boyfriends. She uses virtually the same words Daniel Meyers did when he talked about introducing his father to his friends and lovers. For her, the connection is about sharing people she loves with each other.

Addie (19, f, 16)

I do find myself telling stories about my dad to boyfriends more than most people. They're childhood stories. Things that these boyfriends do remind me of him. I find that there are certain times of my life where I just sort of lose it in general, and I feel like the grief is a big part of that, that it becomes a theme in my life. Sometimes I get sort of caught in a rut of not being able to think about anything else, work, or concentrate, and that's usually when, if I'm involved with somebody, that it comes out just in trying to deal with myself and what's going on in my everyday life. If I can transfer it into something, from something that's really silent and keeping it in, and just being frustrated and not being able to concentrate, to something where I'm actively remembering and talking about it, that's good. And I think the act of sharing it with somebody else helps. Maybe the other reason that I'm talking to boyfriends about this is that the two men, the boyfriends that I've had, did not know him, and I feel like there's a part of me that really wants to share somebody that I love with somebody else that I love. I can't introduce my boyfriends to my father. But I can sort of introduce my father to my boyfriends.

The Arms of Love

We take what we learned in the home of our childhood to the homes of our adulthood: the good, the bad, the sad, the happy, the disconnections and the connections. In the arms of love, we grow up and live our lives. Sometimes we feel we don't belong to anyone. Sometimes we grieve that the parent we did belong to is not here to meet our lovers or our children. And sometimes we feel, in the arms of love, that our "ripped places begin to knit together." In the next chapter, we move from the private sphere, at home, to the more public life of work and school.

8

Working

I knew that in the years following that January night I had been numb with fear at some simple truths: that I was going to have to find a way to earn a living, make a decision about what I wanted to do and how to go about doing it, find a home and make it my own. That was the only response I could find to the scent of death, sticking to my clothes, rising from my hair.—Anna Quindlen (m, 19), *Living Out Loud*

My father hadn't been there to kill the bats; he hadn't been there to explain the photographs of Auschwitz. . . . I understood how much I owed to his death, his absence a force field within which I had become an intellectual. . . . Learning French was connected to my father, because French made me absent the way he was absent, and it made me an expert the way he was an expert. —Alice Kaplan (f, 7), *French Lessons*

As we look at the careers and work styles of adults who lost a parent when they were children, we need to keep in mind Kristy's caution: "See, it's hard for me to answer these questions, because I know no other way. If I had two lives, one with my dad, and one without my dad, I'd say, 'Of course, it's a factor of my life.' But I just don't know what I'd be like if he had lived." Like our experience with intimacy, the connection we make to work—the way we work, how well we work—is determined by much more than a single tragic fact from our early years. When it comes to education and career accomplishments, our class, culture, and gender could very well be stronger determinants. Yet the stories here make it clear: there is a relationship between how we labor and what we lost at a young age.

In fact, research on this connection has uncovered an intriguing phenomenon. In *Parental Loss and Achievement,* editor Marvin Eisenstadt reports that losing a parent before the age of nineteen seems to increase a person's chances of achieving in various fields, especially in literature and politics. Most of the epigraphs in this book came from people who lost a parent before the age of nineteen. Contemporary political leaders Bill Clinton, Aung San Suu Kyi, Yasser Arafat, and Yitzhak Rabin all lost a parent in childhood. Jimi Hendrix's mother died when he was fifteen, and Madonna's mother died when she was five. Barbra Streisand's father died when she was a baby, and Carly Simon's father died when she was a teen. Jane Fonda and Kathleen Turner also experienced the early loss of a parent, as did James Dean and Jessica Tandy. Religious leaders Mohammed, St. Augustine, and Krishnamurti were orphaned in childhood.

One of the theories offered to explain this tendency argues that the child internalizes the lost adult, seeks to restore what was lost, and then generally strives to right other wrongs over which he or she might have some control. The result is often extraordinary creativity and achievement. Filmmaker Ken Burns believes that much of his work has to do with "waking the dead." He attributes his interest in race in America to his anger at injustice that was awakened in him at an early age when he lost his mother. Of course, grief can also leave a person feeling depressed, helpless, and antisocial. But as he or she attempts to heal from early loss, the world may benefit.

In *Darkness Visible: A Memoir of Madness,* William Styron discusses the theory of incomplete mourning offered by social historian Howard Kushner:

> Kushner makes a convincing case not only for the idea of early loss precipitating self-destructive conduct, but also, auspiciously, for that same behavior becoming a strategy through which the person involved comes to grips with his guilt and rage, and triumphs over self-willed death. Such reconciliation may be entwined with the quest for immortality—in Lincoln's

[m, 9] case, no less than that of a writer of fiction, to vanquish death through work honored by posterity.

In "Working," we examine not only creativity and achievement in this context, but also a tendency toward self-reliance and an interest in the helping professions. We asked our subjects how they take care of daily business and their larger career goals and whether they've modeled themselves after the dead parent or have gone in a different direction. Some people reported starting out far away from the parent's profession or career, only to find themselves in middle age working a very similar trail.

"What if" questions both tantalize and torture. Who knows how it would have been if Dad or Mom had survived our childhoods? All we know is that they did not. And as we think about how their early deaths might have affected us, we gain insights into the paths we've chosen in our working lives.

Education

Some people got a better education than they might otherwise have received if a parent had not died early. Several of our interviewees who grew up in the United States said that they could afford college only because of the Social Security benefits they received. Others missed out on educational opportunities, sometimes becoming more resourceful than they would have been if their parent had not died so early.

Although Beto suffered from his grief and a difficult financial situation, he drew close to his family, especially a favorite aunt, during his college years.

Beto (52, m, 14)

College was a very sad time for me, but my brothers and I got real tight. I got close to my dad, too. I didn't date much. Part of it was economics. I had to work. I got very close to my mother's sister in Tucson, where I went to college. For a couple of years, when it was financially tight, I moved in with her and managed to save some money. I gave her money when I was able, but she never begrudged me when I didn't have it. When I needed somebody, she was there.

Mariam, who grew up in a traditional Iranian family, thinks that she might not have gotten to college if her father had lived. Despite her excitement at going away to school, she felt guilty about leaving her widowed mother alone.

Mariam (39, f, 13)

I went to England to go to college. I don't think I would have gone if my father hadn't died. I'm not sure, because he didn't send the girls to go abroad to study, even though he sent my brothers. But then my sister was four years older and, when she was about to finish her high school, my father asked her jokingly, "Do you want to go to England and study?" I don't know if he would have let her, but maybe he would have, because I think he particularly liked that sister. She was successful and she was pretty and she was good in school. Anyway, I wanted to go to England to study, but I was very depressed because I felt guilty about my mother being alone in my hometown. I was worried because I knew how hard it was, how lonely it was, and with me not being there, I knew it would be even worse. I kept worrying—what if she gets sick and all those things. So the first couple of years it was very hard.

Barbara Smith and Gloria Anzaldúa surpassed the expectations of their parents, probably because times changed in ways Barbara's mother and Gloria's father could not have predicted. There is a bittersweet quality to their achievements because their parents didn't live to see how far their daughters have come.

Barbara Smith, writer (49, m, 9)

Being a black person, of my generation—I came of age during the civil rights movement—I saw the dreams that black families had for their children. In some cases we got to do more than they even dreamed of us doing. Instead of going to Spelman, a black women's college in Georgia, I only applied to the Seven Sisters. And Oberlin was my fall-back. Who could have dreamed in 1946 that a child like me would have had a choice to go to Mount Holyoke? The dreams and the hopes that my mother and the rest of the family had for us were expanded by a social and political movement.

Gloria Anzaldúa, poet and writer (52, f, 14)

In those days, in my little town, Chicanas didn't go to high school. I got put on the college track, so I was isolated from the other Mexican kids. My father had always had a strong belief in education, and he had talked about when I would go to high school. I think that my father was more in line with my ideas about the kind of person I should be, in terms of being independent, being autonomous, getting an education, being smart, wanting something more for myself than to be a farm worker or a rancher. He didn't quite articulate that except to say, "I want *mi hijita* to get an education." Or he would buy these pocket books of westerns for me to read. I think that in pleasing myself I was pleasing him, but only up to a point. Probably, it would stop with the B.A.—and I'm now a doctoral candidate— but it would also stop with the sexual preference, with being a lesbian. It would stop with the kind of lifestyle I have, the politics. If I am pleasing him, it's an internalized version of him, and I'm really pleasing myself.

∽

Ken Burns managed to go to the kind of college he knew he needed.

Ken Burns, filmmaker, (41, m, 11)

As far as college went, money necessitated that I go to the University of Michigan, because I could go essentially for nothing since my father was a professor there. But my doctor said, "You need to get out." When I told my father, he got really angry at this doctor, a local doctor and radical politician whom my father admired. I couldn't understand why he was so angry at this man, who was this great man. Then I read in *Newsweek* about Hampshire College. It was exactly the opposite of the University of Michigan. It had just started; it hadn't been going for 150 years. It had a couple of hundred students, not forty thousand. It was going to add a new class, which I hoped would be my class. I *had* to escape the particular gravity of Ann Arbor. So I went to Hampshire. I had quit high school early and worked in a record store and earned enough for one year. I was only going to go for one year and then come back to Michigan. But I loved it. I took a year off from Hampshire, stayed there, and earned enough money, with scholarships, to go through Hampshire for the remaining two years. I took four years to do it, but I was in school for only three of them. It was then the most expensive school in the country, but I came out debt free, having worked my butt off.

Self-Reliance

Depending on specific circumstances and what area of their lives people were discussing at the time, their enforced early self-reliance was seen either as something to lament or something to celebrate. In the world of work and daily business, it more often seemed to give people an edge.

Marc (39, f, 10)

One interesting thing that's got an influence on my life in maybe some indirect way is that the first real job I had was working on a loading dock at a warehouse that my cousin owned. I think, in his attempt at trying to help me out, he offered me this job. Also it might have been trying to be a payback for favors that my father had done for him. Anyway, it taught me about hard work, both physical and mental. I went from being this kid to dealing with the real world, in a very serious way on a daily basis. I was dealing with truckdrivers, unloading their trucks. I learned a lot, real fast, about money and people and jobs. Most jobs you get when you're fifteen don't teach you as much as this one did.

I had to invent myself because of not having a father. At a certain point, when I was feeling that I wasn't the kind of man I wanted to be, or I didn't have the kind of skills I wanted, I decided that rather than cry about it, or be unhappy about it, I had to just become what I wanted to become, and to do that meant acquiring certain kinds of skills. So I decided to try to find these things out by talking to some people, working with a variety of other people, going to books, going wherever I could to pick up information. I would avoid mentoring kinds of situations because I felt that it was somehow a compromise of my independence. It's sort of a fear of dependence, or maybe subordination. I'm not sure that's a healthy thing, or maybe, who knows, this might be the key to what my reaction to my father's death is: that it's because of a fear of death, of being unable to accept that relationship, that position, that I need to learn things away from a father-son type situation. I think it's because I had to become the father. I get a great satisfaction out of helping people learn what I've learned, but I just have a hard time dealing with the other way around.

∽

Martin Yan knew from an early age that, in order to survive, he would have to rely on himself.

Martin Yan, chef, writer, TV personality (43, f, 3)

Although my father passed away when I was very young and I didn't really get to know him that much, I had some kind of image of him that he was entrepreneurial. That gave me the sense that you really have to rely on yourself. To be a survivor. I think by being independent and not having anybody who I could rely on, I was given the opportunity to be self-reliant. I am very independent. I also have a strange sense of confidence because I know that, if I don't believe in myself, I will never make it. Nobody ever really had the opportunity to give me any support, so I know that if I don't take care of myself, nobody is going to be able to take care of me.

Patricia (48, f, 13)

One of the reasons I decided to be a nurse was that I would be able to support myself on the day of graduation. After my father's death, the drive for me has always been, if you can, learn how to do it your-

self. Don't ever have to depend on anybody too much. You can probably figure out how to do it by watching somebody or by reading
about it. His death gave me sort of a drive for self-reliance. It's hard
for me to let other people do things for me, I think, because I cringe
at someone attempting to control me. I have to be pretty flat to the
ground before I'll accept help.

∽

For Deborah Nagle, not having a father allowed her to explore a bold
and independent identity at a much earlier age than most women of
her generation did.

Deborah Nagle, writer (46, f, 12)

I had a lot of successes as a young woman. I did a lot of things because
nobody had ever said to me: "Don't have sex on the first date. Defer
to men. No, you can't own a bookstore. No, you can't own a bar. No,
you can't be a disc jockey." Nobody ever said women couldn't do
those things. Nobody was there to do that.

∽

Danny reports a mixed experience.

Danny (30, m, 16)

I used to go to the grocery store for my mother and see how fast I
could go. I'd time myself. I was real competitive seeing how I could
do things for her. I still feel like I want to excel for her. She did so
much work trying to instill good values in us, including a strong work
ethic, so I feel I kind of owe it to her to do a good job. I work in computer operations at a large health maintenance organization. I'm a
pretty hard worker, and I attribute that to my mom. You know, you
try to move on, but there's always those times when things come up,
and you think, "Man! Why did this happen to me? If I would only
have had two parents in the household." I think that having two parents is a key to a lot of people's being able to be successful. But maybe
it also drives me a little more. I realize that I'm going to have to go
ahead and be my own man.

❦

Daniel Meyers considers how his bent toward independence comes as much from his father's life as from his early death.

Daniel Meyers, filmmaker (34, f, 18)

I've been working since I was sixteen. I've been fiercely independent and on my own, freelance or self-employed, and I think that's largely influenced by my father's own sort of irreverent, almost anarchist stance. For many years, I was a small-time builder-contractor. I was totally independent and my own boss. If I got up one morning and wanted to go to a movie, I would do it. I would take vacations when I wanted. I would work with and for whomever I wanted.

Achievement

The list of eminent people in *Parental Loss and Achievement* who lost a parent before the age of nineteen is impressive. In fact, when compared to the general population, people on that list are twice as likely to have lost a father before the age of nineteen and three times as likely to have lost a mother or both parents before that age. Our subjects, too, tended to push themselves very hard as a result of their early loss.

Shannon's work as a curriculum specialist dealing with issues of race and gender reflects both her ethnic background and her mother's strong love for her.

Shannon (24, m, 19)

I don't see my mom's death influencing my career decisions in exactly what I'm going to do, but I see her and her death influencing them in the way that I'm going to be somebody and I'm going to make a difference. When I finally did get my feet on the ground and realize where I wanted to be with my life, about two years after her death, I knew I was going to do something. I've always known that the part of my job that I have strong feelings about is dealing with children of interracial couples. I do feel like it's more than just a job, it's my life, and it's also dealing with racism and sexism. It's changing schools so that we can change the world. I definitely do take on too much of a burden, but I feel I need to make these huge changes.

Daniel Meyers, filmmaker (34, f, 18)

In general, I have been extremely hard on myself. Much of what I've done has been in some way to please my father. Over the years, it feels like, even with so much of what I've done, there's never enough, it hasn't been good enough. I had to do more and be more and achieve more and suffer more. Maybe some of that was because he wasn't there to say, "Okay, Daniel, that's great." And then, also, as a measure, if I didn't feel like I had the same commitment and passion for something that my father had for poetry, I would feel it wasn't right.

In the story "The Red Shoes" by Hans Christian Andersen, the dancer with the red shoes can't stop dancing. She is driven to keep going on. Ken Burns compares himself to that dancer. In fact, Hans Christian Andersen lost his father at age eleven, and we can't help speculating that he, too, was driven to succeed, responding to the same drive to keep working that propels Ken Burns and others orphaned young.

Ken Burns, filmmaker (41, m, 11)

I work harder than anyone else I know. It's the whole "Red Shoes" thing. I fill my tank with gas almost every day. So there's lots of running. I think my last interaction with my mother was a fight. And that's where so much of the pain is. I think we had an argument, or a disagreement, the kind that an eleven-year-old would have with a mother. It was not significant in any way. But I remember once, in a moment of utter pain, years and years ago, just saying, "I didn't kill her. I didn't kill her." And I think there is this huge sense—and I can't tell whether it was born of this last moment, or just my feeling of failure in trying to keep her alive—that I failed, that I didn't do it, that I wasn't able to use my force. The amazing thing is that my outer life is an absolute example of utter will. There is a circle of twenty-five people who depend on me for their livelihoods. I'm the daddy of all that. I keep a lot of that going.

∞

Rich, who works in arts administration, believes his commitment to finding meaningful work comes from what his mother would have wanted for him. One way to read this is that he has internalized his mother. Another is that he has idealized his mother's perspective on work and made it a goal for himself to honor her.

Rich (36, m, 14)

I think that when I was growing up the sense I got from my father was that no one likes what they do, and you just should be a success. I think that my mother would have supported me in really trying whatever I thought would really give me satisfaction. I keep searching for a vocation. I feel like I'm closer to it than I used to be. I still don't want to buy into the notion that you just should be grateful for having any sort of job. I've never been able to totally, even when being in jobs that are not fulfilling, think of it as just a job. My jobs have tended to consume more of my attention and energy and effort to do the best that I can do, sometimes more than I think is good.

Lauren Muller, writer (34, f, 11)

I remember my mother talking about being with my father as he was dying and that he lost his functions, first the physical, and then the mental. It was hard because his mind was so important to him. I'm just now thinking that this must have had some influence on my being an academic and carrying on a life of the mind. I think that even before my father's death probably a lot of my behavior was aimed at pleasing him. He was pretty strict as a parent, and I guess I internalized his high standards or expectations. I'm sure I continued to carry those on after he died. I probably both idealized him and wanted to make him proud. So I probably tried to be very good at everything I did. I think that school offered a surrogate father in the sense that it was a place where I could perform well for approval or authority. And it had sort of a stability and a structure.

I think the struggle I've been having in graduate school around writing—it feels like my life is at stake—has to do perhaps with the feeling on some level that I am writing for the dead father. And there's a way in which the professor who grades your paper, I think, stands in for that authority figure. I think I was trying—and I think it started in high school—to write papers to please God or something. I wrote my senior thesis using the New Critical model, of course, which came partially from the South. My father was a southern man and very enthusiastic about Christianity. I think there is a way in which teaching and reading did replace the church. I guess if you follow that train of thought, one would then see how in becoming a teacher I would sort of become an authority figure myself, which frightens me a little. I don't want to do violence to anyone.

Creativity

The urge to create can be seen as a desire to invent a world. For those whose world was shattered at a young age, the pull to create, to construct a replacement, is strong. Suzanne Lipsett, Diana O'Hehir, and Brown Miller all talk about a drive to write—not so much to succeed as to give voice to what was lost, replace what is missing, and even communicate with the dead.

Lipsett wants to give life to her mother, buried in time.

Suzanne Lipsett, writer (51, m, 4)

The passionate, driven writing impulse that will not go away in the face of poverty, in the face of impracticality, in the face of rejection, but instead gets stronger, has at its basis the sense of responsibility, to give voice to people who have been obliterated from memory by somebody else. Nobody told me anything about my mother. I had to rediscover her. I do believe that I would not have become a writer to this driven degree if my mother had not died. One part of the drive is to create something, if not beautiful, at least meaningful, out of the raw material that is handed you. The other part of the drive is to give voice to the voiceless. In *Surviving a Writer's Life,* I explore the notion that I could give voice, without even knowing it, to people who have been obliterated. I think I did feel a sense of responsibility about it as a writer to get these stories told. If you live and no one remembers you, that's sad. I closed old issues that had been open for my whole life, and they became old memories that just faded away, and—now here's the really great part about that—as an evolving artist who's married to the truth, the fading away of those themes and issues does nothing but liberate the imagination even more. When those themes are resolved, imagination expands.

∽

O'Hehir writes, in part, to recreate her lost mother. During our interview she gave us a copy of her book *Home Free,* pointing out the poem "I Search for My Mother, Who Died When I Was Four." The last stanza reads: "Memory's hair is black. / The face of memory is carved from stone. / Nothing / Is memory's hallmark."

Diana O'Hehir, novelist and poet (72, m, 4)

My mother wrote poetry and taught. I accumulated the legends in her family about her. She was regarded as the brightest in her family. The only one who had inclinations toward learning and creativity. I was aware of this, and sort of regarded it as part of me, I guess. I think it's absolutely true that people who write do so because they are driven. And it very often is something lacking in the person's life, some unhappiness, that they want to allay in some way. Not even necessarily by talking about it specifically. So I think I'm a writer because my mother died. Maybe I would have been anyway, but I truly think that the extent of my career would not have been as great if she had not died. I really don't think I would have had the same kind of drive.

∽

Miller talks about his drive to communicate, to make connections.

Brown Miller, poet (51, m, 6)

You know, a writer is somebody who tries to communicate. If you think about it, I wasn't able to communicate with my mother; therefore, I had this need after her death to communicate. There's this sense that everything I write is trying to communicate with her. Of course, I'm really trying to communicate with anybody who reads my work, but there could be this unconscious process going on where I'm really trying to communicate with the mother I couldn't communicate with, because she wasn't there.

∽

Laurie, a painter, believes her powers of perception were sharpened by her early loss.

Laurie (38, m, 13)

I think that the bizarre things that have happened in my life probably gave me the distance that it sometimes takes to be an artist, that kind of stepping back and seeing things a little bit differently, not like everybody else says they look.

∽

Kelly, whose mother died giving birth to her, faces an entire lifetime of her mother's history to recover and make sense of. That exploration became the seed for her art.

Kelly (43, m, birth)

When Judy Chicago wrote about our lost history as women artists, and being an artist, that really meant something to me. I guess all the art-making that I did really centered around that loss, and establishing that relationship. When I was actively making art, which was before my kids were born, that was probably my therapy for losing people in my life. It was my period of self-discovery, and my loss of my mother was really central in that exploration.

Daily Business

From the heights of achievement and creativity to the daily tasks of balancing a checkbook or setting up a house, early loss makes its mark. Sometimes we flourish, and sometimes we flounder.

Paul and Rachel, husband and wife, have had nearly opposite reactions to their early losses. Paul has a hard time following through with daily business tasks, while Rachel finds herself energized by them.

Rachel (47, f, 5)

It's a complicated thing to know if it's my father's death or the system of the family, but I am very driven to have a successful business, a clean house, a busy schedule, and I love it. Paul and I completely disagree on this, but I don't feel oppressed by it. I get energized by the fact that there are lots of tasks to do. I don't like it when there's not stuff to do. I still see tasks as pleasure. I see washing windows and lying on the beach as equally joy-inducing.

Paul B. (53, m, 11)

I have trouble going through a process and completing tasks. I get crippled a lot of times with a sense of sadness. And so a lot of times it's more comfortable for me to just sit than to initiate activity. Professionally, I'm fine. It's more around domestic tasks. I can feel a kind of vague sadness when I'm doing things that a lot of other people find fun, like a house project. The same feeling would come out—I would detach. A lot of times I would act like I was having fun, go through the motions. But what I would be feeling is kind of an inner sense of emptiness or sadness.

∽

Jessica's relationship to daily business has to do with decisions and commitments, such as signing a lease. Perhaps because her mother killed herself, she is determined not to let anyone down if she makes a promise to them.

Jessica (24, m, 16)

If I don't know what my plans are, I can't sign a lease. I don't want to get tied into something where I know I'll leave somebody hanging or abandoned. If I'm going to do something, I'm going be fairly sure that I'm going to follow through. When I make a decision, I feel like I have to follow through with it, even if, halfway through, it really is not what I need to do. I want to finish things up, and not leave anything hanging.

Lauren Muller talks about her fear of economic insecurity and how that has affected her relationship to money. Some of it has been based on reality, but more of it seems to grow out of watching her mother lose so much when her father died.

Lauren Muller, writer (34, f, 11)

A sense of taking care of myself was important to me. I went to a public university. I didn't like to spend money at all. Didn't buy clothes. After college, I was living for a year where I cooked meals for a family in return for room and board, and I did volunteer work in all these different places like a state mental hospital and a community bookstore. So I loved this idea that somehow I could live without money. It seems to me only just recently that I've allowed myself a kind of higher standard of living. Maybe it's about not wanting to be in the position my mother was in, being dependent on somebody and not understanding all that. But I always think it's kind of a weird false pride that I would be so particular about not even calling home collect. In retrospect, that seems a little like overdoing it.

David Z. (52, f, 13)

In terms of taking care of daily business, I think that if something is out of your control, like death, you try to live your life by controlling everything, so, to that extent, I try to control fate. I know that life is very fragile. I know that tomorrow something could be gone. In spite of that enlightened knowledge, and although my need to control has diminished dramatically in the last five years, I'm still trying to control most of my environment and my work. I love what I do. The income level I'm at is good, yet in spite of all of that, I'm fearful. I'm thinking as I'm talking now—because this is the first time I really started to think about this—that I am always afraid I will be back in the position my mother was in when my father died. I have these fears even though when my father died he was just about to start that process of earning a good living, and I am now earning a good living. My fear reaction is not commensurate with the reality. Or the history. And it is almost the same fear that my mother conveyed to me when my father died: "What are we going to do now?"

Peggi wonders if a certain sense of impermanence in her household relates to her father's early death.

Peggi (56, f, 19)

I have been in this house since 1968, and I will never sell it. It seems like that's related to the aftermath of my father's death. But I also have never really moved in. I still feel like I'm camping here. Is that because I thought it wouldn't last, or procrastination? I've never had a retirement plan, never thought I would live that long. Although I always had jobs, I never really settled into work until after forty. I thought I should live and do things while I was young, not wait to retire since that might be too late.

Rich shares Peggi's feelings of impermanence, but responds to them somewhat differently.

Rich (36, m, 14)

I was convinced growing up that I'd be dead by the time I was thirty. In those years when I turned thirty and thirty-one, I was sure that I was going to be dead soon. I did not go and get an HIV test until last fall. People told me, "You'll get your negative result back and you'll feel this enormous weight off your shoulders." The exact opposite occurred. I got a negative result, and I plunged into the worst depression I've ever had because there was a part of me that's always believed I was going to die young. I don't know how much to explicitly connect this with my mother's death. The way I handle money is that I don't save because I figure I'm not going to be around. I don't need to establish security. I don't need to have a pension. I don't need to buy a house. Because I'm not going to be here.

A Different Path

Some people feel that the early death of a parent changed the focus or direction in their work lives, even if only temporarily.

Tim (35, f, 17)

Had my father not died, I might be an accountant right now. We went to Germany to visit with my brother two months after my father died, for Christmas. That's the first time I ever picked up a camera and decided that that's what I wanted to do. I had always been analytical with dad, and I was always good at math, so it seemed being an accountant would have been a more logical thing to do. I think my dad's death changed the entire course of my career path.

Walter Liggett, poet (70, f, 11)

If my father hadn't been murdered as a newspaperman, I think both my sister and I might have become journalists. My mother didn't want us to do that because she didn't want what happened to our father to happen to us.

Robin (46, f, 8)

When I accomplish something, when I do well in graduate school, I think of my father. He was a lawyer and then went to school to become an optometrist. He was smart. There were times that I was real aware that my mother was pushing me in a different direction than my father probably would have. I think my father would have wanted me to have been more intellectually involved.

William (54, f, 14)

I'm sure, if my father had been alive, I'd probably be an engineer to-day. Or something like that in the sciences. I think that's almost a given. His father was a civil engineer, and he was a civil engineer who became an architect. I was interested in science. I did well in high school in those subjects. I always had that bent going.

Art (70, f, 17)

If my father had lived, and we had stayed in Milwaukee, I'd probably have gone to school in Wisconsin. I didn't get drafted because I had five people to support, and going into the army would've made going to college easier. I would have had the GI Bill like so many others did. The way it was, my wife and I both worked to get me through what little schooling I did get. I guess the fact that it was impossible for me to get a four-year degree really affected me more than anything else. I worked in a division of a company where education and engineering and scientific skills were how people got paid and got advancements. I didn't have the credentials that most of the people I worked with had, and I've felt I could have gone much higher in the company if I had had a degree. I'm sure it affected my salary to a large extent. But you know, I might not have met my wife if I had gone to the four-year college. You can't play God. I mean there's always good and bad. If you run into one dead end, you go try to find a different way.

Emilia (62, f, 12)

I dropped out of nursing school because I felt insecure. I had these classmates who were a little better off than I was. If my father had lived and had established his own business, it might have been differ-ent. Eventually, I went to Manila and became a secretary, which I don't think I would have done if my father had lived. In some ways, my family gained because we had to work so hard. Also, we had to prove to ourselves and other people that we could make it through even if our father had died.

Blocked Paths

Although Jim eventually got an M.A. in creative writing and another in education, in his early years he felt blocked. Forty years after his parents died, he has returned to teaching with a renewed commitment. He still admits, however, to an ongoing battle with depression, which is only one of the ongoing blocks people talked about.

Jim (61, m, 16, f, 18)

I couldn't concentrate. It was really hard for me to give any long-term energy to anything, because, even though I was probably reasonably intelligent and capable, to make a long-term commitment to anything didn't seem relevant. I would get all enthusiastic, but then my enthusiasm would wane in about three or six months, and I would think, "What's the use? I'm not going to get what I want out of this." Now I'm back teaching again, this time with a certain commitment and a certain enjoyment that I didn't have before. So I must have made some progress, or some growth. But I think there's still a sense of depression I carry that sometimes undercuts my efforts to be a good teacher. I have to fight that a lot. And it's affected by all that death. That's the overriding thing in my life, it's just there, it's like a weight I carry all the time. It never quite goes away.

Terry believes that if his mother had lived he would have more easily pursued his dreams.

Terry (38, m, 6)

I don't want to get too general. But I think that everything affects the next thing, and how my mother's death may have affected me is that out of default I became a carpenter and then over the years developed into a contractor. I say "out of default" because of my inability to stay in school without any kind of support or guidance from my parents. It's hard to say whether or not my mother's death had anything to do with an inability to focus on the future, an inability to focus on reality and dreams and work towards those dreams, but I think that it probably did. I like to believe that my mom would have given me attention, which I never really got, and appreciation and encouragement for me to do what my heart really told me I wanted to do. My sister has always been very supportive of my artwork. I believe that my mother would have probably, just through love for me, wanted me to do what I loved doing, unlike my father, who has said, "You'll never make money in art, and you've got to get a real job."

I think the career that I am in, at this point, has worked out to be a means to an end, but certainly is not the one I would have chosen. What's important in my life is my artwork. That's what I believe in a lot more and really enjoy.

∽

Rachel feels that her father's death has kept her from being as aggressive as she otherwise might have been.

Rachel *(47, f, 5)*

I can see opportunities careerwise that I don't avail myself of, in part, because I don't have good failure mechanisms. I tend to stay on the safe side. I worked for twenty years for Pillsbury and rose to the level of being a director, so, from that standpoint, I was successful there. And I now own a small business that has survived in this economy for four years, so, from that standpoint, I'm also successful. I don't have a sense of being marginalized in any way, but I think I don't go for it, like some of the career women I know. Of course, I always assumed that I was responsible for myself. I mean, it never occurred to me that I would be a responsibility of someone else.

Carrying On Where Our Dead Parents Left Off

Some people feel that they have modeled themselves after their parents. They see themselves as following a similar trail and restoring what was lost, by working in the same area or approaching work with the same style or spirit. It's possible that if our parent had lived, we would also have incorporated some of their traits into our own personality, but we might just as easily have rebelled against them or been less concerned about embodying their styles and attitudes. With their deaths, following their steps becomes a kind of tribute and memorial to our lost loved ones. Usually, this is a good thing, but occasionally we repeat our parents' unhealthy patterns.

Ken Burns, filmmaker (41, m, 11)

I'm a bit of an evangelist. I could've just been a filmmaker, but I chose to move my filmmaking into television, and then I chose not to be a filmmaker whose work was considered, but a filmmaker who was considered along with his work. There is a sense of mission, of destiny, of having to say something, keeping things together as a country, of cohering, of finding what we share in common. I like to think those are traits of my mother. I feel very much my father's intelligence driving both my brother and me, but it's really a spirit of hers that I feel ultimately.

Deborah Nagle, writer (46, f, 12)

I would say my father had more influence than anyone else on how I carry myself. There's an air of sort of intellectual authority that I have through just the way I look that has absolutely nothing to do with education. I'd developed that look years before my actual degrees.

Robin (46, f, 8)

I'm a hearing officer, and I think sometimes how I do my work is affected by my dad, because a lot of it involves infusing a sense of humor into stuff, and trying to get people to see how silly what they're arguing about is, trying to get people to see the absurdity in it. My father had a way of trying to make people laugh, when they were upset or they were angry about something, to just try and humor them.

Teresa (32, f, 8)

As a reporter, I've actually written a little bit about my dad and work. My mom had told me, "You know, your dad really loved his work, he loved making people happy." He really was extremely charming, and he was running a dining room, which he loved doing. When I took a year off between my junior and senior years of college, I got a job waiting tables. Mama told me that my father's attitude was, "You don't sink to the customer's level, you bring the customer up to your level." I remember being very conscious of this when I was a waitress. I remember thinking, "What would Daddy have done in this situation? How would he have handled this?" There's also a certain degree of disengagement that I think I probably do get from my dad. It's a very strange thing, because here my dad was this really charming, popular person, yet I have some sense of there being a part of him that was kept just for him. And I know that I feel that way myself. There is a split that happens when you're a reporter between being really charming and social, and being an observer, reading other people's reactions. That's something that you actually do as a waiter, too. Part of being charming is reading the other person, understanding what it is that they want from a situation, so that quality, whatever that is, is something that I associate with my dad.

Eric Marcus, writer (36, f, 12)

What's interesting about my career is that, as traditional as I thought I was, I am much more like my father than not. I'm not good in the corporate world, couldn't stand that kind of thing. I work for myself. I think I have the life and career my father would have liked to have. I never wanted to grow up and load bags of mail onto trucks like my father. But I admired his artistry, his ability as a painter, and as a writer, which I didn't really know about until I discovered a journal that he had written. I found it when I was about twenty-six years old in a box of his things, and I was stunned by the beauty of his writing.

I think he would have been very proud of my work. He was very antimaterialist, so I don't think he would have been as proud of my commercial success as he would have been of my more serious books, like my history of the gay rights movement and my book on suicide. He didn't care about money. But he would have cared that my history book was reviewed on the front page of the *New York Times Book Review*.

I really feel as if I've lived out some of his ideals: to do good things, to leave the world a better place. I don't know if that's influence or that's genetic programming. But I feel a pretty strong tie to who he was.

Detta (47, m, 17)

My mother said I could be anything I wanted to be. I wanted to be an engineer. That was fine with her, and she helped me fill out my college application. But then she died. I never wanted to do what the aunts were kind of pushing me towards, which was home economics. After graduation, when I got a job as a junior designer, they wanted to know how I was going to make a living at that. I said, "Well, I'm not sure, actually. There are a lot of people that work at this publishing company, they seem to do it." And to this day they're surprised that I can make a living at this. I feel like my mother would have liked what I'm doing. Just because it is doing what makes me happy, instead of what I have to do to get by. You can't always have everything that you want, but you can make the best of what you get. I got that from her.

Peggi (56, f, 19)

My father was a chemistry teacher. And I have had an interest in science. When I first went to school, I was a psychology and French major. I avoided science and math. Maybe because that was what my father did, and I wanted to do something different. To not "compete" maybe. I dropped out and didn't go back until I was in my thirties, and then I was a science student. I thought of my father right away when I got into the science building, with its smells. I felt like "This is home!" or familiar, remembering the pharmacy school where he taught, the smells in the hallways when we would come in, in the evenings, for basketball games. It felt very natural and almost comforting to be in that science department at the university. In fact, throughout my life whatever is associated with my father has had a little extra charge, sometimes a numinous quality to it.

Monica (30, m, 10)

I always wanted to kind of follow in my mother's strong steps, being a single parent and running her own business. When I told my brother that I wanted to come to San Francisco and run this flash repair business, he didn't believe that I had the potential, but here I am, a single parent with my son and my business. My mom influenced me to believe in myself as a woman. With six kids, she managed to own one of the biggest grocery stores in our town, and be very respected by men. Just to see my mom walk into stores and hear people say "Oh, Señora Antonia" gave me a sense of pride. As I look back on it, at the time I didn't even know what I was feeling. Now I work a man's job, I deal with men, and I have learned to get the same respect from men that she got.

But I have found myself doing as she did, not having time for my son, working too much. She worked long hours. I work long hours. I want to break that routine, because I don't want my son to remember what I remember. I used to say, "I'm not going to become a workaholic like her," because I know that her work had a lot to do with her death. And then I find myself being like that.

Marc (39, f, 10)

I saw a therapist when I was in college. I had already decided on photography as a career, and, when I talked about my father, and remembered him always taking pictures and always having a camera, the therapist thought that perhaps becoming a photographer was a way for me to identify with my father. That's interesting—it's hard to say. Clearly, I was not interested at all in what my father had done for a living. I remember when my mom told me, "If you ever want to be an accountant, you are promised a position at his firm." That probably was about the last thing in life that I could possibly do.

I remember, also—this is an interesting thing—I remember, as a young adult, or an adolescent and adult, that I didn't want to be like my father in that he worked nine to five in an office, and then he came home and worked after dinner until midnight every night in a duplicate office he had in the basement of our house. I thought this was the most insane way to live, and I was never going to live that way. I was going to be different. But I have found, in some odd ways—not a complete parallel—that I've wound up much more like that. I have my own business, and often work until three o'clock in the morning. On the other hand, I probably spend more nights at home, while my father basically spent every single night working. Nonetheless, I mean, we're talking about questions of degree here. I still have wound up much more like my father than I thought I would.

Kristy (25, f, 13)

My dad was a famous artist. I felt so connected with him creatively. We did a lot of work together, and he taught me a lot about art. We drew together, wrote stories together. I'd have an idea, and he'd work on it, or he'd write it out. He'd give me a blank sheet and say, "Kristy, okay, now you put your colors on here and let's work with it." I have a lot of memories of Dad's support of my creativity. If I'd build a house, he'd say, "Maybe you'll be an architect. I like how you positioned this." If I'd done a piece, he'd say something about simplicity. "See, if you just take this one out, or you add this one, it changes the perspective." There was so much support on that level. Now he is so present in my art.

Irena Klepfisz, poet and writer (54, f, 2)

I was raised as a socialist, and I kept that very close to my heart, in terms of what I believed and what I thought was right, but I was not involved in the civil rights movement, I was really not involved in the antiwar movement. I really did not become politically active until after I came out as a lesbian. Earlier on, my shyness had been so acute it was pathological. When I started to teach and had to stand up in front of the classroom, it was just a nightmare for me. It took me years to get comfortable. That changed in my thirties, when I first started doing poetry readings. So it wasn't really until my middle and late thirties that I in any way started maybe doing what my father had been doing since he was probably nine years old. But now here I am talking about the Jewish Labor Bund—my father's world. It's puzzling. I mean it sort of makes you really wonder about the unconscious drives. You wonder about what's really willed and conscious and how much control you have over your life, and who you are.

Good Works

Some orphaned children perform the role of the wounded healer. They've taken what they've learned about the pain of loss to help other people deal with their hurts.

Mary Montgomery, writer (61, f, 3)

In addition to the writing I have done for children about grief, I trained as a grief facilitator. I work with grief support groups. I am not a person who can reveal my feelings, but I can soak up other people's feelings, and listen. I think all of that came out of my father's death. Dealing with this whole grief thing, and writing about it, is more trying to understand feelings, and my own feelings, and I guess it's kind of redemptive in that I have never been able to tell anybody how I feel. I understand how difficult it is to tell, so I want to make it as easy as possible for other people to talk.

Jan B. (50, f, 8)

I think that I became a psychotherapist because nobody would listen to me as a child. No one listened to my feelings. Now I listen to people's feelings all the time. I listen to their grief and walk them through this dark passage. I'm sure that's what I'm doing.

Kelly (43, m, birth)

My choice to work with children was not exactly trying to create my own family, but it was creating family in a way, creating a good environment for children to be in. Maybe there's compensation there for the lost family.

Martin Yan, chef, writer, TV personality (43, f, 3)

When I was in Philadelphia not too long ago, a lady came in and shook my hand, and said: "You know, I wanted to come and thank you. My husband just passed away, but when he was in the hospital, dying from cancer, the only time he smiled was when he was watching the *Yan Can Cook* show." There are other stories like that, maybe not so dramatic, but I have been able to make a few people happy, to have an impact on some people, to offer something that gives them courage, that gives them some happy moments away from their suffering. So that's why, if you look at my schedule, I do personal appearances probably more than anybody else in the country, or in the world. Every day I work. I hate traveling. But when I get there and see the people smiling and laughing, it makes me feel that it's all worth it.

Joe (28, m, 12)

I work with homeless and runaway youth a little bit. I've tutored in schools, and I have an intense interest in helping disadvantaged children. I think that comes from losing my mother so young. I felt like I had a bad situation, but I did have those few people who are so necessary to firmly plant a person's life. A lot of people are lacking that, and it makes a big difference. With my parents dying when I was so young, I could have ended up in a lot of different situations. If I didn't have my sister and my brother, I could very easily have been the guy who hangs out at the racetrack.

Beto (52, m, 14)

I think my mother's illness and death made me very sensitive to other people's suffering and pain. And I think that did have a lot to do with my career choice as a poverty lawyer. I did become much more sensitive to people, and drawn to people who were experiencing pain.

Paul B. (53, m, 11)

I was pulled toward a profession where I could rescue. Where I could help. I fantasized being a physician for a long time, but there just wasn't the funds. And I wasn't very good in science, so that was another factor. But I had a need to pull someone back from the brink and rescue them. So I chose a helping profession.

Jessica (24, m, 16)

I knew that I wanted to teach before my mother died. It was a small idea in my head at the time, but it's gotten bigger. I think that now the only reason I relate it to her death is that I feel that I've got to give of myself what is good, and not take that away from people. My mother had all these wonderful things she could've given, and gotten in return, if she had stayed alive. I feel like if I teach and give those things to other people, I'll be a good person.

Deborah H. (45, m, 16)

You know it's hard for me to separate my mother's death impacting my career decisions versus the whole effect of who both of my parents were. She was a nurse and he was a doctor, which probably played a big role in how I landed where I landed. Essentially, when I was sixteen, I was tutoring in the inner city and working in school programs in the summer and pretty much engaged in sort of "servicey" kind of work. When my mother died, I think that intensified. I think my eventual choice to do oncology work is very related to more of the work of unraveling the loss experience, very much so, although not consciously. I went into nursing school to do midwifery and I came out doing hospice and death-and-dying work.

Rob (44, f, 15)

In my practice, one of my specialties is bereavement, so I have to deal with my own stuff all day long. The reason I went into it in the first place is because it was so confusing to me. It was my way of trying to figure things out. I started working with cancer patients. It felt real natural to go and talk to people about getting ready to die, and talk to their family members. I'll never forget the first time I was talking to this woman who had cancer. She said, "I'm going to die, and I'm ready." I just talked to her for hours. Then the family talked with her, and she died, and it was sad. But it was complete.

My own grief was never complete until I was able to do this kind of work. That's what I'm trying to help other people get to. But it's hard because it's not an intellectual kind of thing. It's not like you can teach the head. You've got to be able to teach the heart. It's not like everything will be tied up in this little box and then you put it away on the back of the shelf someplace. Acceptance for me is knowing that my father is dead. And that comes with feelings. That took a long time, because I did a lot to try to hold on to him. My impatience, my beating myself up, that was all an effort to hold on to him, because that's what he did to me. When I started seeing that, I was able to let some of it go. It's a pretty long process, but that doesn't mean it's over. That doesn't mean that those thoughts and feelings never come up again.

Patience is a real important thing. As I work with people, they tend to come back to the same kind of struggle that they're working on; they do it over and over and over again. Eventually, they'll be able to make some movement. I have experienced the same thing. So I have a lot of compassion for that. I went through a difficult period of time—who knows if it will happen again?—when I passed my father financially. I achieved more than he did in his lifetime, and I've found more about what I wanted to do. I felt guilty, and also sad that he wasn't able to find his dream. So there's always a sadness underneath it. That's not going to go away. Nor do I want it to.

Working

Sooner or later, everyone's parents die. But those of us who experience that loss in childhood make a family, a career, a life in which bereavement is a constant ingredient. As we make that life, our early grief transforms itself. Sometimes we're immobilized with regrets or fears; other times our sorrow becomes the driving force of our achievements. Not everyone stays closely connected to the feelings of sadness, but almost all of us, as we reflect on our early loss, know that how we see the world has been affected by the fact that one or both of our parents died before we came of age. In the next chapter, "How I See It," people talk about their personal identity, their worldview, their spirituality, and the gifts their parents left them.

9

How I See It

The death of Jean Baptiste [his father] was one big event of my life. It sent my mother back to her chains and gave me my freedom.—Jean-Paul Sartre (f, 2), *The Words*

I had declined to believe in that apocalypse which had been central to my father's vision. . . . I had inclined to be contemptuous of my father for the conditions of his life, for the conditions of our lives. When his life had ended I began to wonder about that life and also, in a new way, to be apprehensive about my own.—James Baldwin (f, 19), "Notes of a Native Son"

Like tracks made in the snow, first by one animal, then by another, there were two sets jumbled together, mine and my mother's. The work of my life was to distinguish one set of tracks from the other before they all melted away without a trace.—Suzanne Lipsett (m, 4), *Surviving a Writer's Life*

For this book, we asked seventy people to remember their childhood, to go back to the time and place their mother or father died, to relive funerals held or not held, attended or not attended, to recount their experience of loss, devastation, and grief as they moved from childhood into adulthood. Then we asked them to speculate on how the loss of their parents affected their lives now—their family and love relationships, their work lives, their attention to the daily responsibilities of living. Finally, we asked them to sum it all up, to tell us how they see their lives now from the vantage point of anywhere between a few years and three-quarters of a century. We asked them to think about how they view the world, their place and role in it, their spiritual outlook. We asked them to speculate about their parent's death and its continuing influence on their lives and identity.

The very breadth of the questions, not to mention the sundry experiences, ethnicities, and ages of the interviewees, gives this chapter a kaleidoscopic effect. Kaleidoscopes are, of course, multifaceted, changing. Through them we see patterns encompassed in circles. In this chapter, we see bits of people's lives, as the chapter circles from their overall emotional outlooks to their legacies from their parents, and back to looking at their lives in relationship to the event of their parent's death.

We all have heard Descartes's famous dictum, the result of his search for something true beyond the shadow of a doubt: "I think therefore I am." As we talked to them, many contributors groped for words. Often they felt that their parent's death influenced how they see the world and who they are in the world. Yet some had a hard time articulating just how. Some talked about the death, or their constant thinking about it, as the focus of their own search for identity. For others, the death was a fact of life, there among others, influencing them in ways they found difficult to pinpoint. Perhaps the lesser-known converse of Descartes's saying, from Katigiri Roshi, "I am, therefore I think," is more pertinent when we consider how early bereavement influences our lives. We are who we are, and then we think about who that is and how we got to be that way.

We begin this chapter with a section called "Balancing Acts," in which people talk about personal identity and emotional stance, followed by a section in which people talk about how the parent's death has inspired them to take care of themselves. Then we move to "Gender and Sexuality," where people speculate on how their parent's death affected their coming into being as a man or woman and whether that experience continues to affect how they see themselves as men or women. Next we consider "Culture, Identity, and Politics" and "Spirituality," two separate categories that nevertheless overlap considerably. Next we explore how people view death beyond their own experience of it. Finally, we look toward the future, as our interviewees talk about the legacies or gifts they've gotten from their parents' lives and deaths.

Balancing Acts

We asked people whether they see themselves as more open and empathetic or more closed and fearful because of their early bereavement. Not surprisingly, the responses ranged far and wide. In the following pages, parts of the answers to these more general questions become more specific, making their way into the sections on spirituality, identity and politics, attitude toward death, and, of course, legacies. None of us succeeds totally in segregating our emotional selves from our spiritual or political selves. The impulse to find balance is strong.

Monica (30, m, 10)

I believe that we're like a box, or a package, full of energy, that we have negatives and positives, and we can choose. You have to have both, in order for the current to flow. If we have too much negative or too much positive, we should balance it. If we are missing positive energy, we should grab the positive to keep alive. That's why I say my mom—the memory of her love—is food to me. I had too much negative in my life, losing my mother, almost being molested, not being cared for properly by my father. Sometimes when my mom was under a lot of pressure, she hit me. I can choose that negative. I can do like those people on TV who talk about their abuse, but I don't want to be stuck there. I feel pain, I feel sadness, but I can pull out of it and let the energy flow. I think that being stuck on the negative is like being under the ground, in the darkness. The only way the pain is going to stop is when we get more people to listen, when we get more people to understand. We were *buried* in the pain. People told us not to talk about it, not to express it. We need to talk about it, but not get stuck in it. When you're positive, you're daring and adventurous. You need to create this love in yourself.

∽

Jeff B. talks about putting death in perspective, echoing a lot of other people who stressed that a parent's death is just one bad thing that can happen to a child.

Jeff B. (24, m, 18)

I talk to friends about how everyone has shit in their life. Death is definitely one of the biggies. Maybe dealing with my mother's death has made me really focus on becoming an individual. But at the same time, everyone I know has had something traumatic that happened to them, even if it's not losing a parent, or someone, to death. I think it's valuable and important for people, by whatever process, to realize that whatever has happened has happened, and that that definitely is a part of who you are. But for me it's important to find the good aspects and make them work for me. I would find it really frustrating to live life being angry. I choose not to spend my energy that way. There are too many positive things that can happen to you as a person, or you as a parent, or as a husband or wife or whatever, to always be tainted with the sense of that *anger*. It's a costly emotion.

∽

The times when life isn't easy are often the times when thoughts of one's dead parent comes up. Kenyetta has to deal with the fact of her father's murder, and although it has affected her personality, she, too, manages to balance the negative with prayer, family, and friendship.

Kenyetta (20, f, 18)

I'm cautious now. I'm leery, I'm scared of what's going on in the world today. It's not a nice thing. It's horrible for me. I was at a bad point where I just didn't care about myself. I was a lost cause, you could say. But I just woke up one day and said, "This is not me, this is not how it's supposed to be." I feel I've helped myself with the strength of God and praying and talking to my sisters and brother and my friend, and they all just make me strong. I feel I've done a lot for myself. I've come a long way. I've accomplished a lot. I want to keep doing the right thing, and stay on the right track.

∽

Once the worst has happened, there's a feeling of being able to cope with anything. Lisa speaks of the strength she feels as a survivor.

Lisa (28, m, 12)

I just have always felt like losing my mother was one of the worst things ever in my life, and I made it through. So, pretty much when things happen, I may get mad or sad, but I have this hope inside me or assurance that I'm going to be all right, and I kind of get over things easy that way. When things really go bad and everything's coming down on me, I have this attitude that this is the bottom, now I'm going up. And it always works out that way. I don't know if it's because of my attitude or if that's just the way things go. You know, the cliché. Once you hit the bottom, you can only go up.

∽

Danny echoes her sentiments. But that doesn't stop him from longing for a balance that he might have gotten in life had his parents lived longer. (His father died when he was twenty-five.)

Danny (30, m, 16)

I think with my mom passing away, I learned to be on my own, and I developed a confidence that if I can make it through that, which I think is one of the worst things a person has to go through, I can do anything. I think I have a good down-to-earth grasp on things. People sometimes even come to me for advice. When my dad passed away, people from his work said, "You know, I was always able to go to Russell for basic advice, and he would always know exactly what to say." I look back at that and I say, "Yeah, that's great." Then I look at my mom and say she really gave me a work ethic, and she instilled God in my life, although my dad was spiritual in his own sense. But, you know, I see other traits in myself, and I wonder where they come from. I want to ask my parents about the family history, but I can't.

My wife is Navajo, and stories are very important to them. I wish so much of my family history had not been lost.

∽

Tron Bykle describes his effort to tip the balance of his own life away from the kind of regret his father lived with. The day his father died, Tron was on a train platform when he was overcome with sadness, and before anyone told him, he knew his father was dead. He is a different person because his father died—both because he has lived differently than his father did and because he feels fortunate to have had his father for as long as he did. He can, as he says, "use his energy to help me with the loss."

Tron Bykle, artist (51, f, 14)

If anything, my father's death has opened me up. The fact that he lived with some regrets, I think, has prompted me to take the opposite view. I definitely don't hesitate. If there's something I want to do, I do it. I'll plunge into it. I think whatever it is that I've been engaging in, right or wrong, he has been a quiet force in all of that—coming to this country, going to school, and creating a life that I'm very happy in. When I say "very happy in," it sounds kind of saccharine, but I'm very fortunate to be doing what I'm doing. Basically, I feel that I'm fortunate to have known him for as long as I did. I can use his energy to help me with the loss, going back to knowing the moment that he died without my being there and nobody telling me, but my sensing it. Something about the protoplasm of his energy is part of me, and it's made me somewhat available, in a spooky sense, to have this other type of experience, where I can be open to feelings and dreams.

∽

Marc talks about how his life has been, and in some ways continues to be, a search for the part of himself that's missing because his father died when he was so young.

Marc (39, f, 10)

I feel I've been on a search for my father to a certain extent, especially when I was younger. But I don't think it's completely ended. It's not so much a search for the memories, but a search for that part of myself that came from him that I feel I've lost contact with because he died at a young age. In some ways, that search has led me to open up to ideas of the world that I might not have if I hadn't been trying to find those answers. I would generally say that I'm an open person and optimistic. I didn't retreat from the world, hurt and licking my wounds. I am a relatively compassionate person, and able to understand people's feelings and feel for them, and I'm sure that part of it has to do with the fact that I did have an early loss and had to come to terms with those kinds of feelings at a young age.

Terry's story explores another aspect of compassion and empathy. It is not always positive. If we identify too strongly with the other person, we can lose sight of who we are.

Terry (38, m, 6)

I think that I do have empathy and compassion, but I struggle with that. I identify in a way which is sometimes harmful to me. It's almost like, in that kind of chameleon way, I become the other person. By the time I become that person, I am so apt to throw away so much of the more optimistic parts of myself. I don't know if it was the death of my mother or the way that I am anyway, but I can really be fascinated by a lot of the world around me and intrigued. The interest and the compassion and, in a way, the torment are all the same, both positive and negative. It's just a sense of there's a lot more to life than meets the eye. I can look at a person or a house, inanimate objects, and just imagine effects and influences of age and time. Maybe it's just my imagination or understanding the power of how profound events can shape and mold people and things, maybe a sense of trying to make lemonade out of lemons. But my sense of my mother dying is it's opened up this whole other world. It won't go away. Sometimes it's depressing and sometimes it's enlightening.

∽

Where Terry risks losing himself, Brown Miller's paradox is that he can be stingy and overly generous at the same time. Several people raised the question of whether or not we can give people what we didn't get, and if we can, do we give ourselves something in the bargain?

Brown Miller, poet (51, m, 6)

I think in some ways my mother's death made me a more selfish, less generous person. It's almost made me a person who has this paranoia about losing the little bit of happiness that I think I have, and therefore I'm not as forthcoming as I should be. On the other hand, as a teacher, one of the things that I criticize myself for, and other teachers and other people who know me criticize me for, is spreading myself so thin, and extending myself too far. I tend to *over*help, and, just on the brink of overdoing it, I have to pull myself back. It might be that if you didn't get what you wanted at a certain age, you have a tendency to try to give what you didn't get to other people. That's kind of paradoxical. It doesn't make any sense in a way, but in a strange way, in the realm of the mind, things can often be backwards. So I have both. I have this sense that I'm sometimes too selfish, too stingy. But then there's this kind of automatic thing that takes over, even when I'm not intending to. A student will ask a question, or a friend will ask for something, and I'll do way more than they need, or want, sometimes. Sometimes I make a pest of myself.

∽

Janette talks about two different kinds of balance: One is being more sympathetic and less judgmental. The other is becoming more sensitive to being there for people as a direct result of people not being there for her, while still standing up for herself.

Janette (19, m, 12)

Before my mother died, sometimes I would see kids acting wrong, and I thought, "Didn't their mother teach them right?" But when I saw my mom die, I saw that not everybody has a mother or father for that guidance. It made me realize I shouldn't judge people, because I don't know their background. And I feel like people can't judge me because they don't really know me. I try to be there for other people, because I know that when people weren't there for me, it was harder on me.

When I was younger, I used to be more passive and let everybody tell me what to do. I'd always keep my mouth shut about everything, and if something happened, I would just think, "Well, that's going to happen, that's what I deserve." I think when my mom died, it taught me that I shouldn't hold things back, because life is too short to be keeping quiet and letting people control your life. I guess, now, I speak up more. I'll stand up to my dad. A lot of times, you know, if I tell something to my friends, I don't try to hurt their feelings, but if I think they're doing something wrong, I'm going to say so. If it's going to hurt them, I'll tell them, "I'm not trying to hurt you or anything, but you have to look at things from both sides."

∽

For Barbara Smith, empathy makes her able to comfort others in their grief because she knows what she'd want someone to say to her. At the same time, she sees limitations in her ability to do for herself as well as she does for others. Realizing that life is fragile has made her both avoid risks and take them, another sort of balancing act.

Barbara Smith, writer (49, m, 9)

I think that losing my mother made me much more sensitive, in a good way, much more understanding of life and how things work. My age peers are beginning to lose significant people in their lives now, particularly when you look at AIDS. Sometimes people will say to me, "I don't know what to say." I'll say, "Well, call her up." I feel like I know exactly what to say. It's not like it's a little set piece that I spew out, it's that I know what I would want to hear under similar circumstances. When people confide in me, how worried they are about their mothers' or fathers' illnesses, or their imminent death or their actual death, I always tell them I understand. They absolutely believe me because they know that I do.

I've often been complimented by people who I'm close to about how well I am able to take care of others. I'm trying to do as well for myself. My mother's dying made me strong, I guess. It's like, if I can get through that, I can get through anything. But I am a physical coward, I don't take undue risks. One of the reasons is that I know you can die. After a certain point, I never had this illusion that I could do anything and survive, although many people would say that I've taken incredible risks, of other kinds, particularly because of being a political activist, of being a radical.

There is a frustration in Lauren Muller's words, almost a desire to just let go of the story of her father's death, and implicit frustration in her statement.

Lauren Muller, writer (34, f, 11)

I've actually told the story of my father's death, or written it many times. I'd like to create other stories, or let other stories in and let go of this one. But I keep coming back to it. I take everything so seriously, or I did for a long time. And that might be another effect of his early death. It might have been my personality always, but also after his death, it seems I took everything so seriously. I think my need to take on life is connected to my father's death. I think being touched by death made me more open to life, made me want to take it on more fully. Because you touch something that's in the marrow. You cut through a lot of superficiality and are more sensitive to things.

Taking Care of Ourselves

Several people talked particularly about their efforts to take care of themselves, especially at crisis times in their lives, and in ways their dead parents may not have taken care of themselves.

Jessica (24, m, 16)

When I was bulimic, I checked myself into the hospital because here I was given the chance to go away to this wonderful college. And I realized that if I was going to go I had to be healthy. I had to do it for myself, not to please my grandparents, or anybody else, because my decision to go to school didn't please anybody in my family. I had to be healthy to be the good person who could cultivate inner strength and then give what I learned from that to other people, and to myself. That was a big realization for me. I also realized once I was at college that, although I wanted to be like my mom and live the life or give her the life that she never had by doing it for her, that I should do it for myself and do the things that make me happy.

Edward speaks for several of our interviewees, who, as they moved into the next stage of adulthood, began to take care of themselves in ways their parents had not. Edward's aim is to live longer by maintaining a more healthy lifestyle. But talking about his father's physical lifestyle led Edward to speculate on how taking care of himself on an emotional level, especially in not being like his father, is perhaps not so black and white as he thought it was when he was younger.

Edward (30, f, 17)

I've started exercising a lot. A lot of that has to do with turning thirty, but a lot of it has to do with my dad being overweight and pretty fucked up physically when he was in his fifties, and I think I don't want to be like that. He's almost an example of what I don't want to be when I'm that age. I'm just guessing this, but I think he never came to terms with the divorce, never came to terms with his infidelity, and I think that being unfaithful like that is something that, on some level, he probably could never forgive himself for, and that had something to do with his deterioration. In a way, in the past, I guess it made me a kind of a moralist. Now that I'm older and out in the world, I realize how squirrelly everything is, how gray areas are the only areas there are. I guess I tend to be more forgiving now.

Despite efforts to take care of ourselves, there is the frustration of things we can't control and no guarantees.

Detta (47, m, 17)

I'm fearful of things that I can't control. I'm scared of cancer. I'm religious about getting Pap smears, and having mammograms, and having stuff checked out. I had a mammogram a couple of years ago, and they called me back from Ultrasound, and I had a weekend of, "Oh, I don't want to die. I don't want to die like my mother."

Rob (44, f, 15)

I think I really did worry about dying young, because my father did. It wasn't a real conscious kind of thought. But I know that my lifestyle is a lot different than his. He drank coffee around the clock. He ate a lot of red meat. His diet was awful. And he had these raging headaches much of his life. I exercise a lot. I don't drink. I drink a cup of coffee or two a day. I eat mostly real good. I get a massage every other week. I try to take care of myself.

Gender and Sexuality

Gender identification, our roles in society, and our sexuality are complex and multifaceted. When we asked people to talk about what effect their parent's death had on their becoming a man or a woman, we got a broad range of responses. This section looks at how people view their gender in relationship to their parent's death. But it also looks at issues of how, in turn, their gender and sexuality affect their power and effectiveness. It's all tied together.

Marc (39, f, 10)

This is something I'm still coming to grips with, in understanding gender identity, and understanding sexuality. In some strange way, I feel that my father was able to give me a good sense of who I was as a male. I'm not sure how. But I feel that he did. It was a big struggle for me, as it is for any adolescent to deal with these issues, and especially without a father both as a guide and as a model. But somehow

I feel that he modeled it for me as a child, and that model was strong enough to do its job when I needed it.

∽

In this part of the interview, Rob talked about his difficulty, from college age on until almost the present, with finding male role models and mentors. He said he kept choosing people who failed him at some level, as his father did.

Rob (44, f, 15)

It's still real difficult for me to be trusting of men who are older than me. Now men my own age, and younger, I don't seem to have that problem. But what's a man supposed to be? Is a man supposed to be somebody who is unfeeling? I don't remember ever seeing my father cry. Is a man supposed to be tough? What is masculinity? How do you know if you measure up or not? I know all those kinds of questions affected that, and certainly I didn't have any way to ask.

∽

Eric Marcus talked about the strange advantage of not having a father when he was coming out. And, unlike so many of his male friends, he does not have to struggle to live up to expectations based on who his father was and what he accomplished.

Eric Marcus, writer (36, f, 12)

I thought one of the advantages of having a dead father was that I would never have to come out to him. I had many friends who struggled with how they would deal with their fathers. And I never had to deal with a father. It wasn't a worry. On the flip side, I never had my father's support, and I'm assuming I would have in the end and he would've been very proud of me. But it wasn't a worry. I joked about it: "I'm lucky I haven't got a father to deal with." I have friends like one whose father is a very powerful man, very successful. He feels he lives in the shadow of his father. In a sense, I've never had to live in the shadow of anybody.

Tim (35, f, 17)

I think that my father's death made me become a man much quicker than I probably would have, being thrown into being the man of the house, taking care of my mother. All of a sudden, I realized that there's not just doing drugs and drinking and whatever. It steered me in the right direction. Strange to say, it probably was a good thing. I'm sure that, at the time, he really questioned what I was going to be like when I grew up because of who I was at that time that he died. I would really like to show him, just in general, how it turned out, as far as work that I've accomplished, and taking care of my mother.

Deborah H. had her mother's love and support in early childhood, but her mother's suicide separated her from her identity as a woman for a while. Ultimately, grappling with the effects of her mother's death gave her the courage to form intimate relationships, to come out as a lesbian, and to forge a personally felt feminism.

Deborah H. (45, m, 16)

I was pretty male-identified. I think that had to do with my mother not surviving and my father surviving. I think I felt a powerful need not be her, so it also meant separation from my own identity as a woman. But it didn't hit me at the time, at sixteen when my mother died, that this had anything to do with her being a woman. On a psychological level, I think my feminism had fundamentally to do with coming home to myself as a girl/woman and to my mother as a woman and not being scared to connect again with myself as a woman and with other women. I think that finding my own voice and courage from what I dealt with due to the loss of my mother had to do with my being brave enough to come out. It was no accident that I got myself into therapy at twenty-four, that I came out at twenty-four, that I had finally taken in the emotional side of the feminist stuff that I had been involved with for two years.

But Deborah H. reiterated that there were advantages to being male-identified. She got along well with her father and learned from him.

Both Deborah H. and Edward raise the idea that there may be some good fallout from losing the parent of the same gender. Edward had his mother as a primary role model, and even while he pokes a bit of fun at himself for assigning certain characteristics as female or male, he points out the advantages of being able to define for himself what it means to be a man, without any expectations from a demanding father.

Edward (30, f, 17)

I sort of like the way I turned out, so I don't want to go back and meddle with my past. In a way, I feel like it's nice to have the chance at this point to define for myself what it means to be male, rather than having this inherited definition that I have to grapple with. My brother, when we were a lot younger, used to tease me by calling me a "feelings" kid, and it used to bug me. It was when that horrible song "Feelings" was popular, and he used to sing that to me to get my goat. I think, in a sense, I got that from this bond that I have with my mom, which otherwise might not have been there. Now I'm falling into the trap of spewing out masculine stereotypes: men are more intellectual, they're more rational, women are intuitive, women are flighty, women have this sixth sense that men don't have. But those things, for better or worse, intuitiveness and whatnot, have been labeled feminine. I think that my father's death probably led me to connect with my feminine side, more so than I would have otherwise.

∽

Gloria Anzaldúa, Diana O'Hehir, Jane, and Patricia all talk in different ways about how the death of their parent allowed them to see various aspects of strength in women and to incorporate those strengths into their own lives.

At the time of her father's death, Gloria Anzaldúa discovered a power women held that she hadn't recognized before, that had for her an almost supernatural element.

Gloria Anzaldúa, poet and writer (52, f, 14)

When my father died, the women who came to the wake would cry and say the rosary and they would have these masses. This was a time when I think the women and their grief somehow became stronger than the men, because the men couldn't cry, the men couldn't express grief. (My father's family, sisters *and* brothers cried, but I'm talking about generally.) Before, in my eyes, they had just been these women who were oppressed because of their gender, oppressed because they were underclass, working-class, farmworkers, because they didn't have an education, because they were poor. All of a sudden, I realized they had a voice. I realized that's where their realm is, the realm of the dead.

When my father died, I felt like the earth was opening up, that some kind of rupture was happening between this real life I was living and this opening to a kind of reality that was otherworldly, that I was very scared of. It was sort of like when you're driving down the highway and it's very hot in South Texas, and everything shimmers. Before my father died, the sights, the house, the way that I looked at things had been very etched and precise. After he died, things took on that shimmering quality. I felt the life I was living was an illusion.

As a child, I had been threatened with La Llorona, the Weeping Woman. If I wasn't a good little *chicanita,* this terrible ghost who had killed her children would come and take me away. So here were all these women wailing at this wake, and here was this event that had ruptured my reality. So I started making all these ties between the women who were howling, La Llorona, my father's death, and this rupture into the other world. That's when I think I started putting together the fact that women were not quite as weak as they seemed, and that, even though they seemed to be obeying the husband and the father, they were really operating on this other level. In a way, my father did me a favor by dying. If I had not lost my father, I think I either would have rebelled against him completely, which is painful for me to consider, or I would have been a more traditional Chicana.

∽

Diana O'Hehir credits the mother she barely knew with leaving her the feeling of being especially loved. During the interview, she recounts how a therapist pointed out to her that even though she was in crisis—fighting cancer, getting a divorce—she was able to manage, partly because she had strong early mothering.

Diana O'Hehir, novelist and poet (72, m, 4)

In relation to my mother, I do feel a kind of certainty that she loved me and a certainty that I can do things. I have some of the letters that she wrote when I was a new baby; they're very filled with love. My feeling is that, through it all, I have had a kind of strength that I think came from good parenting at a very early age. It had to have been very early. I think I'm more open, more empathetic. I am afraid of separation, but otherwise I'm not afraid. Also, I think I am sympathetic to other women, and that perhaps came from my great need for mother figures in my youth. I was a very popular teacher at Mills, an all-women's college, because I was always interested in what the student had to say about herself, and so I had a long line in front of my door of people who wanted to confide their troubles to me. It's possible that my relationship with my students has been good in a special way, because I understand the need to relate to an older woman.

༄

The death of Jane's father meant that her mother changed, in a way that encouraged Jane to assume more independence as a woman.

Jane (30, f, 17)

I wasn't thrust into adulthood. If anything, I was probably too sheltered. And maybe my dad's death, in some small way, helped me to wake up and see what the world is, what the world could offer. After he died, my mom went back to work and became sort of an independent woman. It helped me to see her do that. I moved up to the cities by myself, and I wouldn't have done that if he was still alive.

Patricia (48, f, 13)

I think my father's death is the single shaping event of my entire life. It happened at the same moment that I was changing from childhood to adult. So it's hard to separate, in some sort of objective way, to understand how that piece of time cracked right down the center, between childhood and adulthood. It's like opening an egg. My life hasn't ever seemed ordinary to me. It's always seemed different from everybody else's. And some of the time I thought my life hasn't been what it was supposed to be, in terms of the culture that says women should do and become and have. I never had children. I didn't marry until I was over forty-five. It made me very self-reliant emotionally. I've gone against the grain, mostly, not that I meant to. It's just that certain circumstances happened, I think.

Teresa (32, f, 8)

I wonder if the way that I relate to men, or deal with men, is connected to the kind of relationship that I had with my father. I have a friend who says you make the family that you don't have. And throughout my life, I've had many, many male mentors, and lots of big brothers. I'm wondering if that's something that in some way I attract. Men will do things for me the way a father would, which is very different from the way a lover would. I do think it has to be something about my demeanor, which is probably more reserved, a more "look how smart I am" as opposed to a "look how cute I am" demeanor.

I think because my dad never said no to me and thought I was endlessly fascinating—or at least that's my memory—I don't have a lot of real terror about men. I say what I want to say, and it wasn't until pretty late in life that I started to realize that other women don't do that. It's really only been since I've started my professional life that I've become conscious of the fact that there could be consequences for speaking your mind. So I'm starting to wake up to "Maybe I should show more deference." But I never learned that. And so it's kind of too late.

I'm wondering how a girl learns to relate to a man in a more overtly sexual way. I think that's probably a tension you deal with when you hit adolescence, getting to deal with your dad being jealous and all that kind of stuff. Some of that affects the way that you go on to deal with men. And I didn't have any of that happen. I had a father who, for the time that he was there, was very open to whatever I wanted, which is a good thing. I might've learned more rules later, as more time went on. It's like the lesson stopped, and maybe it stopped at a good point because I didn't learn a lot of the restricting, diminishing ways of being female.

Culture, Identity, and Politics

Sometimes early loss affects how we view cultural and historical events. We find affinities between our personal tragedies and larger political tragedies.

Relating her own personal loss to the losses of her people, Gloria Anzaldúa is working at restoring some of her culture's history.

Gloria Anzaldúa, poet and writer (52, f, 14)

One of the things I'm trying to do in my writings is to kind of recuperate the Chicano experience by going back into indigenous history and into Spanish history. Mexico sold us to the United States. I always believed that unconsciously Chicanos feel we were abandoned by Mexico. Then we were abandoned by the U.S., by the gringo, because the gringo didn't honor his commitment to us in terms of the language and in terms of the land, and we lost everything. So there is this thing about recuperating and restoring, and what I've been trying to write about is this loss and this mourning that comes not just from personal experience and personal loss, but from the loss that goes back to the Aztec times when La Llorona was heard in Mexico mourning the loss of her children. It was an omen of the coming of the Spaniards. So maybe the coming of the Spaniards was the first loss, and the second loss was the U.S. manipulating Mexico into selling half of its territory and the U.S. turning its back on the Chicanos and the natives and the blacks. Then there was the loss of my father's death and repeated losses as I moved away from the culture. I keep losing it, so that all the writing's about transfiguring these people that I lost, and also recuperating and restoring what was lost. I think this is what Chicanos write about. So the thing about being an orphan comes from way back.

∽

Like Anzaldúa, Ken Burns makes the connection between personal and political tragedy. His films explore the tragedy of racism even when they're not explicitly about that subject. He links his mother's struggle against cancer with the African-American struggle for civil rights, partly because he was watching the violent events of the civil rights movement on television as his mother was dying. When we suffer an early loss, it can be that much more difficult to be aloof or sanguine in the face of others' pain. So, too, the need for family and community has become an important theme in his work.

Ken Burns, filmmaker (41, m, 11)

When I saw Rodney King being beaten, I cried like a baby. I had already realized that my childhood stomachaches had started during the time I was listening to the civil rights stuff, the dogs in Selma, the fire hoses and things like that. So race has become a symbol for me in my work. I've gone from the Civil War to baseball, and now talking about jazz, and doing something on Thomas Jefferson. Also, another incredibly powerful theme in all of my work is this notion of trying to keep family, however you understand that, together. Community. Country. The Civil War is the great traumatic event in the childhood of our nation. It is when we lost 2 percent of ourselves to death, over an issue that continues to bedevil us. It's all connected to my childhood fears of separation. The stomachaches that kept me home. The dreams that we'd be bombed and I wouldn't be able to get back home.

Joe's personal identification with the pain of other people's stories informs his understanding of the world around him and enables him to identify with others on a broader level.

Joe (28, m, 12)

I've always noticed that a lot of people that I've become close to— and it's not a conscious choosing—have been people who had either divorced parents or have lost a parent or so forth. I think that definitely has an effect on sort of feeling like the odds were against me, and that brought out an interest in looking at other people who had different odds against them and what can we do about it. At times, even when I was younger, I had almost a desire to be part of African-American culture, musically and in many ways.

∽

The circumstances of Irena Klepfisz's father's death in the Warsaw Ghetto uprising permeate her views of culture and identity. His life and death have influenced her attempt to reach some kind of balance between the personal and the political in her own life.

Irena Klepfisz, poet and writer (54, f, 2)

It's not easy to be the wife or the child of a martyr. My mother must have felt it in her own way, and I don't want to speak for her, but I certainly have felt, sometimes, like my father abandoned us, that when he came to a choice he didn't choose us. What did it mean for him to go back to the Warsaw Ghetto and to leave a child and a wife on the other side? Was my father really a suicide in that sense, and what did that mean about him? He did make a decision he had to go back; he was in charge of all the ammunition in the ghetto. I could see why he probably couldn't live with himself if he didn't go back. At that point, his sister was dead; his parents had been killed in Treblinka. So it must have been also enormous rage and frustration at passivity. And at the same time, having a wife and a child, it wasn't simple.

I have to say, as I've gotten older, and I've gotten involved in my own political work and my own passions—not that it's anything remotely equal to the kind of decisions he had to make—I can see how sometimes you pick the thing that seems less personal and private. Your partner at home is in a rage, and you're just saying, "Well, I'm going out, I'm going to do it." No matter what damage it does at home, I can see how people are driven.

My biggest struggle was not to live in the past and not to live with the uprising and not to live in the war, but to live now. There were times when I experienced such enormous despair about ever getting into the present. It's hard to stay in the present. I think most of us live in the past and in the future and sort of forget about what's going on now. I think becoming active in my thirties was a way of entering the present. And it was very important that initially my issues, even the lesbian issues, were not connected with Jewish things. It's not that I ever went through self-hate or denial. I wanted to do something on my own that distinguished me in some sense from my father. At the same time, the message all my life was that I was somehow his heir. And the legacy *is* one that I really want to keep. I feel like it's mine and I want to try to pass it on to other people.

Spirituality

Coming to terms with death sent many, but not all, of the people we talked with on spiritual quests that led down various roads: away from childhood religion, and sometimes right back to it. Some replaced early religious training with a spiritual or religious practice they consciously sought out in an effort to make sense of or make peace with their parent's death.

Beto (52, m, 14)

I think ever since my mother died, I just did not consider myself a Catholic, and I didn't even think I was a Christian. And then I went to Nicaragua about ten years ago and found out that I'd always been a Catholic, and I'd always been a Christian. But it was a different Catholicism than I grew up with. The pope and the ceremonies and all the dogma were relatively irrelevant to that process. It's much more ecumenical. It's liberation theology. There's a line in liberation theology that the poor are closer to humanity. And I've always found it to be true. I came to that conclusion a long, long time ago, so when I saw a church that was living those principles and actively talking that way, I just fit right in. It fit my entire system of beliefs, so now I consider myself a Catholic. But the pope has nothing to do with it. I do have a Christian perspective, but it's a very different way than most people use the word. It's ecumenical and leaves a good deal of room for other beliefs. I'm also lately getting into indigenous religions. It's just really interesting to me that the Athabascans in the North Pole have the same basic religious principles as the Mapuches in the south. Really, it just blows me away. I just found out about a tribe in Borneo— being completely ruined by mining and oil drilling— who believe that the land doesn't belong to them, they belong to the land. So the responsibility goes to the land. That's exactly what the Athabascans, the Sioux, the Navajo, the Yaquis, the Mayans believe. And these people live in Borneo.

In thinking about my mother's death, I guess I'd say that death is a great leveler. Maybe part of my respect for the people, the poor, especially humbler people, I can attribute to that. I think it's a sense of what's important. All I know is that my mother's death affected me profoundly, but I don't think I've been able to articulate how profoundly it did affect me. But again it's just something that happens.

Doreen (36, m, 10)

I keep an altar in the bedroom now. That's my spot. I've been really talking to the ancestors in the last few years. I've been asking for ancestral help, and I've been getting some very interesting things in dreams, information from those who've come before me.

Walter Liggett, poet (70, f, 11)

Soon after moving to Brooklyn, following our father's murder, my sister Marda and I began attending a Lutheran church. I sort of accepted it in a shallow way, then I became an agnostic, never quite an atheist. In 1955, I became a Unitarian, and then I joined the Baha'i faith in 1959. I've remained a Baha'i ever since then. Some Unitarians believe in God, but it's optional. I had to go beyond that.

Nan (79, m, 13)

I got mad at God when my mother died, and then I got mad at him again when he took my husband. I think that's a part of the grieving process. But I have to say that a big thing in my life has been my faith. I feel like I'm lost without it. I don't know how people don't live with some sort of spiritual guidance. I think I have felt strong spiritually because of my mother and the influence that we grew up under.

Teresa (32, f, 8)

To what degree did being Catholic help? The whole thing of one day you will see this person again, you know, the belief in angels, all that sort of thing? Those things do help. The sense that dead people are out there watching you or nearby. This sense of having a sort of ongoing conversation with a dead person, that's something I suspect I got from being Catholic. It has actually been a helpful thing. You *do* learn a lot of stuff about endurance, and you're sent these challenges, and you have to find a way to live with these challenges. We were sort of living in the shadow of Kennedy, and the Kennedys being assassinated, and also Martin Luther King, Jr. I remember a couple of different nuns saying, "You should look to their example." We had this sort of reputation or aura or whatever of being the stoic, noble Hopper children. It wasn't until my brother Sam died that my sister Elizabeth and I admitted to each other we'd felt that we had to be strong and noble and put a good face on things growing up and were sick of it.

My parents converted to Catholicism, so we didn't have years of being Catholic, and years of understanding of what being a Catholic is about. I do think that to a large degree I was making up my own interpretations for a lot, like the lives of the saints, all the martyrs, feeling persecuted and feeling like an outsider or having a horrible weight to bear, feeling alone. That was stuff that I really internalized, and I really had the strong sense of "If I can survive this, this is a good thing, and I have other models for surviving this kind of thing."

Kristy (25, f, 13)

I remember reading Kahlil Gibran and really getting into Krishnamurti. I think I was fifteen. At that time, I really dug deep, and there was a lot of sadness. I definitely think my father's death has affected my life, because when I get into situations I tend to get pretty deep in them, whatever I'm doing, especially if I'm passionate about it. I know that when I feel so happy I feel so sad, too. But when I'm in the moment, I'm always okay, no matter what's going on. The image that's been coming up a lot for me is just digging. Part of that has to do with it getting deeper and deeper. My father's death has given me a lot of insight. I think I focus a lot on death, and what does death mean. With death, there has to be life. It's letting go. Where death means an ending of something, there's always something new.

Melissa (28, m, 9, f, 9)

I see the world as undergoing constant change. One of the things that helped me with my foster parent's born-again religion of fire and brimstone—because I felt really guilty all the time—was the idea that the end of the world happens every single moment. Every single moment somebody's world is ended, and a new world is being created. I take that so much to heart because my world really did end when my parents died. It was completely over. Talk about Armageddon—it was the apocalypse. But, if we look at the apocalypse as continuing change, it's happening at every moment. And somebody's dying in every moment, so their end is happening. So when really huge things come up in the news, it's always the apocalypse. We're building up to an end that's happening right now.

∽

Barbara Smith reflects on how an early religious life can affect an ongoing ethical way of living. Even when we make different choices than our families might expect, those choices can be based on early religious training.

Barbara Smith, writer (49, m, 9)

I would want to show my mother that I have tried to live, to the degree that it is possible in a political context like this one, as ethical a life as I possibly could. I feel that those values that I put in a category called church or religion I was taught at home. I always feel so good now when friends of mine compliment me on my ethics. I would want her to know, despite the fact that I made different choices than anybody in my family could *ever* have predicted or expected, that the core stuff about how you treat people, and what is absolutely right and wrong, I've stuck to.

∽

The spiritual realm allows Kelly to have an ongoing relationship with the mother she never knew in life.

Kelly (43, m, birth)

I probably have constructed my spiritual outlook around the fact of my mother's death and the relationship that I've developed with her spiritually. I believe that our spirit continues after death, because I do feel such a strong connection with my mother, and that the knowledge of her has come to me in such a timely way, that it seems more than coincidental. I feel that there is a spiritual source of energy that animated the human being that was my mother. When she died, that didn't dissipate. Perhaps it lost its physical limits and flowed into new channels. I feel like I have access to that source of energy. Whenever I experience meaningful coincidence in my life, I suspect my mother's hand in it.

∽

In Chapter 6, "The Floating Bridge," Horace Silver told of times when he has felt his mother's presence. Although he doesn't refer to that experience here, that kind of natural incorporation of the physical with the metaphysical permeates both his music and his spiritual outlook.

Horace Silver, musician (66, m, 9)

I don't belong to any one religious group. I dabble. I'm a student of metaphysics. I've read a lot of metaphysical literature, and I take out of it what I can use and the rest I leave behind. So, in a sense, I make my religion. In terms of religions, I'm a conglomerator. I do that with my music, too. I'm a jazz musician, and proud to be, and I always will be. My influences, in terms of my playing and my writing, basically stem from other jazz players, but I keep an open mind because I like classical music and if it's something I can borrow, I'll try to borrow it. I listen to folk music. I love Broadway theater music. I listen sometimes to American Indian music, East Indian music, African music. I've borrowed little tidbits here and there from some of those types of music, and put them into *my* music. So I don't like to pigeonhole myself into one little slot. And that goes with my religious philosophies, too. You know, I was impressed with Thoreau. I read *Walden Pond*, and I came to realize that that's the way he formed his religious beliefs, too. He didn't belong to any religious group. He studied a lot of different religions. He took from that, and he put it all together, and made a philosophy of his own. And then he lived by that. And that's what I do. I take what I can get from here and there and put things together, and I try to live by that.

Suzanne Lipsett, writer (51, m, 4)

I see the world full of random events that can get you at any time. I'm very fatalistic that way. I don't have much of a God these days. I'm softening to it, though. I mean you have to think about these things with cancer. I believe that everything passes and that there's a greater beauty that everything gets swallowed into. I think that is a spiritual resource that I can retreat into and get comfort from. So just that confidence is deepening. The more scary or the more threatening my own life becomes to me—I've had three horrible cancer episodes now, and right now it's touch and go—I know that I'm blessed with this confidence that just the beauty of the landscape endures, people go through the Holocaust and they come out the other side and they have lives and they have, some of them anyway, the capacity for joy sometimes. Things pass.

Attitude Toward Death

As grown-up orphans, if we know one thing, we know death is inevitable. At different times in our lives, we experience the inevitability differently. For some, the struggle with mortality is about the parent's death, while for others it's the fear of one's own death or the death of loved ones.

Tim (35, f, 17)

Dying scares me, there's no question about that. I want to live and see my kids grow up and go off to college. I think it's really again because of the elephant-in-the-living-room kind of thing that for me death was something you *had* to talk about and doing so made me accept it more and made me more aware of what death is and how life goes on after death and the things you need to do. I think about dying young a lot, not just thinking about getting older, but about having the baby at around the same age my dad was when I was born. It's tough because you don't know what to expect. I'm thirty-five years old and my dad died seventeen years from now, and it's just amazing that those thoughts are not ever going away.

Paul B. (53, m, 11)

After my mother died, I thought that it was some kind of message from God that I was a bad little boy, and I fell under the spell of my father's kind of fundamental religion, and really struggled a lot with guilt and sin and those kinds of issues for a long time. But her death has always kept me thinking about death, and in recent years it's helped guide me into more of a spiritual perception about life, the life cycle, and life and death. Her death was an ending that created great pain, and, yet, over the long haul, the journey helped me be empathetic to the suffering of others. It's helped me confront death. And I've given up the fundamental religious kind of sin-and-guilt stuff, and feel pretty good about it. I can see now how the long-range effect of her death has been ultimately positive for me.

How a parent dies inevitably will affect some parts of how we think about life and death. There is no doubt that suicide carries a complicating charge.

Deborah H. (45, m, 16)

I think the fact that my mother's death was a suicide, and all of the figuring out I had to do about why she chose to end it, has had a very, very long-term and profound effect on me, in terms of everything from philosophically how I think about life and what it means to me to how I feel about other people's choices to rationally choose to end their life, and probably most vividly, how I approach all the ethical choices that come up in my work doing oncology and AIDS nursing. I feel like I have some added chapters in my life of having worked so hard and long to unravel what I think of as life's mysteries. I don't have any more answers than anybody else does. I just feel like I've been at it longer than most.

Wendy (27, f, 16)

I tend to have more suicidal tendencies than I care to think about. I don't know if I have suicidal tendencies because it's a genetic thing or because it's an easy out like my father took. I worry a lot about it because I can feel a pull in that direction. I've gone to therapy because of it, because it's just gotten to the point where it's a stronger pull than anything else. It has overwhelmed me at times.

Irena Klepfisz, poet and writer (54, f, 2)

What I'm focused on now is the total bewilderment of being in my fifties. I used to worry that I wouldn't live past thirty. Now I wonder what my old age is going to look like. I had always assumed I would die violently in a war, that I would die as a result of somebody wanting to kill me. It never dawned on me I could possibly die of old age. I've been caught totally unprepared for this moment. Everybody who has died in my life has died violently. My close friend committed suicide. I've been thinking an enormous amount about death, and it's not in the same way that I thought about it for decades. It's not about war. It's not about violence. It's about what does it mean for your body to age? What does it mean to not feel anymore who you are, not recognize yourself in the mirror? It's a very different sense of death than I ever had.

Jamie (45, m, 19)

I guess I have always felt that there has to be some part of us that's more than the part that we walk around in, and I've always had the sense that if I found a place of stillness, then I could at least feel some communion with my sense of my mother, that there has to be on some spiritual level a connection that never goes away. I can't say that

I'm not afraid of death, and I can't say that I understand it, and I don't think that I'm prepared for people to die. It's still the great mystery, but it's not this completely unknown thing.

Emilia (62, f, 12)

Death is just like being born. It comes when God wants you. I accept death. If somebody dies, it's time for them to go.

Gloria Anzaldúa, poet and writer (52, f, 14)

I began to see my father's death was just a cycle of life, and I got more into trying to puzzle out my relationship to death and "What was death?" What did it mean? Was it a stage to something else? Was it the final stage? Was it just a thin barrier that you crossed over and there my father would be? Was it a continuation of life? Was death the mutating of the body? I did all that. Then it was okay that he died, but it was awhile. I had to read a lot of philosophy and do a lot of writing before I could come to that.

Suzanne Lipsett, writer (51, m, 4)

This whole thing of "She's dead so she doesn't exist and that's over now" is just wrong, because people live in memory. I think it's kind of a technicality that you're alive or dead. Maybe that's just my hysteria. I think there is an element of hysteria in my writing to make a mark for my children, knowing that the cancer that I have is just advancing. I know that my best self is in my books, so if they read them, I'll be available to them.

Brown Miller, poet (51, m, 6)

When I started writing poetry, so many of the poems contained the word "death" and were about death, not necessarily my mother's death, but just kind of death in general. The main thing that I am proud of writing, a book about the bombing of Hiroshima, I picked partly because it involved a lot of people dying at one time. That book includes a lot of poems about my mother. I certainly picked Hiroshima because it had political significance. I immediately began to integrate that with my memories of my mother and things about my mother. My mother's death caused me to see the world as vulnerable, as very fragile. Of course, there's that thing about mother and Mother Earth. I look at environmental concerns and think, "If the Earth is our mother, well, it's really important to me to not risk the life of that mother." I've already lost one mother. In a sense, maybe you might say the human species is no more than about six years old, or a very young child, and we could lose our mother way before we're mature. The human species right now is not mature, or just barely. We're like a little kid playing with big weapons and toxic waste and all. Probably, if I sat down and read through everything I've written, I could find lots of examples of that theme.

Daniel Meyers, filmmaker (34, f, 18)

In Pompeii, I saw a dog and people frozen two thousand years ago and I thought, "My God, this is death, forever frozen, this is real life, this pain." You're dead forever and you'll never come back in any form. Over the years, I had these panics. In the middle of the night, I would jump up with this fear that I was going to die. Then one evening I went with a friend to an audience-participation play. The actor showed us the world of death. Later my friend asked me, "What are your images of death?"

I said: "Well, it's forever, and you'll never come back. And my father went through pain in those last moments, his gasps, blood trickling down his cheek, slowly breathing, fading away, his body becoming nothing but body, no spirit, the chemistry no longer working. Pretty gruesome." She asked me if I had any good associations. I told her that when I have trouble sleeping, I think to myself, "When I'm dying, I'll sleep very well. There's something that's calm about it, relaxing." She said, "Try to visualize those things before you go to sleep."

So I went to sleep. It didn't work. But the next night, after looking at a book about Pompeii, I tried it again. I dreamed that a group of people and I were being taken on a journey by this guide. We were all excited and cheerful. Then we all got silent, because we realized there was this trapdoor to the otherworld. We were going through to the other side, the world of death. But we weren't afraid, because we were just visiting. The guide opened the door and we walked down this staircase into several rooms, all white, with columns and arches like Pompeii. The air was like liquid. I realized I could float in it. I kind of kicked up my feet and levitated. Then I swam and glided and coasted through the air of these chambers, and other people started doing the same. It was so beautiful and so calm, and we all felt so at peace.

When the time was finished, we quietly filed out through the doorway, back up to the staircase, out the trapdoor. We were transformed. I was one of the last three people, and we stopped and said, "It's so lovely down there, let's go back and enjoy it for a little more time." The other two people filed down. I was about to go down, too, but the trapdoor had shrunk, and I couldn't get through. I was disappointed because they were swimming around and enjoying it. I figured I couldn't go back upstairs, because somebody might come by and accidentally close the door and they'd be trapped down there. So I had to wait and kind of guard the door until they were finished and came back up. Then I woke up and took the scenes of this dream in, image by image. It was very simple. I realized, then and there, that I no longer was afraid of my own death. It is what it is, it will be when it comes, and I will feel free. I'll just breathe slowly and relax and expire.

David Joseph, poet (40, m, 14)

I think when a parent dies when you're young you may have a consciousness about death in the sense that anyone can be taken away from you at any time. In combination with another experience from my very earliest days, I have a certain view of death. When I was about four, we went to the beach. After my father got tired of playing with me, I got caught in the surf and I got carried out into the water. I was just turning any which way, with no idea of what direction was what, completely surrounded by water and surf. I had this picture of myself as being unplugged or something. It was like things running out, and then the picture just shuts off. The next thing I knew was that I was getting revived on the beach. My father had gone in the surf, swum, got me back out, given me mouth-to-mouth resuscitation, and saved my life. As a consequence of that and my mother dying, I always have a sense of death, of my own or anybody else's, as being maybe about five minutes away. I think that people who nearly died when they were very young have a very different sense about life. I have a preoccupation with it as a theme in writing, and maybe less of a fear of death, and maybe less of a fear of life.

Horace Silver, musician (66, m, 9)

I have no fear of death. Nothing dies but your body. Your spirit and mind go on. The body is a vehicle. The real person is the spirit and the mind. The body is only an instrument, which you occupy on this earth plane to experience life and learn your lessons here. A lot of people make the mistake, they get so wrapped up in materiality, that they look on the body as being themselves. I am not this body that I'm in. This is just a vehicle that I'm using. But I am my spirit and my mind is me, in this body. So when this body dies, my spirit and my mind are eternal, they'll never die. Death is only a door to a new life. We don't prepare anybody for dying. We should teach them about death. Then they won't fear it. We all need to learn more about the death process.

Doreen (36, m, 10)

I think people who lose a parent early are kind of lucky, in a weird way. We're lucky that we've gotten a chance to have that crisis happen early. As I've looked at other peers of mine who have not experienced a close death, I see a certain immaturity. I know that I've already dealt with death. I don't fear my own death. I know it's better than life. I know that what comes after is really something amazing.

Continuing Legacies

Doreen's idea that we are lucky takes us from looking at attitudes toward death to considering what gifts we received from our parents, in their lives and in their early deaths. After all, we are lucky, in a way. We learned to appreciate what we do have and to find the meaning in loss at an earlier age, and often at a more profound level, than people who did not experience the early death of a parent.

When we asked people to talk about the gifts their parents' lives and deaths had given them, almost no one, even people whose lives as children were a litany of horror and catastrophe, was at a loss for words. Some people described clouds with silver linings, and others talked about being liberated, despite the horror of their parent's early death. The theme of self-reliance, which appeared in the previous chapter, came up again. Earlier in the book, we discussed the tendency in our culture to look at grief as something that will get done, that we'll be over at some point. The Altschul study on bereaved children, for instance, talks about integration. At some point, the theory goes, the child integrates the fact of death into her life and then life goes on. Well, yes and no. The idea that grief is something to be dealt with, that we somehow achieve a state of grief resolved, of integration, implies that grief is a noun. We have chosen the subhead "Continuing Legacies" to describe what we heard from people: that grief is more like a verb or a process.

In the same way, the legacies we inherited from our dead parents are a living process. While our interviewees feel they have received a gift from the parent that they will always have, it's not a trophy or a souvenir to put on the mantelpiece and look at now and then. It's more often a sense of liberation, of the ability to survive, and it will continue to grow and change as we do. These gifts are ongoing. They continue to reveal themselves. If we talked to these people five years from now, they probably would say that the gift is still with them and has manifested in their lives in yet a different way.

Rich (36, m, 14)

I think that I became stronger and more self-reliant, and I also think that it did give me permission to invent myself again. This is something that scares me to say. In a way, my mother's death at that time provided me with a certain opportunity to create myself again. She was the only one I was close with, and when she died, my father and sister just sort of ignored me. If she had been around when I went to high school and started to make friends, I wonder if the sort of clinging part of me would have held me back in some ways.

Laurie (38, m, 13)

We have this little kitten, and our older cat—both of them are fe-male—started bringing in birds and mice and putting them down in front of the little kitten. She was teaching the kitten how to hunt. That's the thing I didn't get by my mother dying when I was so young. But the funny twist is what I have gotten from not having a mother: hunting my own way, and creating my life without having to think about pleasing. Being a lesbian, for example, is relatively easy because I don't have to worry that my parents are going to have a problem with that. In a lot of ways, being an orphan has given me a freedom to create myself.

Doreen (36, m, 10)

My mother's death made me much more of a risk-taker than I ever was going to be. When I was younger, I was crying all the time. At the drop of a pin, girlfriend was Tiny Tears. I was a real good girl. I think it was because my mother was very fearful. That's where she op-erated from a lot of times, especially regarding us. For ten years, she gave me plenty of caution for which I'm grateful. But then I got ten years of my father. He encouraged me to just go do it. That combi-nation gave me the oomph and the ability to go off on my own in a reasonable way. When I left home to go away to college, except for summers, I never lived at home again. And I blossomed outside of that place.

I would have never known my father the way I got to know him. And I guess in a way that's her gift to me, also. He was a really won-derful person, very supportive of me. He allowed me to be who I was. We could talk, we could really get there. You know, by the time my father died about six years ago, he and I had gotten through all our stuff. That's what my mother's death taught me to do. It taught me to say everything I wanted to say when I had to say it, because we don't know—someone can be here one day and gone the next.

∽

Detta's sense of self-reliance comes not so much from being forced to invent herself and rely on herself as from having a vivid image of her mother telling her she couldn't fail.

Detta *(47, m, 17)*

While I don't actually think that my mother is my guardian angel, I think that that's the kind of belief system that allows me to do things, knowing that somewhere along the line, something will keep me from failing fatally. I don't know if that's just optimism, or if that's just knowing that you grew up very well loved. When I think about it, I feel confident enough to do stuff. Under other circumstances, I might say that I am just like every other woman who grew up in my generation, that I lack a certain amount of self-esteem. But the fact is that my mother taught me not to say, "Oh, I don't know how to do anything," but to enumerate what I did know how to do. And she said, "When you just feel really bad, just say to yourself, 'I can cook, I can wash dishes, I can twirl a baton, I can lace up my own shoes.' And she said, you know, "You can do whatever you want."

Detta was older when her mother died and never literally mistook her mother for an angel. Ariel, on the other hand, remembers behaving well because her father could be watching. Detta was more confident, Ariel lost a confidence. It's important to note their age difference at the time of their bereavement, surely a contributing factor.

Ariel *(27, f, 3)*

I probably have a higher moral standard because there was always the possibility that my father could be an angel and that he might be watching me. But, on the more serious side, I think I lost a certain confidence in myself and a sense of stability about the world. When I was a little kid, I used to walk off down the street. I had confidence in the world, but that was destroyed. I'm trying to rebuild that sense of confidence and stability. My father believed in serving people, that it's important to choose something that's not only for yourself but that contributes to the community somehow. I think because of that I'm attempting to make more committed career choices, but that's also connected to a growing confidence in myself. That little girl who walks off is my part of the Camelot myth that I can use as a personal fetish. It enables me to continue to grow towards that sense of confidence.

There was always a sense of magic about the time before my father died. It's funny that as I've made the transformation from a child to an adult, I feel like I'm in the magic again. I think I've taken my history, my legacy, and decided to do something positive with it. It's all I've got. My dad had a sense of adventure, this image of this man and a horse galloping over the horizon. Sometimes I call upon my father's sense of adventure to get me through certain situations.

Eric Marcus, writer (36, f, 12)

My father left quite a legacy, actually two legacies: his high ideals and his suicide, which was not exactly a happy one. But I think I'm using it to the most constructive ends possible. Even if he wound up being disillusioned, I grew up with a man who was very idealistic. He thought the world could be a better place. He was white and had black friends at a time when other people he knew didn't. He wasn't afraid to experiment. He was the kind of brilliant child everyone took credit for until he turned eighteen and developed schizophrenia. And he really couldn't manage anything other than a physical job. He was brilliant. But I never wanted to be brilliant in the way he was. He was somebody who would really give the shirt off his back to help someone, often to a fault. He could help others, but could never help himself. His idealism about the world was admirable. Unfortunately I knew him mostly during his period of disappointment and disillusionment, when he realized the world was not going to be what he wanted it to be.

Deborah Nagle, writer (46, f, 12)

I keep a picture of my father with four other heroes on my bathroom wall: Albert Einstein, Louis Armstrong, Marilyn Monroe, and Benjamin Franklin. My dad, in some ways, remains a romantic figure to me. He was successful early on, as I was. I would say that what my dad gave me was a very real sense that people could make a difference, that ordinary people can make a difference. I recognize my father as a voice that has been extremely useful to me. But I wonder if my dad just checked out because of disappointments. I wouldn't do that. I think it's worth it to endure through a lot of disappointments. I've certainly had moments of despair, but I'm stronger because of seeing my father give up too soon. I think he became brokenhearted and alcoholic because he was disappointed in seeing betrayal and dishonesty in people he worked with. All of this made me turn out to be a tough guy with a sentimental, romantic streak.

William (54, f, 14)

I think a big gift of my father's death was that I think it was sort of character building in a sense, somehow, greatness thrust upon us. Even though I know I've led a fairly charmed life, I would have had it cushier and that sort of thing. It would have been a long time before I was thrust into any kind of responsible position or earned my way up the ladder. I was put into that much sooner than I normally would have been had he lived. I think that was actually useful to me to have the experience.

Teresa (32, f, 8)

On the one hand, you might resent the situation that makes you alone, or it's your occasion for being noble, and so, on the other hand, you do sort of embrace it too. It was horrible that my dad died, but, if anything, there is a certain strength that comes from that. I do think that it's hard not to see yourself as part of something, see yourself as different from people who have both of their parents. It is not unlike being somebody with some kind of disability, and to the degree that you compensate for that, you can link those things, but, if you're young, there are certain things that you can just never know. How much of how I am is how I would have been and how much is because I'm trying to compensate for this thing that's missing in my life? And if you end up stronger in some ways, then maybe it is because of that, but it's hard to know.

Patricia (48, f, 13)

I think I could survive anything. I remember the day of my father's death, and the following evening and the next day. I mean I've written it, I've talked about it, I could probably walk through it on a stage again. I remember those moments because I made decisions then. I think what those twenty-four to forty-eight hours taught me was that I can think through a crisis. I don't have to respond altogether emotionally. I can hold some of that back and use it later, that those feelings don't have to cripple me. My own history was happening and I had a sense of it when it was happening. I can remember when John Kennedy died. I had a great deal of empathy for Jackie Kennedy, because I think she experienced the same thing. She knew history was happening and that she had to do certain things. She had to make decisions. So she looked almost cold, but what it was was a person who could function in a very difficult situation. I think, as I look back at the death retrospectively, I'm proud of myself. When the plane's going down, when other people are screaming "Oh my God!" and being hysterical and carrying on, I can fiddle with the dials. Or say, "Oh the hell with this. I can take it or leave it." But I think, in many ways, I'm not as emotional as I view other people being. And it doesn't upset me. But I do believe that there's a difference. And I would think that that's about pure survival. The instinct for survival is very, very strong.

Sandy (46, f, 16)

I think the early loss made me much more open to people's problems and people's tragedy. I'm aware that life is tragic. Also, I feel I'm stronger. I've been in difficult situations, and then I say to myself, "Look at what you've been through. You will survive. And if you don't survive, that's okay too. It gives you a sense of an ability to endure. I'm a tough bird. I've been through a lot of hard times. And it gave me a kind of strength that I never knew I had. I think my dad's illness and death helped me to learn that lesson about myself.

Ken Burns (41, m, 11)

I think most of all, my mother's greatest gift has been dying. I would not be the person I am if she had lived. It's so hard to say that. But the gifts I have, and, I hope, have been able to share are gifts that have been incubated in the suffering of my mother's death.

Paul J. (28, f, 11)

My father was very aggressive but at the same time very sensitive. And I've sort of emulated those qualities in him. You know, I guess it's the combination of the sports and the poetry. He even wrote a few poems and, additionally, he was very loving towards me. He would always kiss me goodnight, and that's something that my friends' fathers would not necessarily do. And the way I treat my cats and my wife or my future kids, I believe, will be much the same way. Also, when I was a late teen, I started to realize what I had been through in my life, and nothing else seemed unconquerable.

Marc (39, f, 10)

My father had a lot of integrity. He was a very honest man, a very solid man, and those are things that I definitely wanted, and still do want to emulate. I try to hold his character up as exemplary and try to live up to that example. He had a great sense of personal responsibility and social responsibility. Of course, when I was a child, his armor did appear chinkless, and it pretty much was. I don't feel that I have completely lived up to what I consider to be his best characteristics, but it's not been a great source of frustration because, as an adult dealing with the real world and its gray areas, you wonder how chinkless the armor was. You know, you hear a lot about the Great Santini, where there's this man of steel that no one could live up to, and it wasn't like that. I felt that I was relatively realistic about who he was. On the lighter side, my dad was very organized—well, my computer program's organized, but I'm not. I guess he had sort of a gentle sense of humor and teasing that I do have. And I think that he's given me, either through his genes or through his example, not only a sense of humor about the world but also an inquisitive intelligence. He gave me a feeling of perseverance, not quitting, working very hard to get what you want.

Jeffery K. (22, m, 8, f, 18)

About five years ago, I was very deep into rap music. And at a time when there was only gangsta rap, talking about shootings and selling drugs, I was more of a hip-hop evangelist. It was more political rap, and I definitely got that from my dad. His values. His belief system.

Martin Yan, chef, writer, TV personality (43, f, 3)

If I had the opportunity to actually work alongside and learn something and be taken care of by my father, I am quite sure it would be a good experience. I was told that he was a very generous guy and very helpful to other people. If I could talk to my father, I would probably tell him, "Look, I know that through your life and your career you have helped a lot of your relatives and other friends and people that you knew, some of the people that you knew from the village." And basically, it's very admirable. This is the same virtue that I like to carry on. Not only, I should learn from you, but also I would pass the same virtue on to the kids. Or anybody that I know.

Monica (30, m, 10)

You know, I think that we adults who lost our parents when we were kids kind of belong to one unit, one world. We belong to this whole room, and we have something that others don't have. I appreciate people. If somebody gives me something, anything, I don't want to lose it, so I don't. When you lose something so important, you learn to appreciate whatever gifts you are given.

Nan (79, m, 13)

I didn't realize it at that age I was admiring what my mother was doing, but I did. I would stand beside the sewing machine and see how she sewed and basted. Now we pin it and stitch it. Sometimes, when I'd be at the machine sewing—of course hers was a pedal with the foot and mine was electric—I could just see her sitting at the sewing machine doing what I was. I think, so many times, if she was in the car with me now, like I'm going seventy miles an hour, she would die! Yes, I think of her a lot.

Jamie (45, m, 19)

It occurred to me how much my mother had given me and how grateful I was for that. There are so many things I don't even think about, knowing how it's appropriate to dress or how to act in a situation even if you're not quite sure what the situation is. Also, she shared with me her insecurity. She was petrified when she found out she had to do entertaining when she and my father moved to new bases. But she let me know you do whatever you can to get everything ready as best you can, and then once you open the door, concentrate on your guests and hope for the best and *don't apologize*. I was in the kitchen one evening helping her finish up dinner, and she grabbed the wrong spice and threw it into this pot of something that none of us much cared for anyway. She said, "Oh, what have I done?! Oh my god." And then she said, "Don't you tell anybody! It could be a new recipe." I thought, "There's a good attitude." I also think she gave me a very good model of being a person. And I hope that if I were ever ill, she gave me a wonderful model for dealing with being ill. You know, one of my brothers just about started crying one day. We were doing something in the kitchen, and he turned around, he had tears in his eyes, and he said, "You remind me so much of Mom."

Brown Miller, poet (51, m, 6)

I think often just in daily life, if there's a problem, or if I'm trying to help somebody else with a problem, I sometimes very consciously, very deliberately, in my mind, refer myself to my mother's death and her personality. It's funny. The tiny bit of her that I still have access to, through memory, has an exaggerated importance. It has more power than it normally would. I'm sure if she had lived, I probably wouldn't even think about any of these things, or very few of them. But, with her dying so young, they became sort of force fields of inspiration. Even the painful, sad memories help me sometimes to think about a problem, or communicate with somebody who needs help, or at least to understand them. I mean it helps me empathize with people.

I have this visual image in my mind right now of a person holding some glowing marbles, or little gems, in his or her hand, and those are my memories. These little glowing gems. And you can reach down into your pocket and touch them, or even get them out and look at them sometimes and say, "This will give me power to go on. Or this will give me some sort of hint as to how to deal with this situation that's giving me a hard time."

One of the things I'm in love with as a writer is paradox and ironic kinds of things, and I think my mother's death kind of made me, at an early age, think in convoluted terms. So I like riddles and paradoxes. I probably would have anyway, but I think maybe having my mother die at an early age reinforced that or invigorated that sense of paradox.

Lawrence (35, m, 2, f, 16)

I'm trying to get more of the family together now. I try to do this once a month, to either get together or at least talk on the phone. I need to pass on what my mom gave to my oldest sister and what she gave to me. My goal is to try to get myself together so I *can* reach out to help my family. We need to forget about our differences and just come to the table and love each other. That's what my mom and sister would have wanted.

∽

At eighty-seven, Rose is the oldest of the people we talked with. She offers the wisdom of many years passing: the surety that you never forget, and that you do learn and change. We give her the last word.

Rose (87, m, 13)

I didn't idolize my mother. I did not raise a statue. I loved her. In some ways, I wanted to be like her. I would hear her giving advice, and I used to say, "You know, if I could do that, that would be nice." And it was interesting, in later years, my friends would talk to me about everything. I think I tried to emulate her—how she dealt with adversity. How she dealt with her illness. Seeing how she would try to put on a pleasant face when we came to see her.

I think my mother's death gave me a larger, broader view of what can happen in a lifetime. It was not a protected childhood. I learned you have to fend for yourself wherever you can. Growing up quickly taught me a lot. I think you learn from the pain. From disappointment. Not having your mother at graduation. Going to see her in the hospital in your graduation dress. You learn from those things. You learn to be compassionate. You learn to be sympathetic. You learn to listen. You learn to enjoy the good things you have in life, not dwell on the sorrows because they don't help. With heartache and suffering comes understanding. It's not a utopian world. But it's important not to hate. Things can get better.

How I See It

And so we've come full circle. It's important to learn balance and to know things can get better. It's important to hold on to our legacies for five, ten, twenty, fifty, or seventy-five years. This chapter—and this book—is a slice of time, a photo or an album from the particular point in time, the date and place we talked with people. Their lives have changed, and will change. How they, and we, see the deaths of parents in our daily lives will no doubt evolve as we encounter new experiences. After all, it was the death of another parent, Addie's father, that led us, Jan and Leslie, to think more about our own losses and to write this book. In the next, and final, chapter, we return to our stories, and our experiences of writing this book.

10

Coda

The Japanese have a word, aware, *which speaks to both the beauty and pain of our lives, that sorrow is not a grief one forgets or recovers from but is a burning, searing illumination of love for the delicacy and strength of our relations.*—Terry Tempest Williams, "A Downwinder in Hiroshima"

Silences

(Jan)

I woke on a recent summer morning, half a continent away from the summers of my childhood, with the word "silence" in my head. I remember summer mornings before my mother died, waking to silence. Sometimes soft sounds—a mourning dove, the *slup, slup* of coffee percolating on the stove, my mother's voice on the telephone— broke these silences. These were the gentle, friendly silences, and the ones I grieved after she died. There were others: the cold silence that inevitably followed my parents' screaming matches and lasted for a childhood eternity. The admonitions to whisper and walk quietly when Mommy was sick with one of her frequent headaches she treated by binding her forehead in a handkerchief saturated with Vicks. The silence of her absence and the hushed voices of the adults when she had yet another miscarriage.

I wake to silence and I think of the silences on the transcript tapes I have been working with this week—the hard questions people have willingly considered and the pauses, sometimes as eloquent as the answers that follow them. "Did anyone talk to you about your mother?" "After your dad died, did anyone tell stories about him that made part of him come alive for you?" "On balance, are your memories or lack of them a burden or a gift?" "Does anyone ever say how like or unlike him or her you are?"

Some are pleased to name themselves like their parent, others just as pleased to name their differences. Some are puzzled. How can they tell if they are like or unlike a parent they never knew in adulthood, a person no one ever talked about? Others smile in the silence, and then say, "Oh, yes. I remember a story my mom told after my dad died." The silences are different in intensity and texture, but always eloquent.

May 1959

This is the silence reflected in a snapshot of my family the spring after my mother died. It is a snapshot I unearthed during the course of working on this book. Black and white. We are a sad and motley quartet. My dad is smiling. In fairness, on that particular occasion it may not have been a cockeyed drunken grin. But it often was. His arms try to contain my infant brother, who even in the stillness of photography seems to be straining away from him. Next to him, my eight-year-old brother—white shirt, crooked bow tie, pants hitched up high, face set in a familiar adenoidal solemnity—stands slightly pigeon-toed. A quarter inch from him in the snapshot—which translates to what, half a foot? in real life—I stand, glasses askew. My dress, I think it was pink, is too short in the waist. The only dresses ever long-waisted enough for me were the ones my mother made. If my mother had been there, she would have reminded me to suck my potbelly in. As it is, I stand, the defiant ugly-duckling daughter of the beautiful mother who abdicated. Except for my father and the baby, none of us touch each other. None of us, except my father, are smiling.

None, that is, except my mother. Just perceptible, in the background, sitting on the built-in buffet next to a statue of the Blessed Virgin and a vase of flowers, my mother smiles from a formal portrait taken before any of us were born. It must have been May. Although I have no memory of doing so, I must have made the altar, as my mother and I did all the Mays of our lives together. No one else in my family would have done it.

We did not talk about my mother that day. I know that not because I remember that day—I don't—but because we never talked about my mother. Silence. A scant year later, my father remarried. My baby brother Phil now has a mother of his own. The rest of us, in deference and denial, learn to call her Mom.

Seventeen years later, when my father has his first heart attack and we think he's dying, he calls my brother Paul and me into his hospital room. He is adamant: he wants only the two of us.

"I suppose you wonder why I haven't talked about your mother all these years," he says. "It's because it made Mom uncomfortable. She wanted to think you were her own."

It takes me a minute to interpret this mother/mom business: Phyllis who birthed us is Mother; Mildred, our stepmother, is Mom. I do not for a minute believe this is Mildred's wish, this pretending, this denial. I was nearly thirteen, Paul nearly eleven, when she married my father. It is the story my father would like to be true. It is the story he has tried to make true with years of silence.

A short time before Dad's heart attack, Paul asked to meet with him to talk about his lack of childhood memories, particularly from around the time Mom died. Dad agreed he would do that and then canceled, more than once. In frustration, Paul came to me. I was older. I did have some memories, and I shared them, but tentatively, furtively. Silence dies hard. I give Paul credit for trying. When I went in search of memory, I never went to my father.

Finally, seventeen years after that, when I'm at work on this book, when my "baby" brother Phil is expecting his first child, I talk with him. We begin to break the silence.

Breaking the Silence

My father did not cry at my mother's wake or funeral and forbade us to do so as well. I saw my father cry only once, at my brother Phil's wedding. Dad made it as far as the back of the church, after the ceremony, and the dam broke. He put his arms around me and sobbed. "I just kept thinking," he said, "about the night he was born. About how she cried out, and then she was dead, and he was born. I just kept praying today that she would think I'd done a good job."

How many times had I wanted my father to cry with me in the past thirty-odd years? With me: not to me, at me, in front of me. His crying now seemed maudlin, self-centered, making a scene in the glow that follows a wedding, when members of the newly joined families are supposed to be hugging, kissing, and congratulating. I wanted him to be quiet. I wanted to collude in silence. I was afraid of his emotion after all these years. Later that day, I colluded in a different kind of silence. We put his outburst down to medicine and heart trouble, of the physical kind.

In 1994, my father and stepmother both died. She died in May. My father moved to an assisted-care facility. A temporary measure, he kept saying. By September, he'd sold the house he and my stepmother had lived in for thirty-three years. Phil and I, our nephew, and a few others from our biological and chosen family cleaned out the house and supervised the auction. At the end of that day, I drove my father back to his room. I could not stop crying. I cried during the fifteen-mile drive; I sobbed as I helped him out of the car and up to his room; I settled him in. I was, by this time, crying too hard to speak. Finally he seemed to notice.

"It will be okay," he said to me. "Don't worry, it will be okay."

It wasn't much. But it felt like a crack in the silence. It was the last time I saw my father.

I do not remember the last time I saw my mother. Many memories have returned to me in the course of writing this book. Not that one.

Presence

It is October now, a month in which anniversaries pile up for me. Peter died on October 11, one week after his forty-sixth birthday. My father died on October 13. That was my mother's birthday.

As I work, I feel Peter's supportive presence. I feel that I have done good; I can do good; I will do good. As I work, I've longed for my mother's presence, too, but it has been elusive at best. In the second summer of working on this book, I took a camping trip with a friend to the Mendocino coast. On Sunday afternoon, on our way home, we stop at a beach. I fall asleep, nestled in a dune. I dream a wisp of a dream. My mother appears offshore, the point girl, I suppose you would call her, of a forties-style synchronized swim team. She is wearing a red fireman's hat. She is smiling, grinning really. She has come to entertain me, I think.

Shortly after my father died, I felt another brief flicker of my mother's presence. Not a dream, but a daydream. My father, my stepmother, and my mother are sitting around a table in heaven, a sort of outdoor café in the sky. The three of them, finally, pooling their enlightened state, nod their heads in unison and say, "Ah, now we see what her life is about. Now we see what she's doing." Almost childlike in its wishful thinking. But so comforting. It is their affirmation of my life, so different from the ones they chose, from the one they would have chosen for me, and so different from anything I ever felt from them when they were alive.

I think the biggest gift writing this book has given me is that I can echo the sentiments of Eric Marcus and so many others when I say that my mother's death changed my life. I struggle painfully, as others do, at the very idea of saying "My life is better because she died." But it is. Yes, I struggled for years, still do in some ways, *against* the circumstances. I won't be mired down in grief. I won't let any church dictate my behavior. I will, to the best of my ability, be awake to my life, responsible for my own decisions. I will do the things she did not do.

Yet, in the course of writing this book, I've come to feel a new empathy for my mother. For many years, when I told people of her death, I described it as a sort of suicide. The doctor said she shouldn't get pregnant again. The church said she couldn't practice birth control. And so she chose not to live. Her first baby died in 1942. I was born at the very end of 1947. More miscarriages and dead babies followed me. Recently, I've begun to feel how these griefs must have burdened her life. She was physically sick a lot. How could she—or anyone, including my father, it now occurs to me—bond with and love the children she had when she'd lost so many? I cannot echo Diana O'Hehir or Terry or others who say that, even though they have few memories of their living mothers, they did feel a sense of connection and love. I have more memories and less sense of love. Acknowledging that I did not have that unconditional love has allowed me to count and name and value what I did get from my mother.

All this: Someone read books to me from the time before I can remember. Someone told me stories of her childhood, embellished and dramatic. Someone engineered imaginative games, in which I ran stores, took trips, taught school, painted pictures, wrote a newspaper. Someone told me I was smart and that mattered. My mother. When she was there, she was really there.

The problem, of course, was that she was so much more frequently absent in her illnesses and grief. But some things that really matter to me in this life—books and ideas, writing and reading, a sense of imagination and playfulness, creativity, intelligence, humor—I can trace to my mother's life.

Learning connection, empathy, honesty, and how to break the silence: those things I can trace to my mother's death and my hard work that followed.

In the very last weeks of working on this book, Leslie and I talk again about my mother and what her life must have been like. About her struggle to make something in this world, against the odds of her body, against the odds of her culture and religion. This fight marked her as a woman of her time, nothing more and nothing less. In expressing her empathy for both my mother and me, Leslie somehow brings a picture into focus so that I, too, can feel empathy for my mother. And by acknowledging the depth of my mother's sorrow, I can acknowledge the depth of my own loss.

Leslie and I have this conversation one day after what would have been my mother's seventy-seventh birthday. I am now seven years older than she was when she died. I now look older than she ever did. I have more and more gray hair. She had none. I have lived to see my daughter off to college, to the verge of adulthood.

I walk to my car, late that night. The streets are silent. And in the balmy quiet, I feel my mother's presence. I am grateful.

Holding My Breath

(Leslie)

Every sorrow suggests a thousand songs, and every song recalls a thousand sorrows, and so they are infinite in number, and all the same.—Marilynne Robinson, *Housekeeping*

After my father died, six weeks before I graduated from high school, I held my breath for a while. For almost a year to be exact. And then I split open. The tears I wouldn't cry, out of fear I'd never stop, pushed out. Originally plugged up through holy will, the patched wall would no longer hold, and air broke through. The tension started to build right after I returned to college in January of my freshman year. I think it had to do with going home at break and facing the shock of my broken family.

My dad was gone, and so was I. My mother, who had always been my great support, even through adolescent dramas, had just lost the love of her life. My young brother, ever the wise comic of our little family, remained strangely quiet. And the gray Chicago winter seemed to wrap the house in a stubborn sorrow. I had fallen down some stairs at school. We went to a doctor, who said I was okay but that the nasty bruise on my back would hurt for a pretty long while. My father had had a bad back. I was beginning the slow and dangerous process of turning myself into my father—a dead man.

As I look back on those first few months after I returned to school, I realize that I was desperately trying to hide my sadness from myself: in the therapeutic vernacular, I was repressing grief. I substituted sadness with a vague fear. If you start to feel that bad, my subconscious must have told me, you will never stop. It will take over everything. There will be nothing else.

When I approached the first anniversary of my father's death, I started a wild, nervous spinning, ending in a brief and healthy breakdown. I began my deeper grieving, and, from that process, grew the eventual conviction that I could face whatever came my way.

With that grieving and growth also came a new identity. Stories of my father trailed me everywhere I went. If you were to be my friend or lover, you'd listen. I wore those stories well, sharing them with my brother, who needed them more than all the near strangers I laid them on. They became myth and mantra. But I never named my father in a poem, until my brother almost died. Then I said "My Father" in writing. It was all I knew to do. And then, at a certain point, I thought I was done with grieving. I'd gone on with my life.

But somewhere along the way, I started to hold my breath again, and somewhere else, I found I could no longer remember my father's voice. Horrified, I went over the story I used to help me remember it, but the story no longer worked. I've read about how people who lose their vision recall what things look like for only so long and then the world of solid objects begins to fade. Painful to imagine, but not difficult to comprehend. Our memories remain ethereal. We cannot fasten them down, and when they lift, they're gone, leaving only traces, which, in time, also disappear. I thought writing this book would help me get the memory of my father's voice back. It hasn't. But something else has happened. I can retell my story, and this time, not so desperately. I'm no longer trying to keep from going with my father to his grave or looking to woo you somehow to my side. Now when I tell it, I can breathe deeply, the way I should.

May 2, 1965

I am on the floor of our small dining room, right where it opens into the kitchen, on my back, doing sit-ups or something. My father passes by. It is a Sunday. He is wearing slacks and a polo shirt, the kind with a little collar, and an alligator over the heart. I don't know it now, but this will be my last visual memory of him alive.

The next time I see him is later that day, at the other end of the dining room, where it opens into the living room. This time *he* is on his back, with his mouth and eyes stuck open. I know he is dead. I am seventeen years old. I have just picked up my ten-year-old brother at the park. He remembers that part somewhat differently. Anyway, we come in the house through the back door. Marc is still in the kitchen when I discover our father's body. I don't remember saying anything.

I only remember pushing Marc back, trying to keep him out of sight of the body. I want him to go outside into the backyard. I think he does. I call our grandfather, who lives in the neighborhood. He calls an ambulance. But I know it is too late.

I go back into the living room and see a neighbor, Mickey Shames, bent over my father's body. I guess she is trying to give him mouth-to-mouth resuscitation. I think about how kind that is of her to try. I don't know how she got there. Maybe Marc has called her. I don't even know how she got into the house. Did she come through the back door? Did she walk past me? Where am I now? Am I still in the dining room? If I am, what do I do there?

I've always meant to ask Marc how Mickey got there, but we've never really talked much about that day.

Memory Revisited

I used the opportunity of the twenty-fifth anniversary of our father's death to talk with Marc. But a funny thing happened on the way to my playing all-remembering big sister. I found out that Marc had kept track of a memory of that day which I had shut out: my screaming. And along with sound, he remembers light—lots of it. I remember neither.

The conversation with him brought back a memory I had of my father's father, just before he died. A formerly six-foot-tall man severely deteriorated from Parkinson's disease, my grandfather greeted my shy five-year-old self with a kind, soft voice. But mostly I remember a strong light from the window filling the small room, almost as if it were emanating from his bright white hair. People told my father that he shouldn't bring a young child to see a sick person so close to death, but I'm glad he did.

I wasn't sorry, though, that I had kept—or at least *thought* I had kept—my little brother away from our father's dead body. I've always believed that in my crazed, panicked state, I did at least one thing right. But setting myself up as the strong, older sister may have been a defensive maneuver and a big mistake for both of us. By assigning myself to the mission of taking care of my brother and remembering our father for him, I also gave myself a way to hide from my own grief.

Doing the interview with my brother for this book, I finally faced more of the truth of the day my father died.

The Blank Tape: March 17, 1994

Of course, it's every interviewer's worst fear—that the tape will screw up. And so when it did—with my most important interview, the one with my brother—I panicked. Marc remained calm. Although we managed to get the cassette out of the blasted box in which it had jammed, the tape tore. My brother performed a careful, almost loving, splice job, but when we played it back, the dread sea sounds of a blank tape washed over our ears. Apparently, we had been talking to each other with no one listening since the start of the interview.

Although Marc readily agreed to return and go through the questions again, we both knew we'd lose some of the initial spontaneity. Worse, we'd lost the amazing turn the interview took when it was more conversation between sister and brother than between writer and informant. That's when we made the discovery that allowed me to see the day of our father's death from a new perspective, so much so that I'd have to go back to my story and modify it or, at the very least, indicate where it contradicted Marc's version.

First, I thought I had picked him up from the park, but the way he remembers it is that we met, accidentally, at the corner near our house and walked home together by chance. No big deal. Just a slightly different version of the same story, except that my version keeps me more in charge. He does confirm that I entered first and discovered our father's body—he had stopped to return a ball to a friend's house—but he says my screaming brought him into the kitchen, and then—while I was phoning our grandfather—into the dining room where our father's body lay. *This* is the fact that I had blocked for nearly thirty years: *Marc saw the dead body.* And I thought I had shielded him from it. Even after he told me, five years ago, of the light in the room, even after I wrote a poem about his *memory* of the light in the room, I refused to see him seeing the body.

Now he describes it for me: the sunlight, the late afternoon, western light moving across the carpet and over our father's body. As Marc speaks, I think of photography, his chosen art form, the art form which plays with light. Together we try to imagine where Dad was headed: Into the bathroom for medicine? No. He always carried his medicine with him. Into the kitchen toward the phone? That would make sense. But why was he on his back? Did he fall forward as Marc says you do with a heart attack, gripping your chest—Marc had a heart attack when he was thirty—and then roll over onto his back during the last moments of his life? These grim questions chill us: And then we pause at how we have never had this kind of conversation before. I draw a diagram of the room and a stick figure of where I remember the body lying. Marc places his stick figure in a slightly different part of the room. There is some crazy spot inside my head that believes if we can just agree on the precise location of our father's body, we might be able to revive it.

Was the tape absent for a reason? Did we need to talk about this and then talk again? I know it was a good interview. Marc was very open, and his phrasing had a kind of poetry to it in parts. But it's all disappeared into the air now. And as he played with the tape, trying to coax it out of the jealous machine, I thought: "Well, it's all right. It's just a tape. The real loss is our father." There goes death again— focusing the light on what's important and what's not. But I wish I had those fresh, new sentences in which Marc reconstructed for the first time whose house he returned the ball to, and how he probably yelled for help, which is most likely what brought our neighbor to the scene. I ache, knowing I almost lost this story, this connection to my brother. And so I wish I had his exact words—with the pauses and hesitations and the excitement in both our voices. But I can rationalize that maybe the memory of the discovery will sustain a deeper feeling that specific facts and sentences might obscure. It's true that sometimes the only way to remember is to fill in the blanks the way you *think* it goes.

Anyway, there is a way in which tapes and photographs steal our memory, providing us with a false sense of accuracy. And, now, of course, computers with fancy graphics programs can cheat on any fill-in-the-blank or true-false exam. I guess it's one way they resemble our brains. Our gestures and phrases will never be completely frozen again. Instead, they will remain fluid in time. Advanced technology only shows us how much we'll never know. Now calling himself a "digital artist," my brother has computers with more memory than my hard disk could ever imagine. My brother, whose memory I perhaps tried to steal, has taught me a little about these fancy tricks of advanced technology. And my little baby brother, the one I tried so earnestly to protect, has taught me more, much, much more than that.

The Dream

During the month of May, thirty years after my father died, in the middle of writing this book, I had a dream in which he appears, with his signature curly hair and mustache. He has grown a trim beard, and he is standing on a stage in a small jazz club, playing guitar. I turn to the friends I have come with and say, "That's my dad; isn't he good?"

Although my father never played an instrument, there was no doubt this young man was Dad. But he was a dad I never knew. Something in the dream told me he was twenty-eight years old, the age of my father eight years *before* I was born. When I told the dream to my husband, he joked, "Maybe it's your father reincarnated. After all, twenty-eight would give him time to get accustomed to being dead, and then come back." My brother took the joke one step further and offered to go look for the guy in local jazz clubs. My mother, who doesn't always like our jokes, was horrified. She doesn't believe in reincarnation.

Who knows? All I can say is that soon after the dream, I encountered a young jazz guitarist, twenty-eight years old, with the hair and the mustache and the beard, my father's first name, and the same gentle teasing manner I'll never forget about the dad I knew for seventeen years. During the month Jan and I finished this book, I went to a jazz concert and watched this talented young man play.

Tell the story any way you want. It *is* Charlie Simon reincarnated. Or it's Leslie Simon having a predictive dream. Or it's Leslie Simon losing it. The last version is the one my friends back in Chicago might subscribe to. But maybe everyone can buy the version I'd like to settle on. That love persists. Through stories and dreams and jokes. Through memory and imagination.

The Future

As my daughter approached the age I was when my father died, the idea for this book came to me. Some kind of fear, I think, was working on me. I needed to remember that I survived the age of seventeen, and I needed to know that I would live long enough to see my daughter's high school graduation. I don't know if I'll live longer than my father did, but I do know that his early death, while a deep injury, did not destroy me. Often, if we're lucky enough to survive our wounds, we can grow stronger from the lives we've put together in their aftermath.

The week I finished writing this last piece for the book, I was involved in installing an exhibit on rape in the student art gallery at the college where I teach. For the last ten years I have worked as a rape prevention educator and through that work, of course, have met many survivors of sexual trauma. Part of the exhibit consisted of interviews with rape survivors, and, as I was listening to one of the taped interviews, I realized that my work with survivors is yet another element in my life that brings me to this book. Perhaps working with these strong women—and some men—and witnessing their healing has taught me to understand my own grief process. Working with them became a kind of floating bridge for me.

You're never completely finished with grief, but grief does not have to finish you. Instead, you can revisit your sorrow when you need to, let it come up when it will. At times of great joy or deep sadness. Through stories and jokes and poems and paintings. With friends and intimates, with children, and by yourself.

I look at the hands of my son. Ten years ago, I started to see in his small five-year-old palms and fingers the graceful shape of my father's hands. There has always been something about hands that intrigues me. The power to hold another human being in them, for healing and hope. The gestures you make. The caresses you give. The power to express yourself. And the power to stir memories.

As I talked with one of the survivors whose story is part of the rape exhibit, I confided in her that I was worried that her participation in the project might have stirred up some of her old pain. She'd been feeling pretty strong but now seemed to be confronting her abuse again. She said to me, "Leslie, it doesn't matter. It would have come up another time anyway. It's something I need to deal with. I'll be okay."

At the exhibit several women cried. Some of them had experienced great injury at the hands of people they should have been able to trust, and something died in their hearts when that happened. As it is for any one of us confronting a deep loss, contemplation of the effects of that loss—through an art exhibit, a book, or simple reflection—can heal us and bring us back to life.

This book shows us that the circumstances of our lives may be very different, but our sorrows connect us. We can't feel another's pain or know exactly what her or his loss feels like. But we can know the great capacity human beings seem to have for repairing serious damage. And going on. Surviving.

All of Us

In this book are bits and pieces of the stories of seventy-two people. But in those bits and pieces are the stories of others: our surviving parents, our siblings, our extended families, our friends. It would be difficult to tally a final count of the people whose lives have touched the making of this book.

Our hope is that it will be equally difficult, even impossible, to tally the number of people's lives who will be touched by this book. We wrote it for a number of reasons. We began because we were dealing with the grief of a recent death. We continued because we realized, early on, that the recent death brought back our old griefs. We finished because as we did the interviews and sifted through them, we saw the glimmer of transformation, the evidence of what people could, can, and do make of their grief. That is what we want to share.

The people in this book are in various stages of their life's journeys. They are also, by and large, whole, healthy, functioning adults. They are survivors. This is what we learned from them, and from ourselves, in the process of writing this book:

Childhood bereavement lasts a lifetime. The pain of grief fades; the grief does not disappear. There is nothing any adult can do to erase a child's grief. Yet, memories and stories, even when they are incomplete or painful, bring insight and fullness into our present lives.

We could make a list of the common—although not universal— traits that adults who were orphaned in childhood share. That list would include worrying about something happening to loved ones, increased empathy for the suffering of others, a feeling that death is never very far away, an urge to live as fully as possible, the frustration of not being able to do so, and a sense of early independence—especially that. But no matter how many lists we made, there were always people who said, "I never experienced that." Or: "And what about X, Y, or Z that I *did* experience?"

In the end, we decided against such a list of common traits. No checklist of shared experience is ever going to help as much as reading the stories of others. We can identify with these stories. They comfort us and spur us to remember more about our own experience, and to make sense of it in ways no one of us could ever have invented on our own.

Something died in our hearts, and, with this book, something else came alive.

Suggested Reading

Starred entries are sources for the epigraphs in this book.

NONFICTION

Ainley, Rosa, ed. *Death of a Mother: Daughters' Stories.* San Francisco: Pandora, 1994.

Ajjan, Diana, ed. *The Day My Father Died: Women Share Their Stories of Love, Loss, and Life.* Philadelphia: Running Press, 1994.

Altschul, Sol, ed. *Childhood Bereavement and Its Aftermath.* Madison, Conn.: International Universities Press, 1988.

Aung San Suu Kyi, et al. "My Father." In *Freedom from Fear and Other Writings.* New York: Penguin, 1995.

*Baldwin, James. "Notes of a Native Son," In *Notes of a Native Son.* Boston: Beacon Press, [1955] 1984.

Bogart, Stephen Humphrey. *Bogart: In Search of My Father.* New York: E. P. Dutton, 1995.

Breslin, James E. B. "Terminating Mark Rothko: Biography Is Mourning in Reverse." In *The New York Times Book Review,* July 24, 1994.

Dorris, Michael. "Father's Day" and "Growing Up." In *Paper Trail.* New York: HarperCollins, 1994.

Edelman, Hope. *Motherless Daughters: The Legacy of Loss.* Reading, Mass.: Addison-Wesley, 1994.

———, ed. *Letters from Motherless Daughters: Words of Courage, Grief, and Healing.* Reading, Mass.: Addison-Wesley, 1995.

Eisenstadt, Marvin, et al. *Parental Loss and Achievement.* Madison, Conn.: International Universities Press, 1989.

Ellroy, James. *My Dark Places: An L.A. Crime Memoir.* New York: Alfred A. Knopf, 1996.

*Fast, Howard. *Being Red: A Memoir.* New York: Laurel, 1990.

Furman, Erna. *A Child's Parent Dies: Studies in Childhood Bereavement.* New Haven, Conn.: Yale University Press, 1974.

*Gifford, Barry. *The Phantom Father: A Memoir.* New York: Harcourt Brace, 1997.

Gordon, Mary. *The Shadow Man: A Daughter's Search for Her Father.* New York: Random House, 1996.

*Grealy, Lucy. *Autobiography of a Face.* New York: HarperCollins/Harper-Perennial, 1995.

*Hammer, Signe. *By Her Own Hand: Memoirs of a Suicide's Daughter.* New York: Random Vintage Books, 1992.

Harris, Maxine. *The Loss That Is Forever: The Lifelong Impact of the Early Death of a Mother or Father.* New York: Dutton, 1995.

Henderson, David. *'Scuse Me While I Kiss the Sky: The Life of Jimi Hendrix.* New York: Bantam Books, 1983.

*Hurston, Zora Neale. *Dust Tracks on a Road.* Urbana: University of Illinois Press, 1984.

Jacobs, Harriet. *Incidents in the Life of a Slave Girl.* Edited by Jean Fagan Yellin. Cambridge, Mass.: Harvard University Press, 1987.

James, John W., and Frank Cherry. *The Grief Recovery Handbook: A Step-by-Step Program for Moving Beyond Loss.* New York: HarperCollins, 1989.

*Kaplan, Alice. *French Lessons: A Memoir.* Chicago: University of Chicago Press, 1993.

Kubler-Ross, Elisabeth. *On Death and Dying.* New York: Macmillan, 1970.

Lewis, C. S. *A Grief Observed.* New York: Bantam Books, 1976.

Lightner, Candy, and Nancy Hathaway. *Giving Sorrow Words: How to Cope with Grief and Get on with Your Life.* New York: Warner Books, 1990.

*Lipsett, Suzanne. *Surviving a Writer's Life.* San Francisco: HarperSan Francisco, 1994.

*Mori, Kyoko. *The Dream of Water: A Memoir.* New York: Henry Holt, 1995.

*Quindlen, Anna. "In the Beginning," Mother's Day," and "Mothers." In *Living Out Loud.* New York: Ballantine Books/Ivy, 1988.

*Sartre, Jean-Paul. *The Words.* New York: Vintage Books, 1981.

*Shilts, Randy. *And the Band Played On: Politics, People, and the AIDS Epidemic.* New York: Penguin Books, 1987.

*Styron, William. *Darkness Visible: A Memoir of Madness.* New York: Vintage Books, 1990.

*Thomas, Dylan. "A Refusal to Mourn the Death, by Fire, of a Child in London." In *Collected Poems.* New York: New Directions, 1953.

Vozenilek, Helen, ed. *Loss of the Ground-Note: Women Writing About the Loss of Their Mothers.* San Diego: Clothespin Fever Press, 1992.

Wakerman, Elyce. *Father Loss: Daughters Discuss the Man Who Got Away.* Garden City, NY: Doubleday, 1984.

*Williams, Terry Tempest. "A Downwinder in Hiroshima." *The Nation,* May 15, 1995.

*Woolf, Virginia. *Moments of Being.* New York: Harvest, 1985.

FICTION

Agee, James. *A Death in the Family.* New York: Grosset and Dunlap, 1967.

Ballantyne, Sheila. *Imaginary Crimes.* New York: Penguin Books, 1982.

Brontë, Charlotte. *Jane Eyre.* New York: Signet, 1988.

Camus, Albert. *The First Man.* New York: Alfred A. Knopf, 1995.

Carpenter, Alejo. *The Lost Steps.* New York: The Noonday Press, 1989.

Fleischer, Leonore. *Shadowlands.* New York: Signet, 1993.

Gibbons, Kaye. *Ellen Foster.* New York: Vintage Books, 1988.

*Hansberry, Lorraine. Quoted from *The Sign in Sidney Brustein's Window: A Drama in Two Acts* in *Great Women Writers,* edited by Frank N. Magill. New York: Henry Holt, 1994.

Hegi, Ursula. *Floating in My Mother's Palm.* New York: Vintage Books, 1991.

————. *Stones from the River.* New York: Scribner, 1994.

*Kenney, Susan. *In Another Country.* New York: The Viking Press, 1984.

*Kincaid, Jamaica. *The Autobiography of My Mother.* New York: Farrar, Straus and Giroux, 1996.

*————. *Annie John.* New York: Signet, 1985.

Kogawa, Joy. *Obasan.* Boston: David R. Godine, 1984.

Lerner, Alan, and Barton Lane. "Camelot." In *Camelot.* New York: Warner, 1960.

Lipsett, Suzanne. *Remember Me.* San Francisco: Mercury House, 1991.

Miller, Brown. *Hiroshima Flows Through Us.* Cherry Valley, New York: Cherry Valley Editions, 1977. (poetry)

Morrison, Toni. *Jazz.* New York: Alfred A. Knopf, 1992.

Nichols, John. *The Wizard of Loneliness.* New York: W. W. Norton, 1994.

O'Brien, Tim. *In the Lake of the Woods.* New York: Houghton Mifflin Company, 1994.

O'Hehir, Diana. *I Wish This War Were Over.* New York: Washington Square, 1984.

————. *The Bride Who Ran Away.* New York: Washington Square, 1988.

————. *Home Free.* New York: Atheneum, 1988. (poetry)

*Perec, Georges. *W, Or, The Memory of Childhood.* Boston: David R. Godine, 1988.

*Robinson, Marilynne. *Housekeeping*. New York: Bantam Books, 1989.

Silko, Leslie. *Ceremony*. New York: Signet, 1978.

Simpson, Mona. *Anywhere But Here*. New York: Vintage Books, 1988.

Smiley, Jane. *One Thousand Acres*. New York: Fawcett Columbine, 1992.

Styron, William. "A Tidewater Morning," in *A Tidewater Morning: Three Tales from Youth*. New York: Random House, 1993

*Villanueva, Alma Luz. "The Edge of Darkness." In *Weeping Woman: La Llorona and Other Stories*. Tempe, Ariz.: Bilingual Press, 1994.

Woolf, Virginia. *To the Lighthouse*. New York: Harcourt Brace Jovanovich/ Harvest, 1955.

FOR CHILDREN

Krementz, Jill. *How It Feels When a Parent Dies*. New York: Alfred A. Knopf, 1993.

LeShan, Eda. *Learning to Say Good Bye: When a Parent Dies*. New York: Macmillan, 1976.

Index